D1328246

Other Books by Jeff Smith

Published by Cartoon Books

BONE One Volume Edition Paperback (in the original Black & White)
BONE One Volume Edition Hardcover Slipcase (in Full Color)
BONE: CODA
RASL Book One: The Drift
RASL Book Two: Romance at the Speed of Light
RASL Book Three: The Fire of St. George
RASL One Volume Edition Hardcover
TUKI Book One: Fight for Fire

Published by Graphix (an imprint of Scholastic)

BONE Color Series
Bone Volume 1: Out from Boneville
Bone Volume 2: The Great Cow Race
Bone Volume 3: Eyes of the Storm
Bone Volume 4: The Dragonslayer
Bone Volume 5: Rock Jaw, Master of the Eastern Border
Bone Volume 6: Old Man's Cave
Bone Volume 7: Ghost Circles
Bone Volume 8: Treasure Hunters
Bone Volume 9: Crown of Horns
Bone Handbook
Bone: Rose (Written by Jeff Smith, Painted by Charles Vess)
Bone: Tall Tales (Written by Jeff Smith and Tom Sniegoski, Illustrated by Jeff Smith)
Bone: Out from Boneville Tribute Edition
BONE Adventures (Featuring Finders Keepers & Smiley's Dream)

Published by Toon Books

Little Mouse Gets Ready!

Published by DC Comics

Shazam! The Monster Society of Evil

Available in fine bookstores and comic shops everywhere
For more information visit us at boneville.com
Facebook: The OFFICIAL Jeff Smith Page
Twitter: @jeffsmithsbone
Instagram: the_official_jeffsmith_insta
Tumblr: theofficialjeffsmithcartoonist
YouTube: The Official Jeff Smith YouTube Channel

For more information about the BONE color series visit: scholastic.com/bone
For more information about Little Mouse visit: toon-books.com

TUKI
Fight for Family

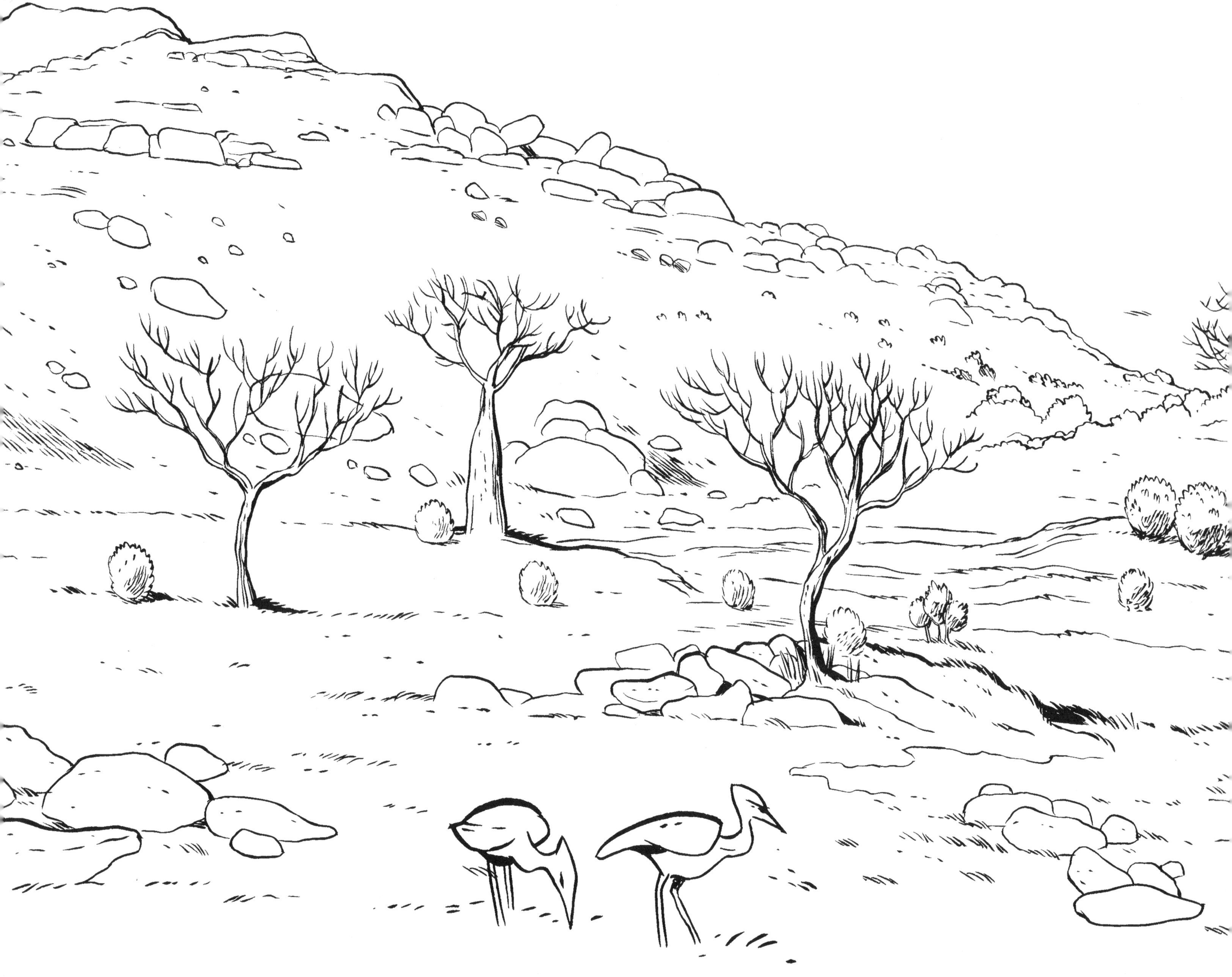

Fight for Family by Jeff Smith

Cartoon Books
Columbus, Ohio

TUKI™ Fight for Family is © 2022 by Jeff Smith
All rights reserved. No part of this book may be reproduced or utilized in any form or by any means, electronic or mechanical,
including photocopying, recording, or by any information storage or retrieval system, without written permission except in the case of reprints in the context of reviews.

Cover Art by Jeff Smith
Cover Color by Tom Gaadt

For information write:
Cartoon Books
P.O. Box 16973
Columbus, OH 43216

Softcover Regular Edition ISBN: 978-1-888963-77-9
Hardcover Regular Edition ISBN: 978-1-888963-83-0
Softcover Special Edition ISBN: 978-1-888963-82-3
Hardcover Special Edition ISBN: 978-1-888963-84-7

eISBN: 978-1-888963-78-6

10 9 8 7 6 5 4 3 2 1

Printed in Canada

Table of Contents

A Note on Paleoanthropology

Evolution, unlike the neat bumper sticker that shows a single line of primates slowly standing upright,
was very messy and scattershot. Isolated groups evolved separately over hundreds of thousands
or even millions of years. 1. 8 million years ago, multiple human species existed together during a period
of catastrophic climate change, including the great traveler & fire starter Homo erectus, our forebearer.
Each of the characters in TUKI is based on a human species known to have existed at that time.

HUMAN SPECIES ALIVE AROUND
2 MILLION BCE

Australopithecus africanus
Paranthropus boisei
Australopithecus sediba
Homo habilis
Homo rudolfensis
Homo erectus

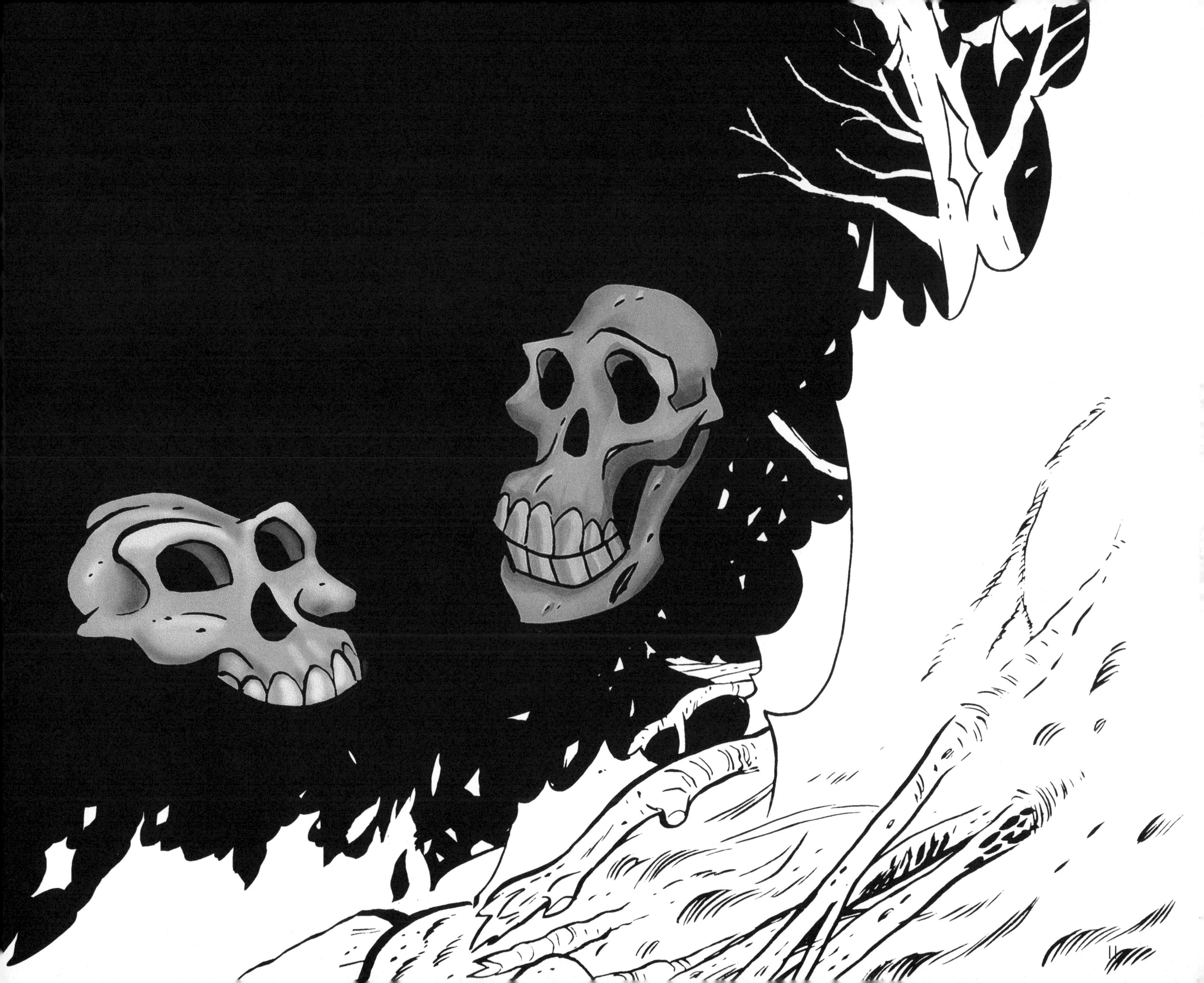

Near the dawn of humanity, three lost children meet a mysterious traveler named Tuki. Together, their search for the Motherherd of all Buffalo leads them far north through the dangerous territory of a rival species called the Habiline. The Habiline hunt and kill anyone found using fire. Tuki's reputation precedes them and soon they find themselves at the center of unwanted attention not only from Habiline warriors, but from gods and giants!

Part Two

2 Million BCE

One

The Old Habo's Grotto

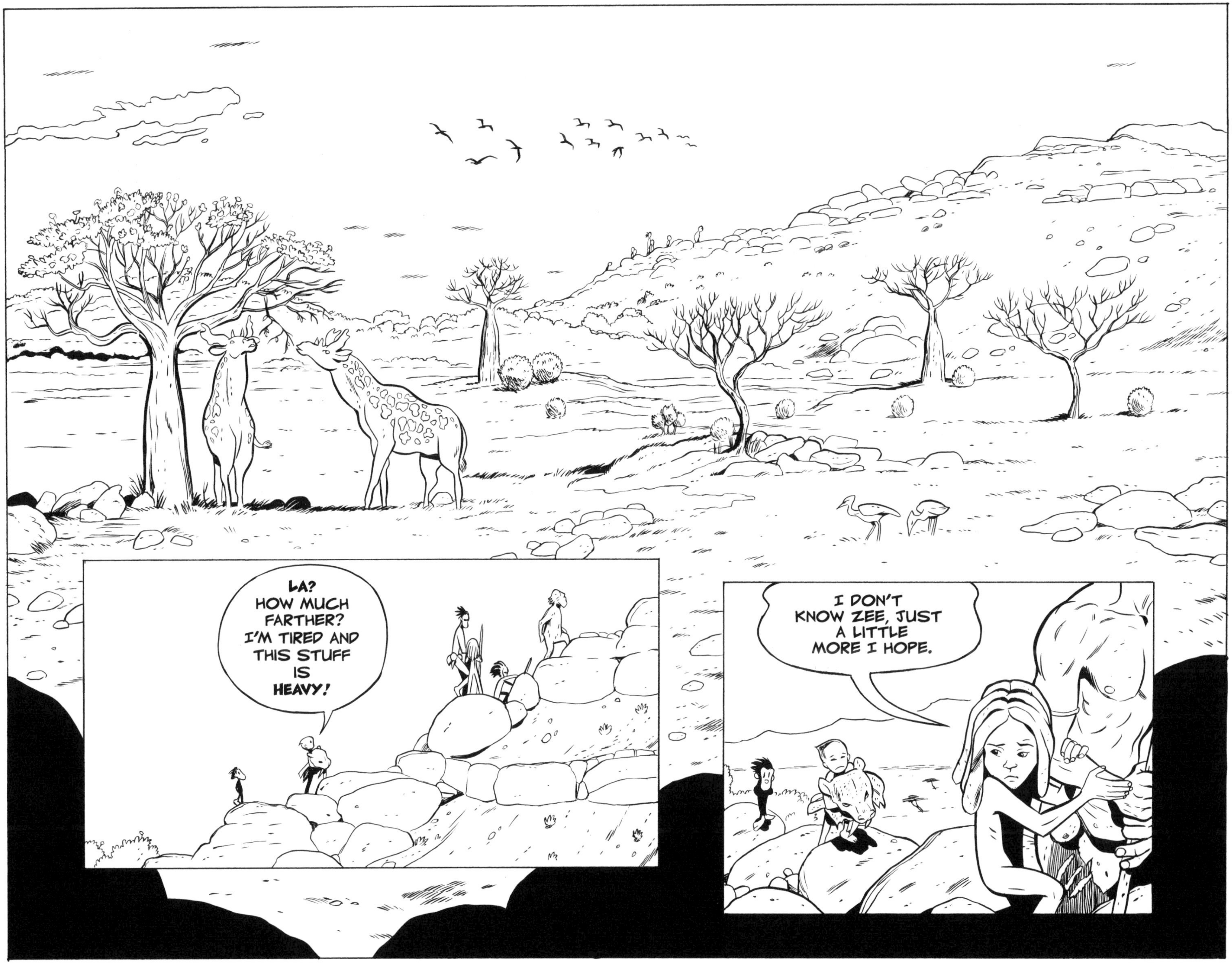
LA? HOW MUCH FARTHER? I'M TIRED AND THIS STUFF IS HEAVY!
I DON'T KNOW ZEE, JUST A LITTLE MORE I HOPE.

HEY! OLD TIMER! HOW MUCH FARTHER IS THIS GROTTO? TUKI'S LEG IS GETTING WORSE!

NOT FAR! VERY CLOSE NOW!

TUKI'S LEG WAS INJURED IN BATTLE WITH A **GIANT** - -

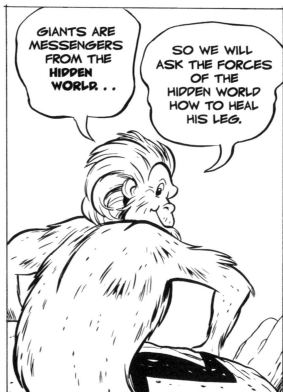

GIANTS ARE MESSENGERS FROM THE **HIDDEN WORLD**. . .

SO WE WILL ASK THE FORCES OF THE HIDDEN WORLD HOW TO HEAL HIS LEG.

THE FORCES OFTEN VISIT ME IN MY GROTTO, AND I **COMMUNE** WITH THEM!

WHAT KIND OF FORCES?

OH, THE BIG ONES - - **IMPORTANT** ONES! LIKE THE **LIGHT OF THE FOREST!** OR THE FORCE THAT ROLLS THE STARS AROUND AT NIGHT!

ALTHOUGH I HAVEN'T MET **HIM** YET!

IS THIS SAFE? HOW WELL DO YOU **KNOW** THIS TWO-FOOT?

I DON'T LIKE IT WHEN HE GETS THAT LOOK IN HIS EYE.

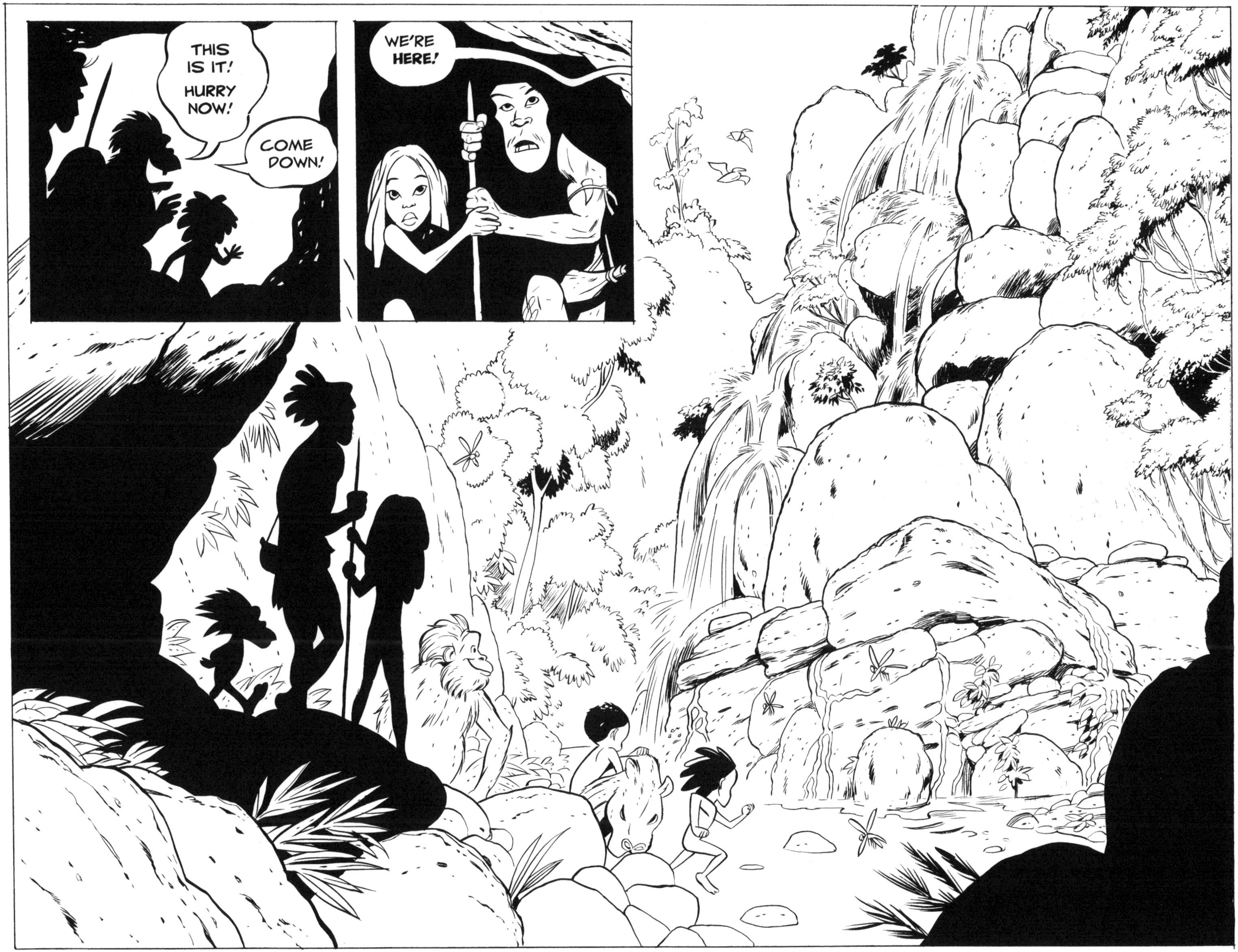
THIS IS IT! HURRY NOW!
COME DOWN!
WE'RE HERE!

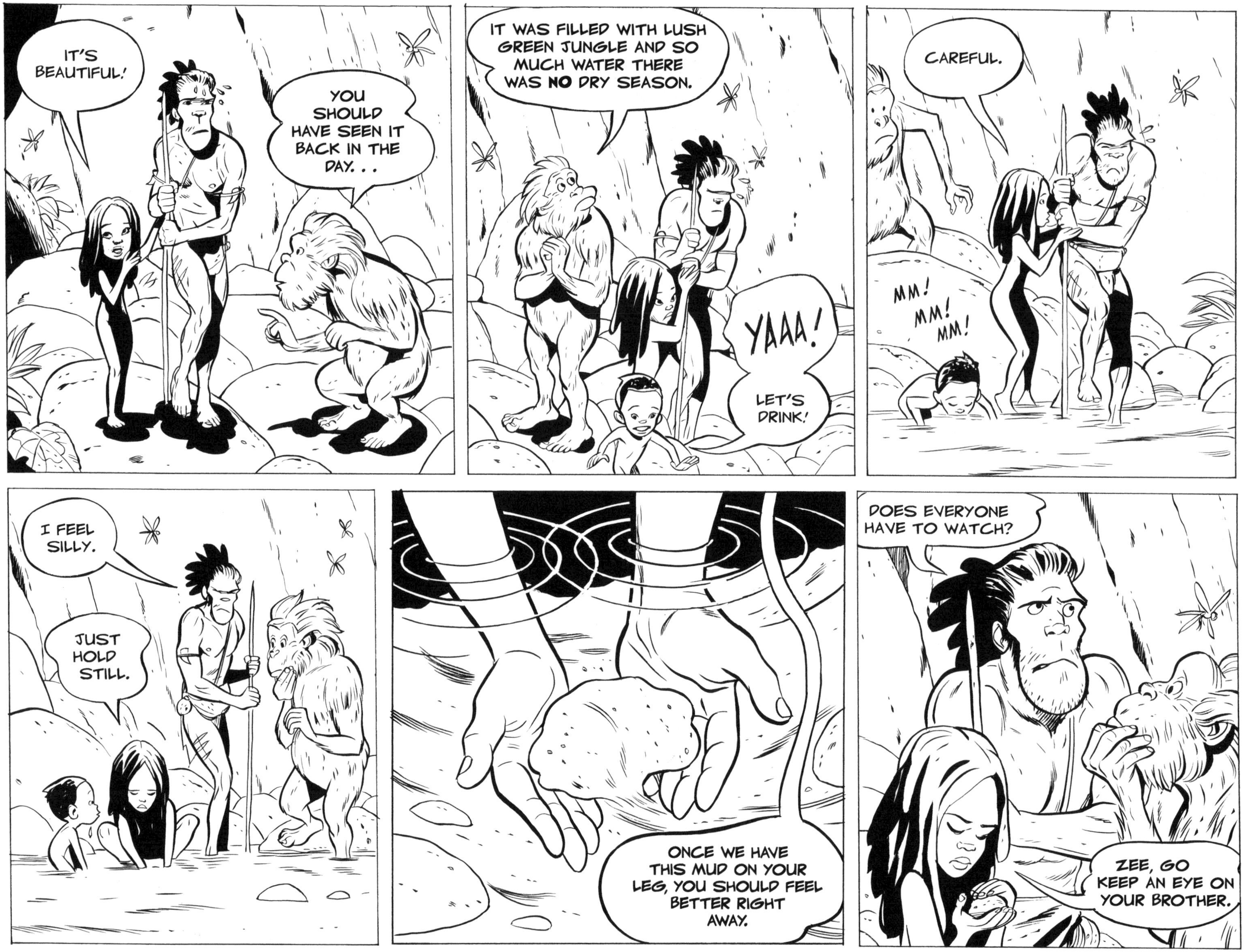
IT'S BEAUTIFUL!
YOU SHOULD HAVE SEEN IT BACK IN THE DAY. . .
IT WAS FILLED WITH LUSH GREEN JUNGLE AND SO MUCH WATER THERE WAS NO DRY SEASON.
YAAA!
LET'S DRINK!
CAREFUL.
MM! MM! MM!
I FEEL SILLY.
JUST HOLD STILL.
ONCE WE HAVE THIS MUD ON YOUR LEG, YOU SHOULD FEEL BETTER RIGHT AWAY.
DOES EVERYONE HAVE TO WATCH?
ZEE, GO KEEP AN EYE ON YOUR BROTHER.

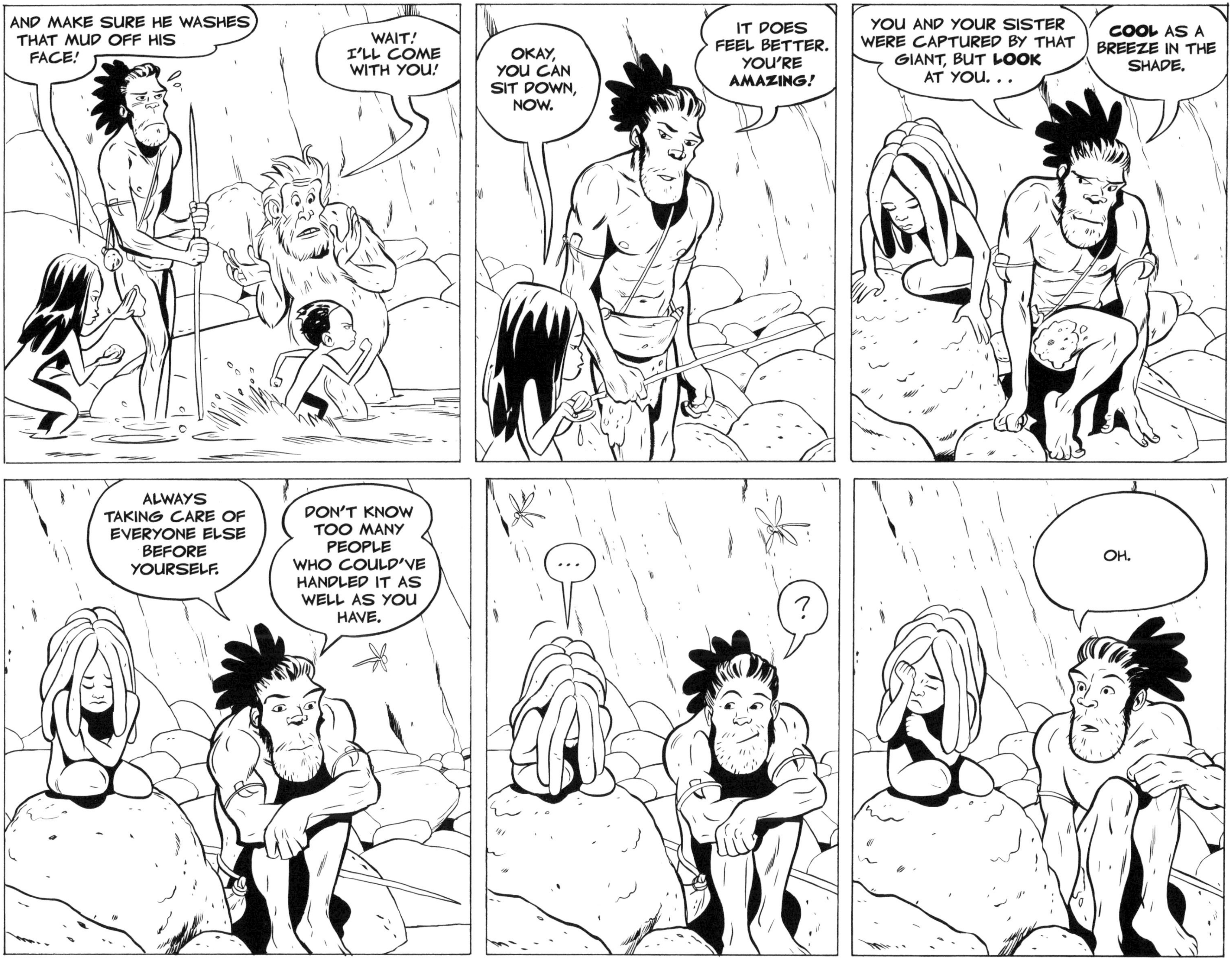
AND MAKE SURE HE WASHES THAT MUD OFF HIS FACE!
WAIT! I'LL COME WITH YOU!
OKAY, YOU CAN SIT DOWN, NOW.
IT DOES FEEL BETTER. YOU'RE **AMAZING!**
YOU AND YOUR SISTER WERE CAPTURED BY THAT GIANT, BUT **LOOK** AT YOU. . .
COOL AS A BREEZE IN THE SHADE.
ALWAYS TAKING CARE OF EVERYONE ELSE BEFORE YOURSELF.
DON'T KNOW TOO MANY PEOPLE WHO COULD'VE HANDLED IT AS WELL AS YOU HAVE.
. . .
?
OH.

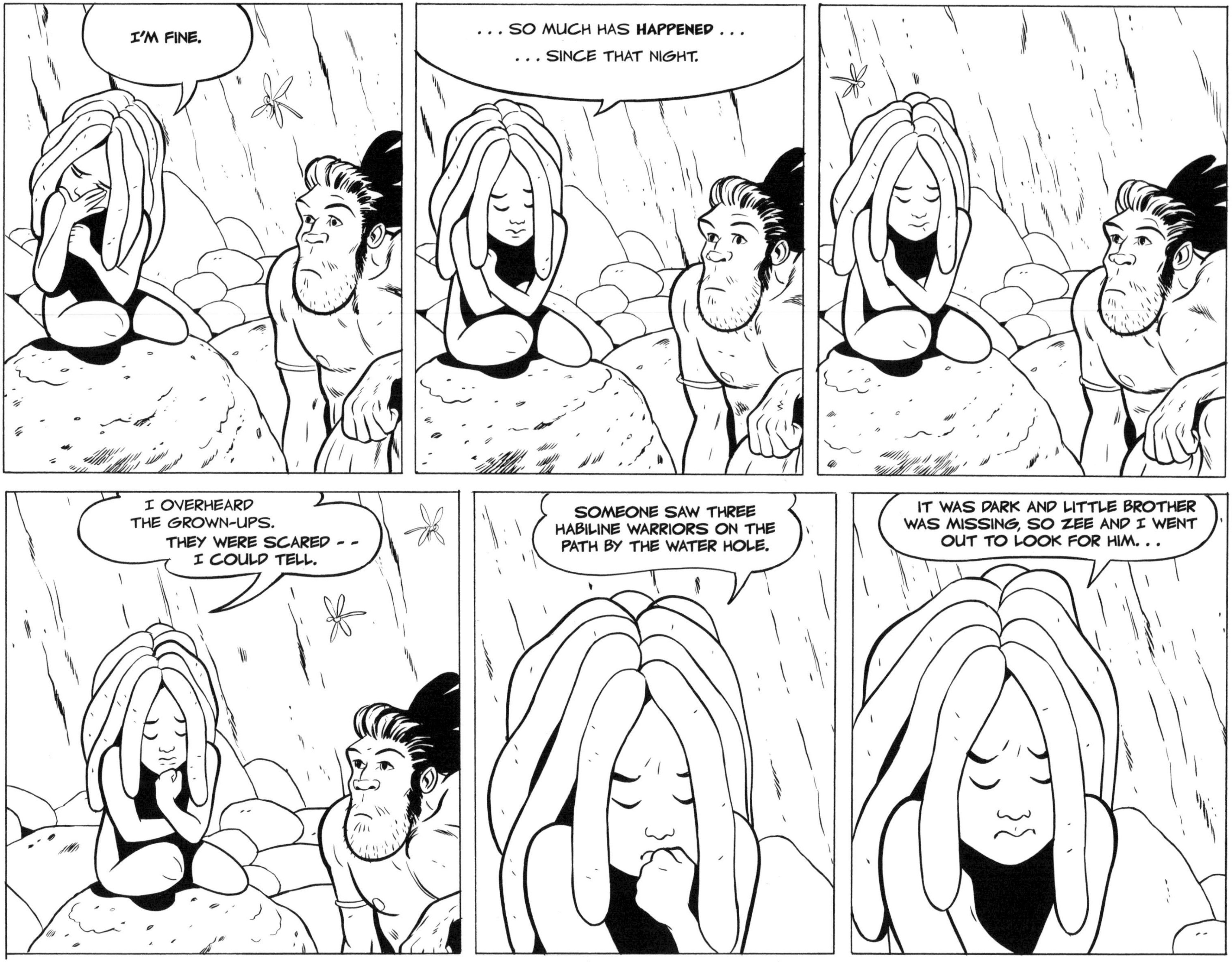
I'M FINE.
. . . SO MUCH HAS **HAPPENED** . . .
. . . SINCE THAT NIGHT.
I OVERHEARD THE GROWN-UPS. THEY WERE SCARED - - I COULD TELL.
SOMEONE SAW THREE HABILINE WARRIORS ON THE PATH BY THE WATER HOLE.
IT WAS DARK AND LITTLE BROTHER WAS MISSING, SO ZEE AND I WENT OUT TO LOOK FOR HIM. . .

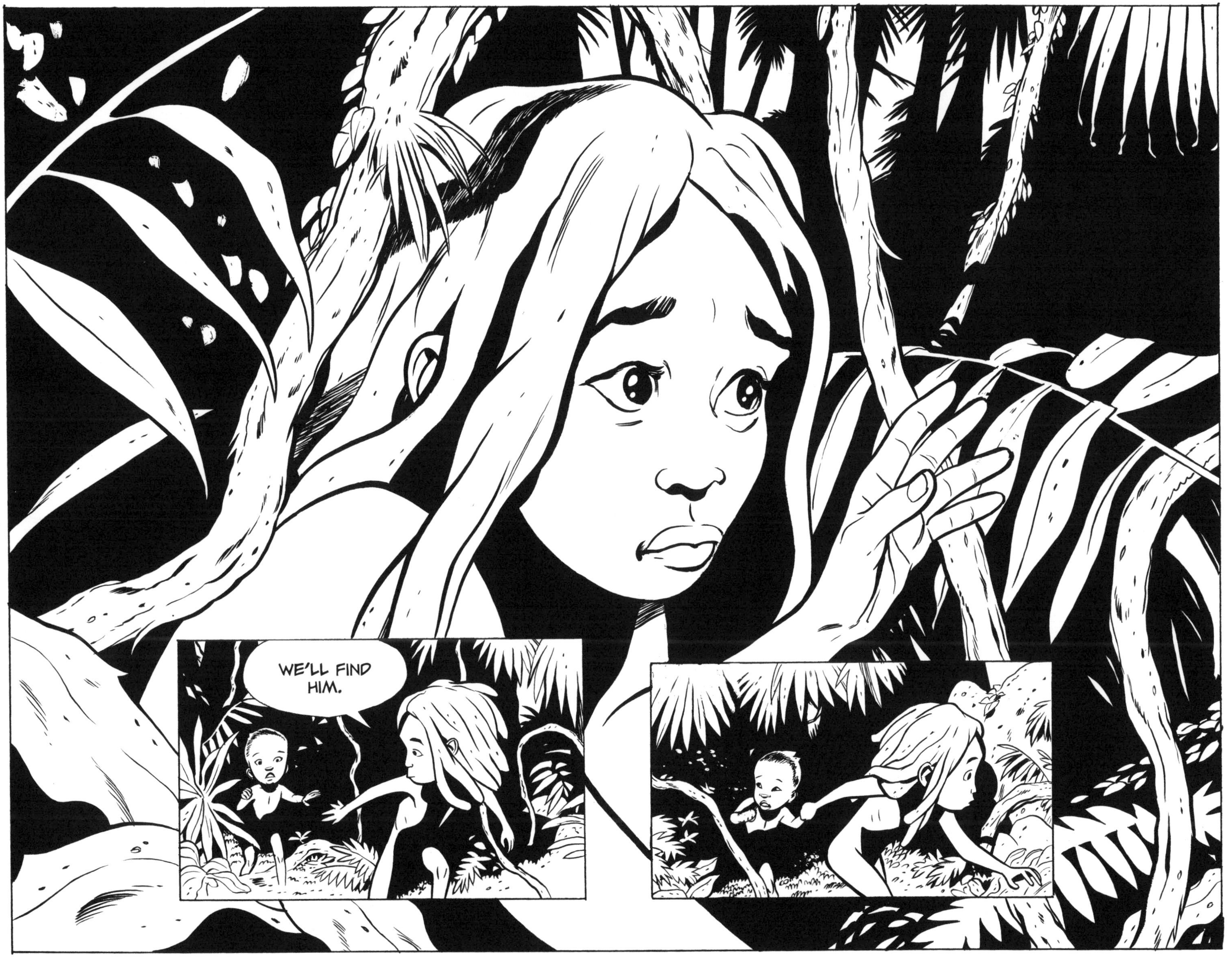
WE'LL FIND HIM.

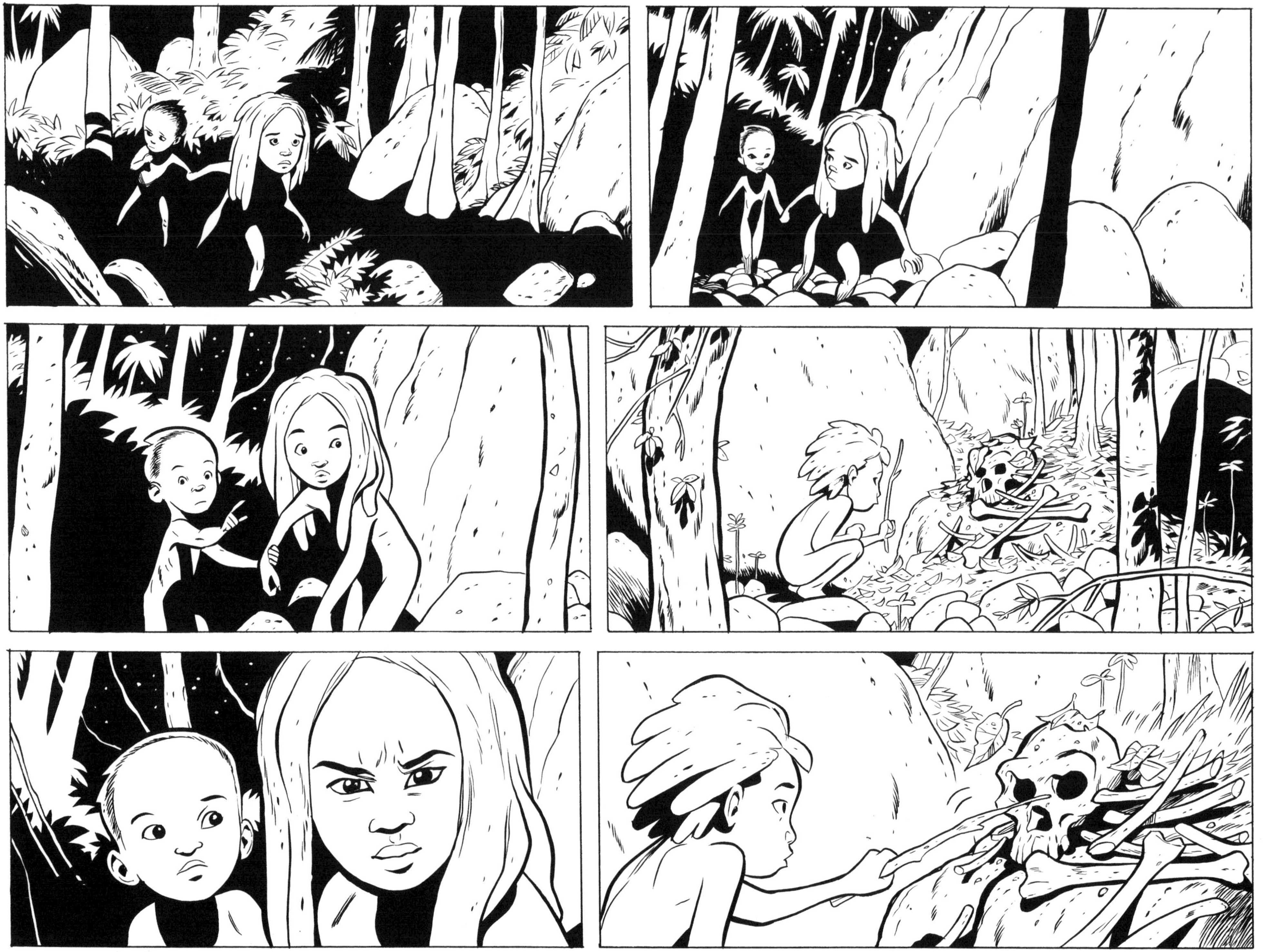

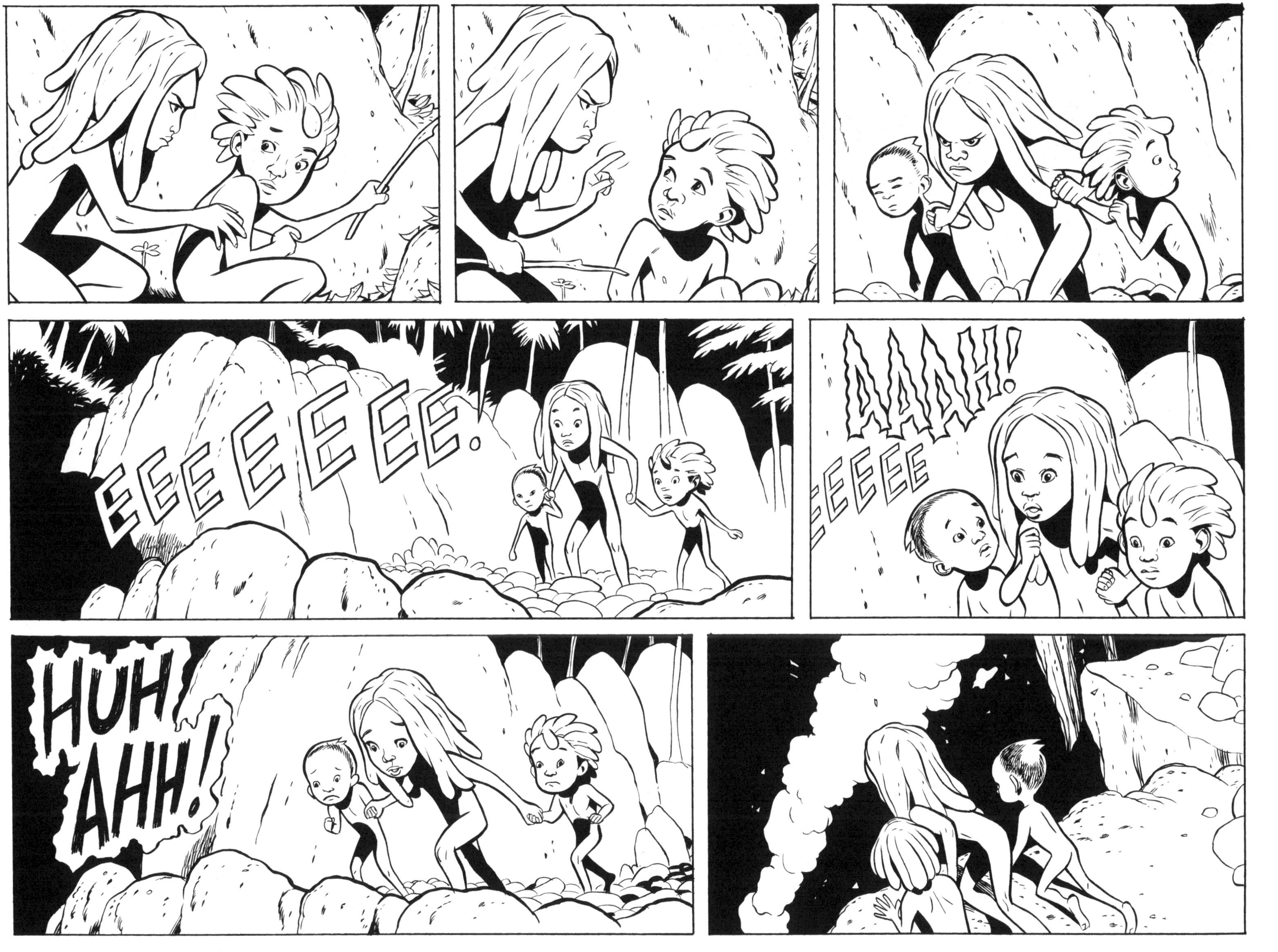
EEEEEEEE!
AAAH!
EEEEEE
HUH AHH!

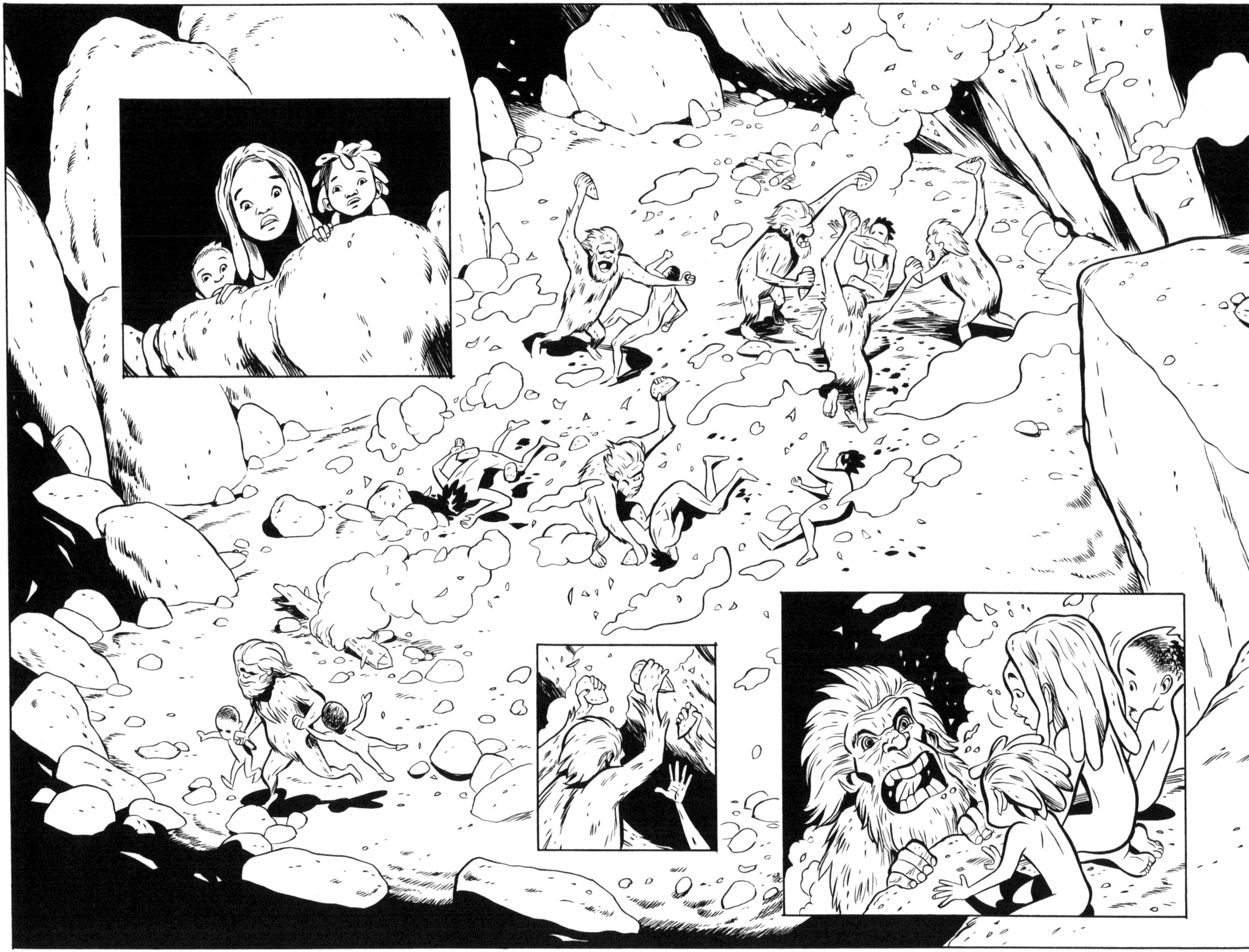

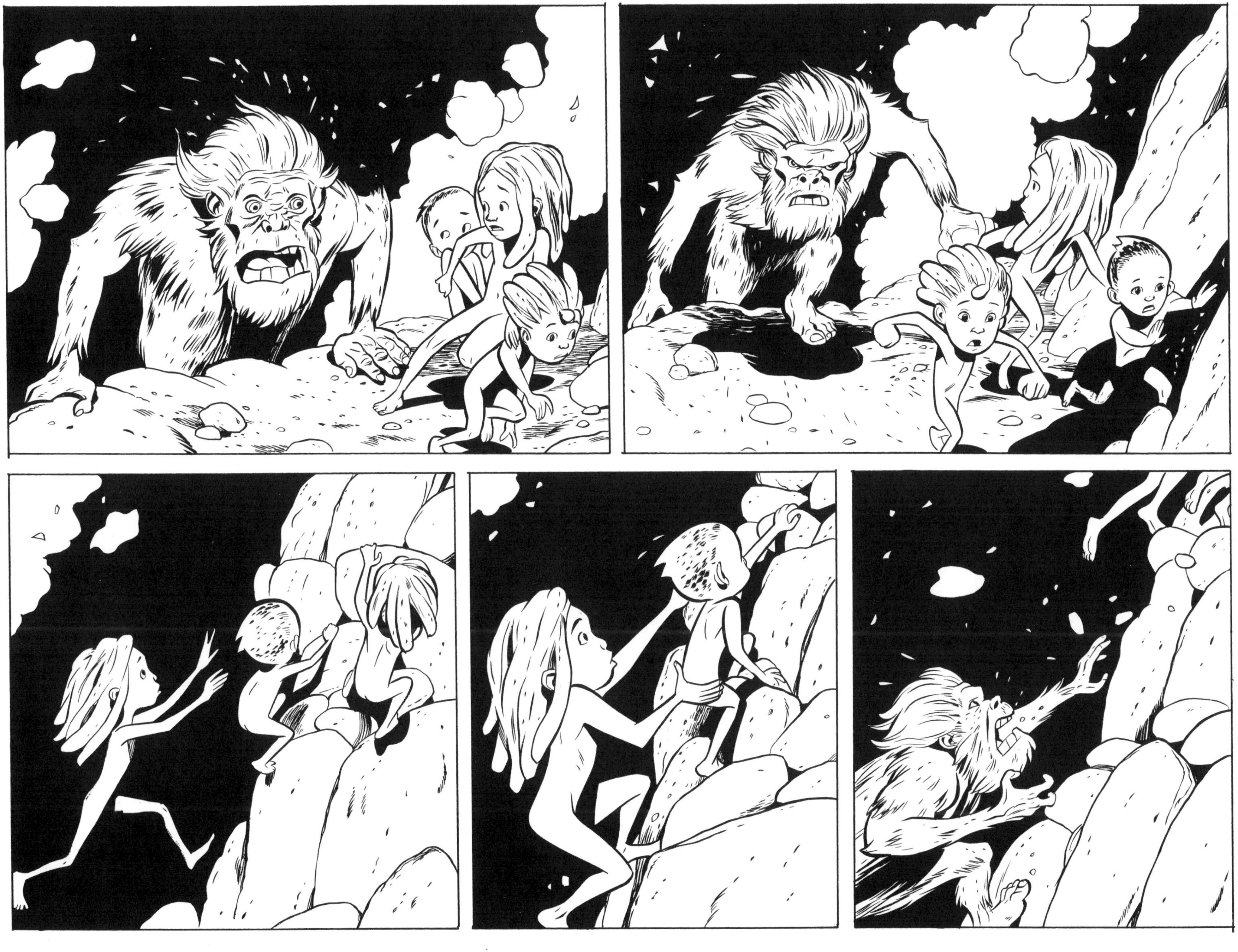

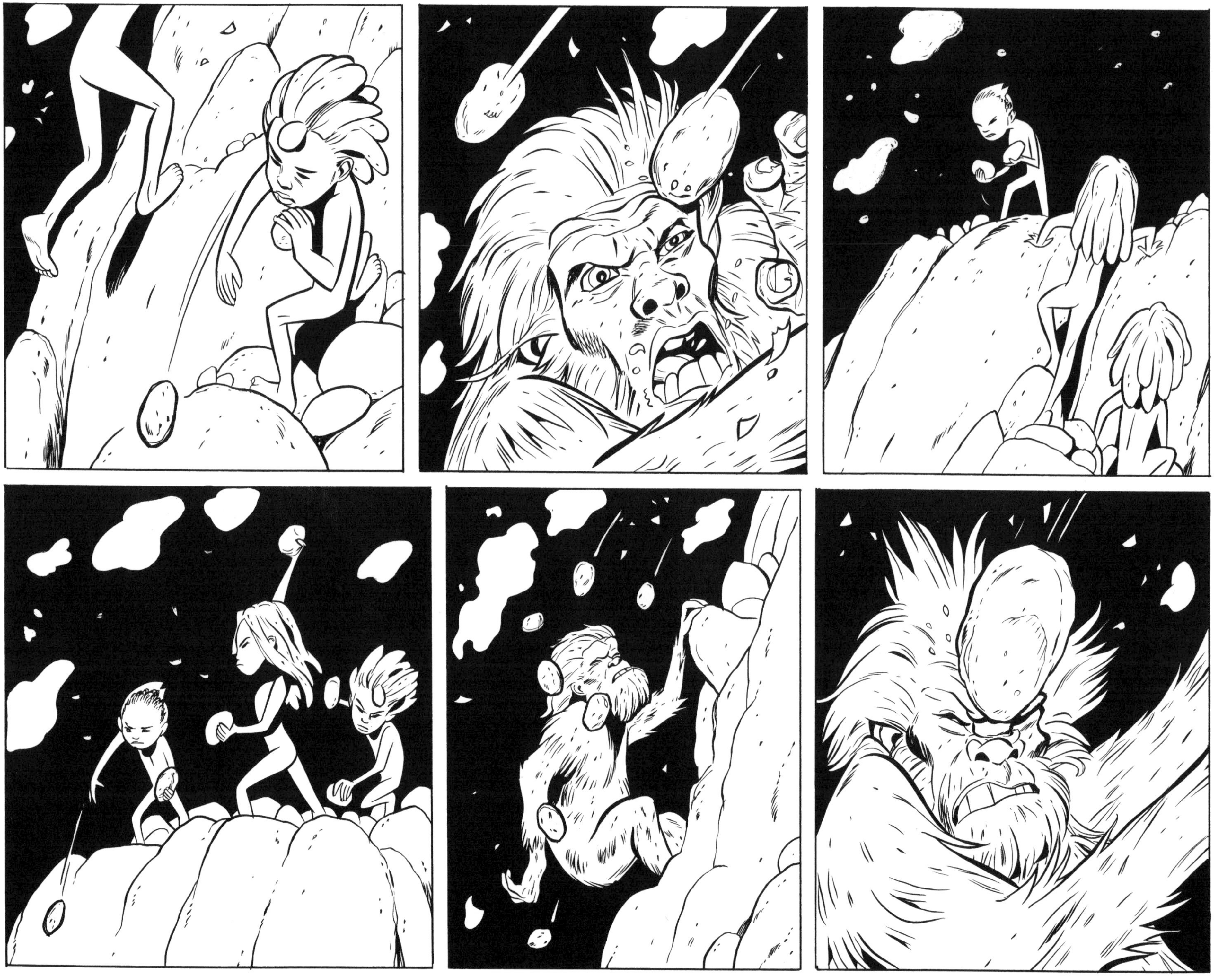

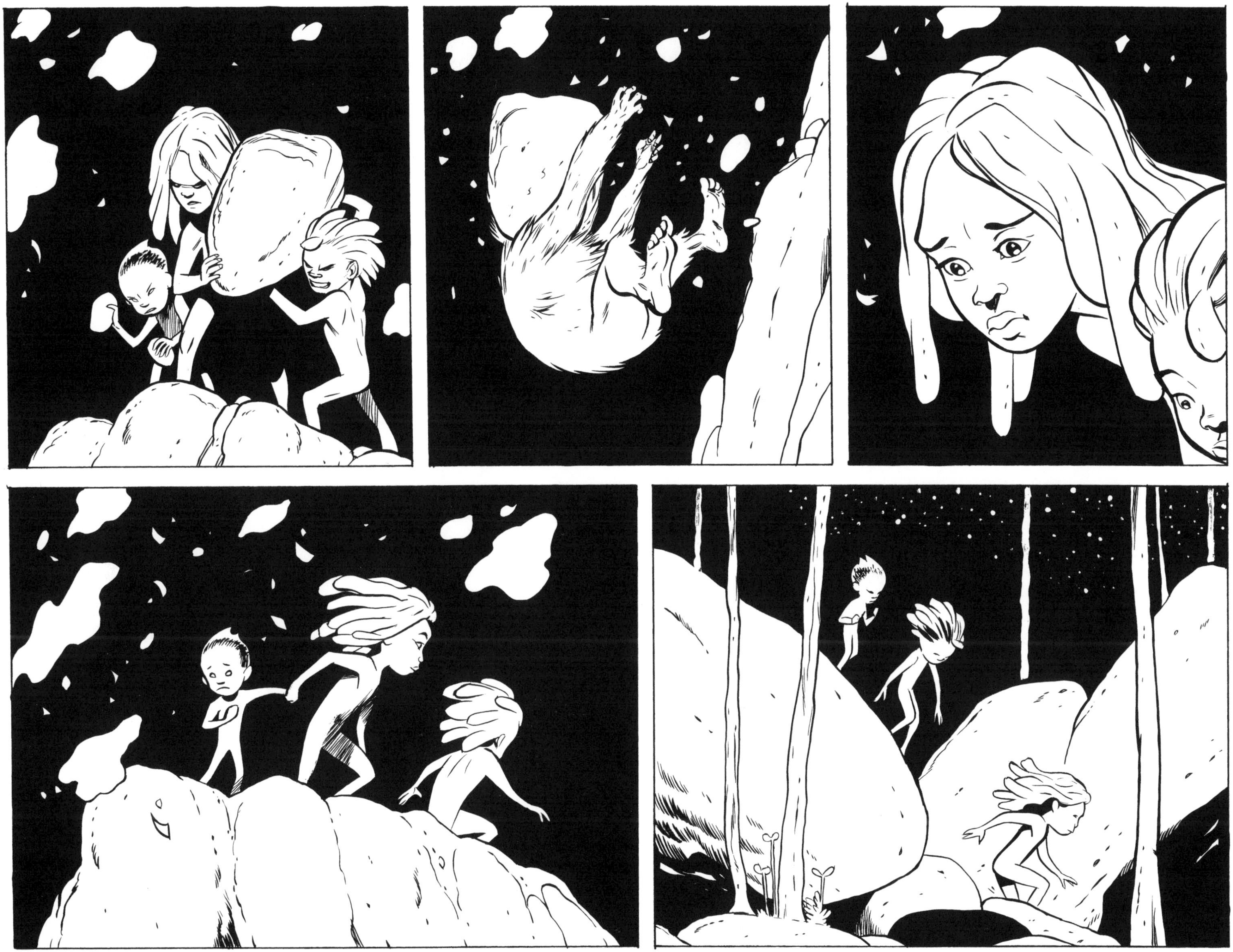

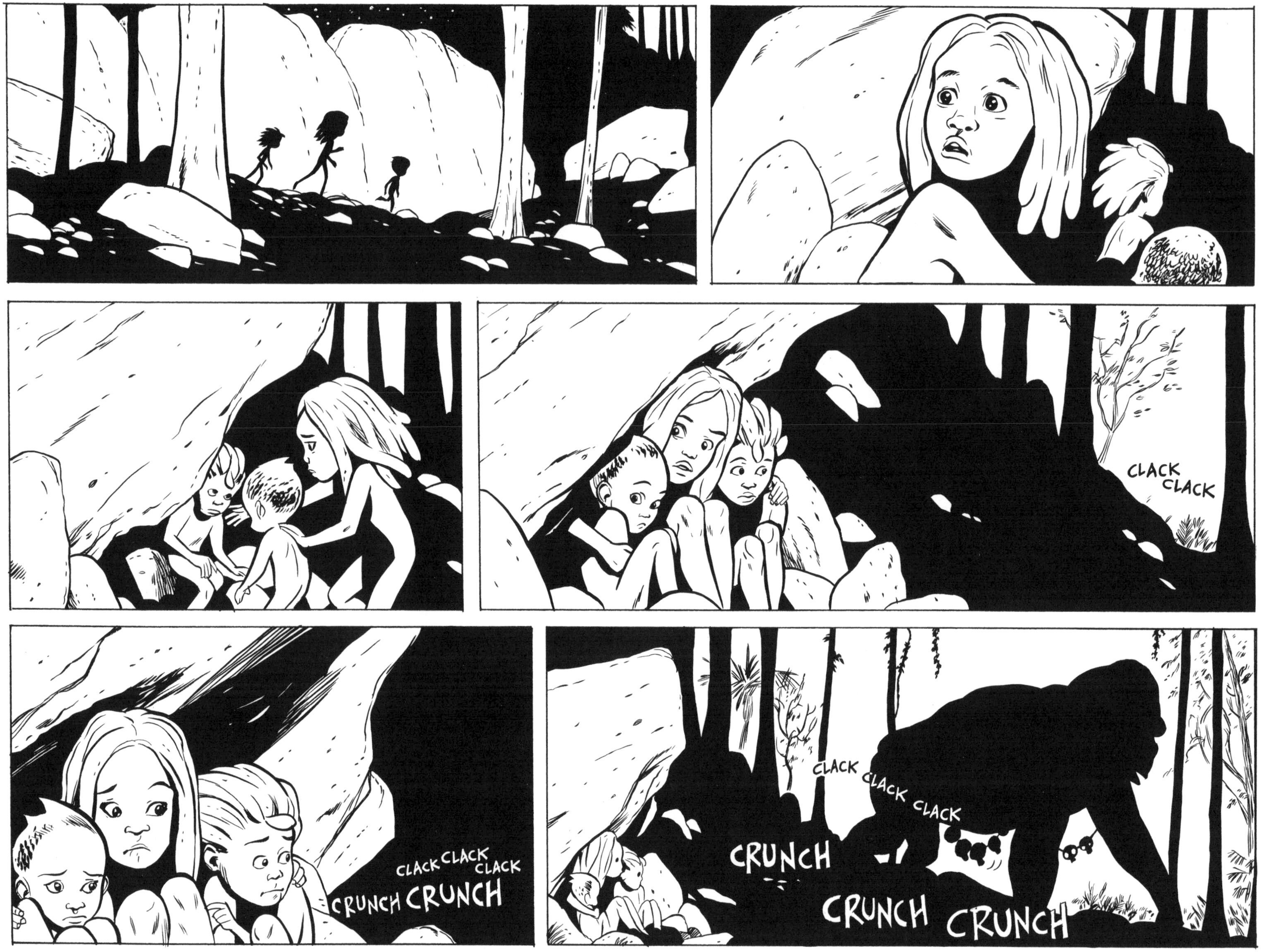
CLACK
CLACK
CLACK CLACK
CLACK
CRUNCH CRUNCH
CLACK
CLACK
CLACK
CRUNCH
CRUNCH
CRUNCH

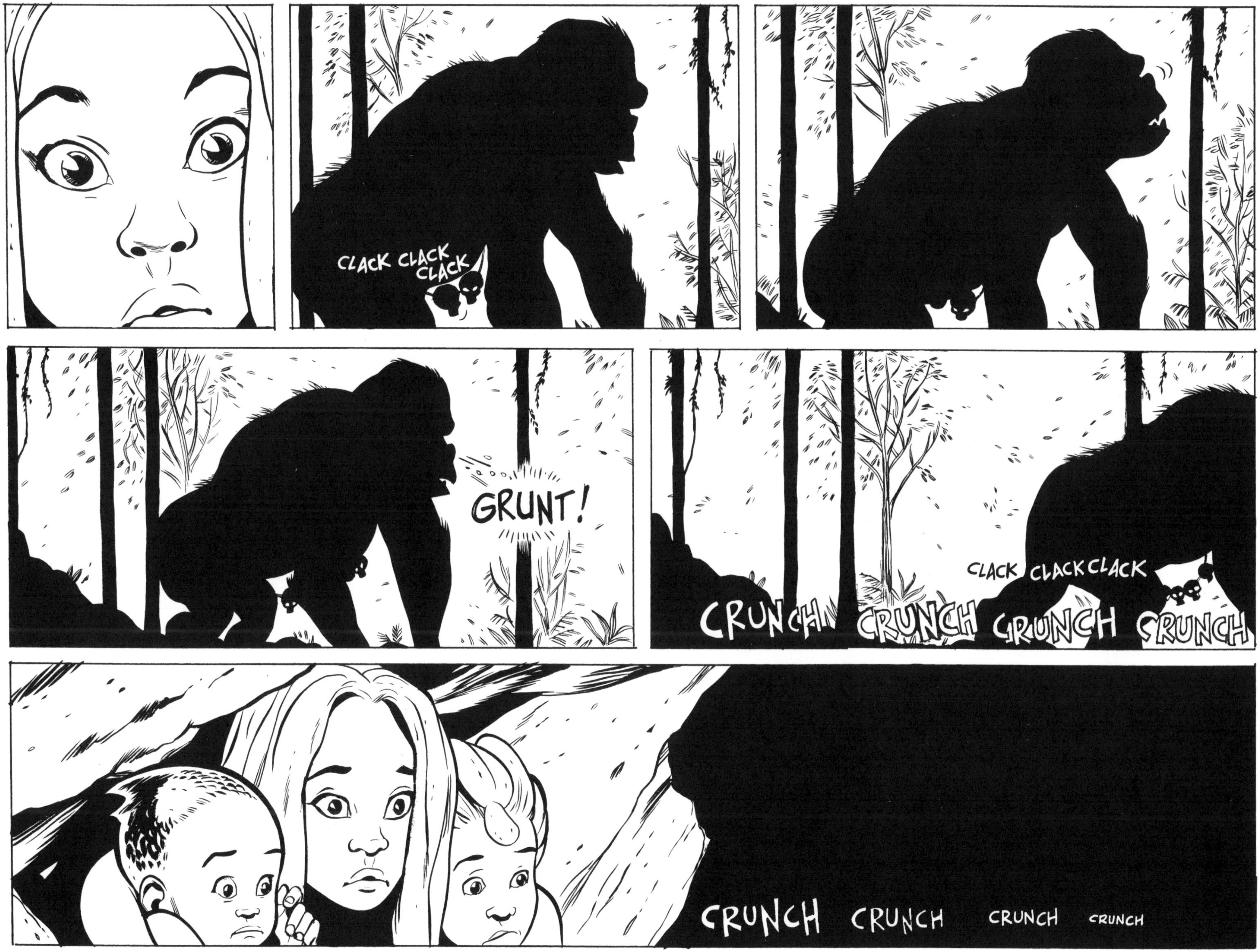
CLACK CLACK CLACK
GRUNT!
CLACK CLACK CLACK
CRUNCH CRUNCH CRUNCH CRUNCH
CRUNCH CRUNCH CRUNCH CRUNCH

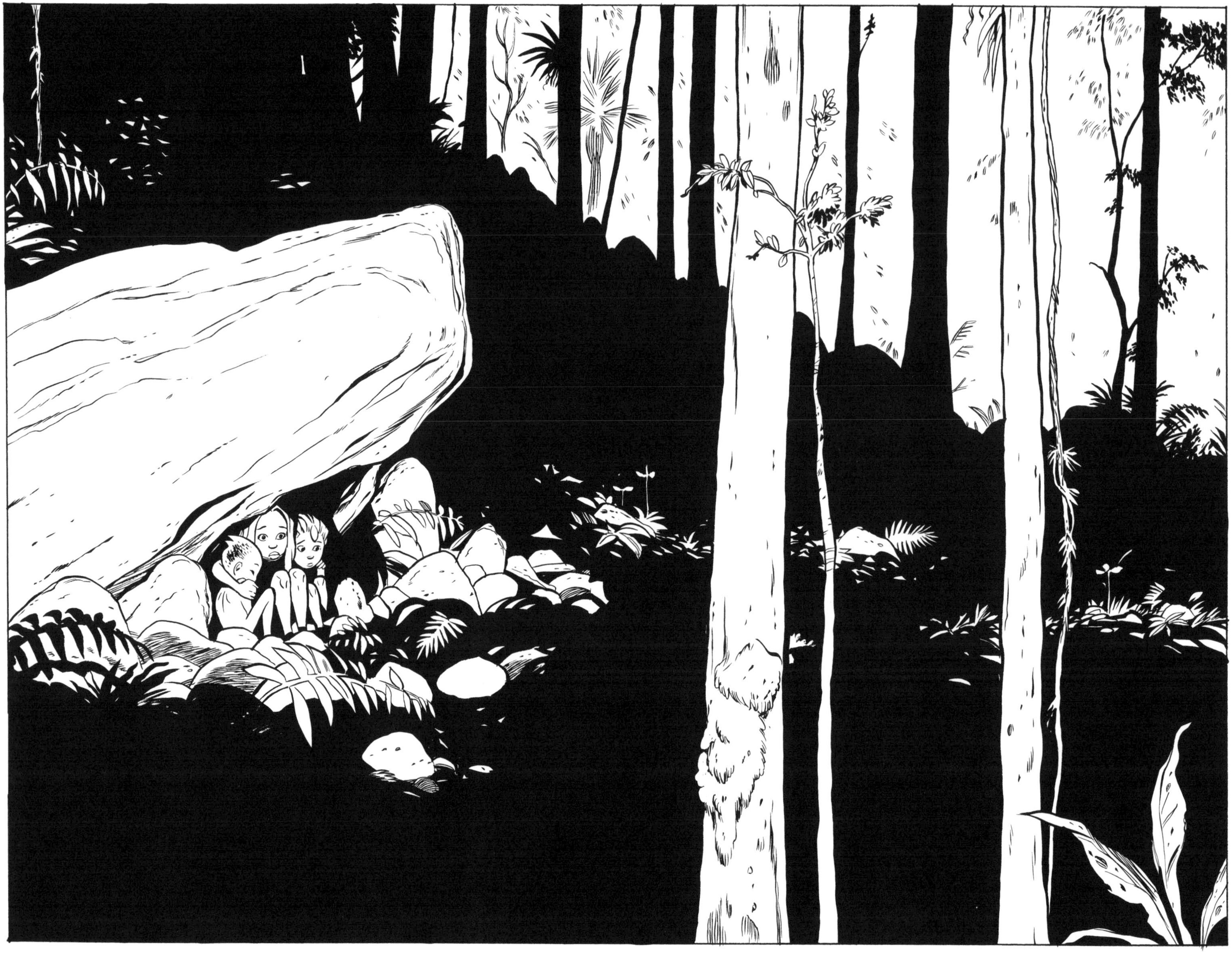

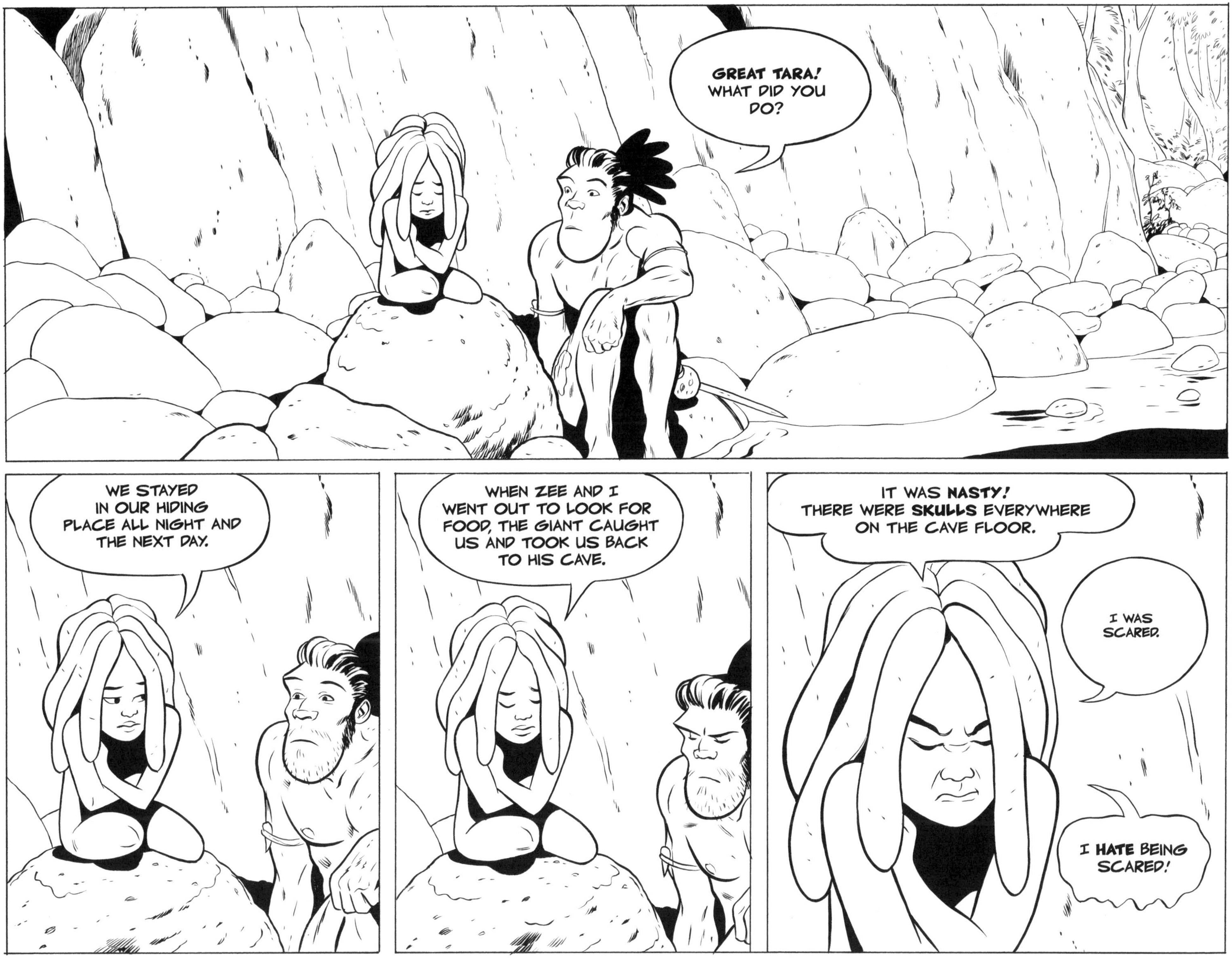
GREAT TARA! WHAT DID YOU DO?
WE STAYED IN OUR HIDING PLACE ALL NIGHT AND THE NEXT DAY.
WHEN ZEE AND I WENT OUT TO LOOK FOR FOOD, THE GIANT CAUGHT US AND TOOK US BACK TO HIS CAVE.
IT WAS NASTY! THERE WERE SKULLS EVERYWHERE ON THE CAVE FLOOR.
I WAS SCARED.
I HATE BEING SCARED!

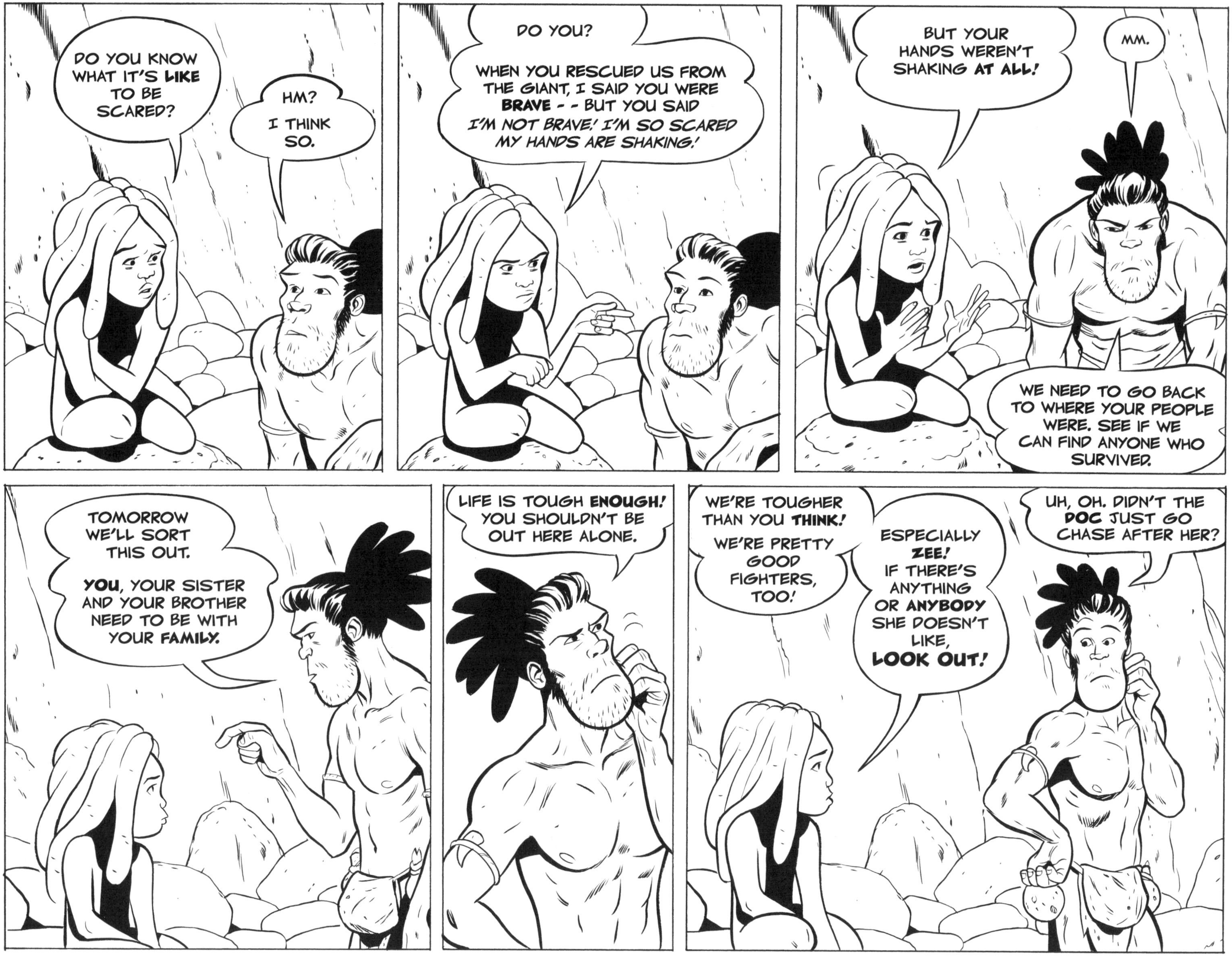
DO YOU KNOW WHAT IT'S **LIKE** TO BE SCARED?
HM? I THINK SO.
DO YOU? WHEN YOU RESCUED US FROM THE GIANT, I SAID YOU WERE **BRAVE** - - BUT YOU SAID *I'M NOT BRAVE! I'M SO SCARED MY HANDS ARE SHAKING!*
BUT YOUR HANDS WEREN'T SHAKING **AT ALL!**
MM.
WE NEED TO GO BACK TO WHERE YOUR PEOPLE WERE. SEE IF WE CAN FIND ANYONE WHO SURVIVED.
TOMORROW WE'LL SORT THIS OUT. **YOU**, YOUR SISTER AND YOUR BROTHER NEED TO BE WITH YOUR **FAMILY.**
LIFE IS TOUGH **ENOUGH!** YOU SHOULDN'T BE OUT HERE ALONE.
WE'RE TOUGHER THAN YOU **THINK!** WE'RE PRETTY GOOD FIGHTERS, TOO!
ESPECIALLY **ZEE!** IF THERE'S ANYTHING OR **ANYBODY** SHE DOESN'T LIKE, **LOOK OUT!**
UH, OH. DIDN'T THE **DOC** JUST GO CHASE AFTER HER?

Two

The Doctor & Miss Zee

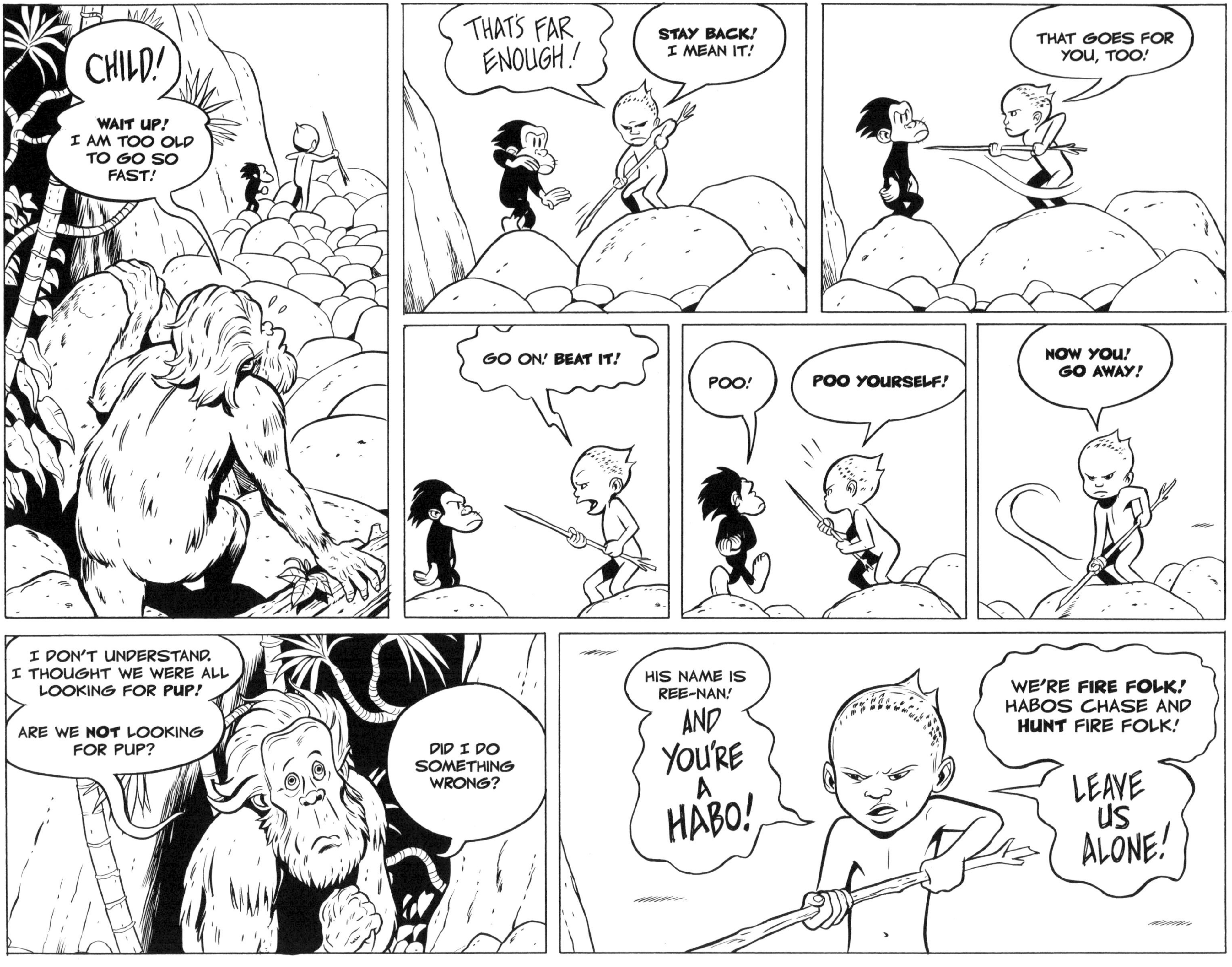
CHILD!
WAIT UP! I AM TOO OLD TO GO SO FAST!
THAT'S FAR ENOUGH!
STAY BACK! I MEAN IT!
THAT GOES FOR YOU, TOO!
GO ON! BEAT IT!
POO!
POO YOURSELF!
NOW YOU! GO AWAY!
I DON'T UNDERSTAND. I THOUGHT WE WERE ALL LOOKING FOR PUP!
ARE WE NOT LOOKING FOR PUP?
DID I DO SOMETHING WRONG?
HIS NAME IS REE-NAN!
AND YOU'RE A HABO!
WE'RE FIRE FOLK! HABOS CHASE AND HUNT FIRE FOLK!
LEAVE US ALONE!

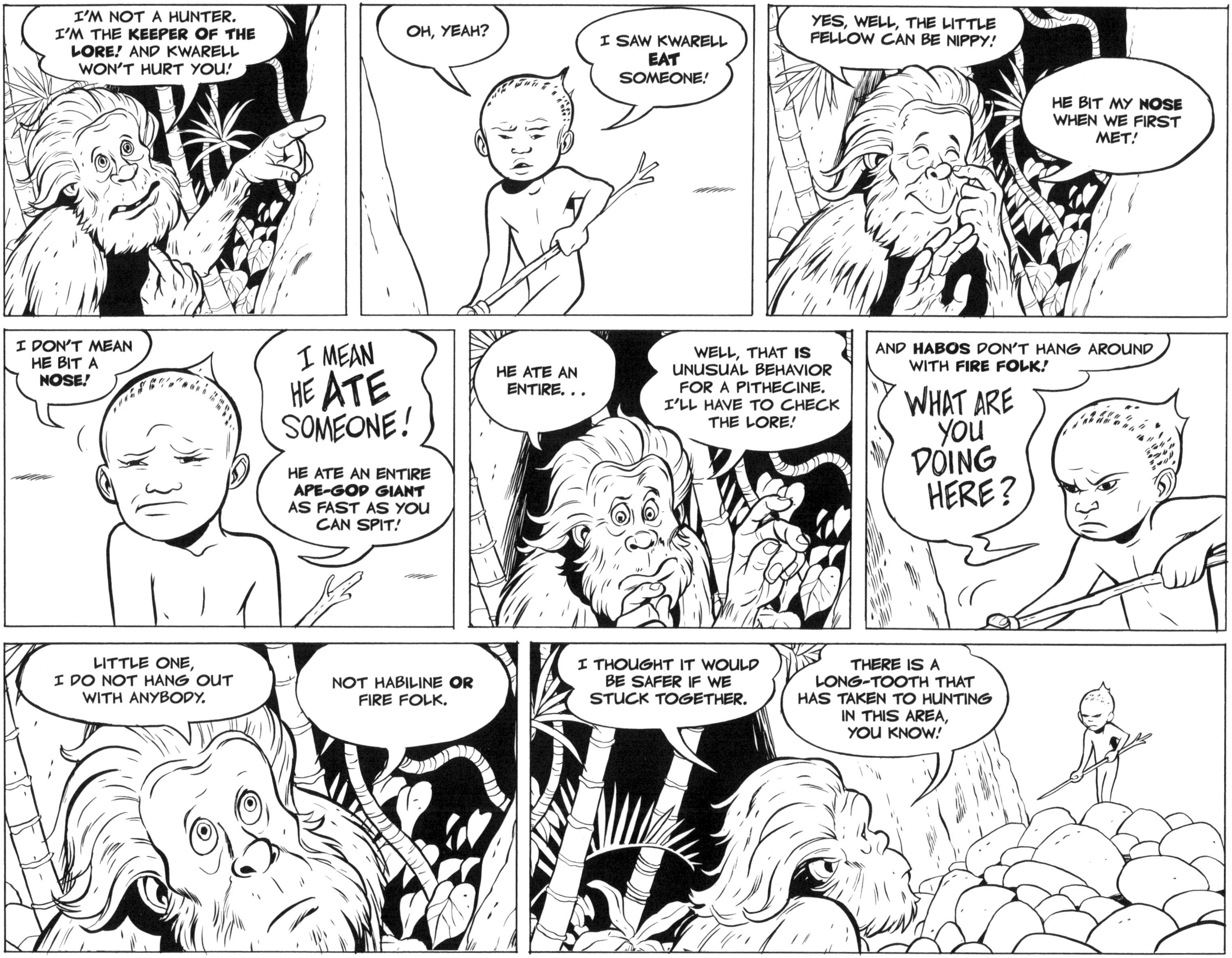
I'M NOT A HUNTER. I'M THE KEEPER OF THE LORE! AND KWARELL WON'T HURT YOU!
OH, YEAH?
I SAW KWARELL EAT SOMEONE!
YES, WELL, THE LITTLE FELLOW CAN BE NIPPY!
HE BIT MY NOSE WHEN WE FIRST MET!
I DON'T MEAN HE BIT A NOSE!
I MEAN HE ATE SOMEONE!
HE ATE AN ENTIRE APE-GOD GIANT AS FAST AS YOU CAN SPIT!
HE ATE AN ENTIRE...
WELL, THAT IS UNUSUAL BEHAVIOR FOR A PITHECINE. I'LL HAVE TO CHECK THE LORE!
AND HABOS DON'T HANG AROUND WITH FIRE FOLK!
WHAT ARE YOU DOING HERE?
LITTLE ONE, I DO NOT HANG OUT WITH ANYBODY.
NOT HABILINE OR FIRE FOLK.
I THOUGHT IT WOULD BE SAFER IF WE STUCK TOGETHER.
THERE IS A LONG-TOOTH THAT HAS TAKEN TO HUNTING IN THIS AREA, YOU KNOW!

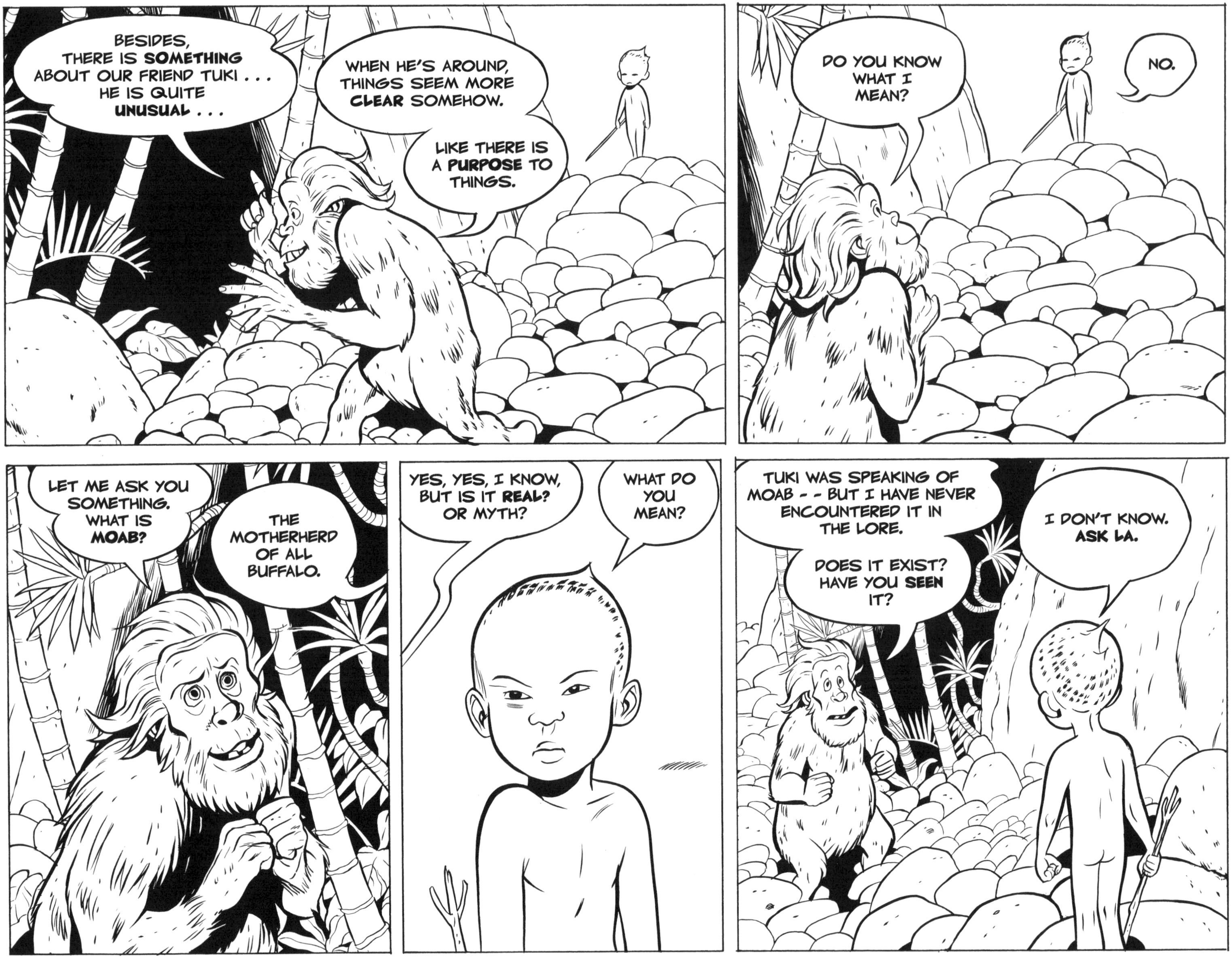

BESIDES, THERE IS **SOMETHING** ABOUT OUR FRIEND TUKI . . . HE IS QUITE **UNUSUAL** . . .
WHEN HE'S AROUND, THINGS SEEM MORE **CLEAR** SOMEHOW.
LIKE THERE IS A **PURPOSE** TO THINGS.
DO YOU KNOW WHAT I MEAN?
NO.
LET ME ASK YOU SOMETHING. WHAT IS **MOAB?**
THE MOTHERHERD OF ALL BUFFALO.
YES, YES, I KNOW, BUT IS IT **REAL?** OR MYTH?
WHAT DO YOU MEAN?
TUKI WAS SPEAKING OF MOAB - - BUT I HAVE NEVER ENCOUNTERED IT IN THE LORE.
DOES IT EXIST? HAVE YOU **SEEN** IT?
I DON'T KNOW. **ASK LA.**

YES! I WILL TALK TO LA! BUT FIRST I MUST SPEAK TO THE FORCES OF THE HIDDEN WORLD!
IF YOU WILL EXCUSE ME, I WILL GO NOW TO COMMUNE WITH THEM!
WHATEVER.
CHILD?
PLEASE DON'T CALL ME HABO. IT DOES NOT SOUND NICE WHEN YOU SAY IT.

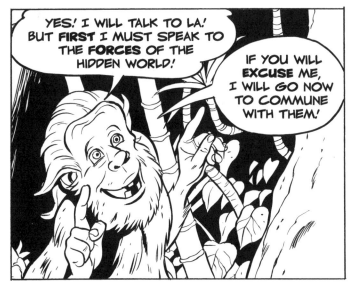

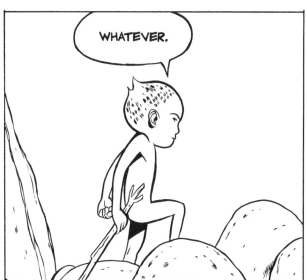

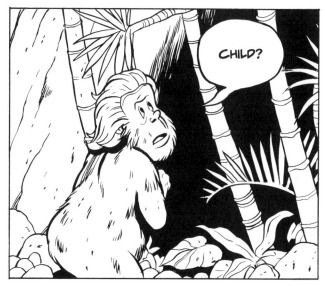

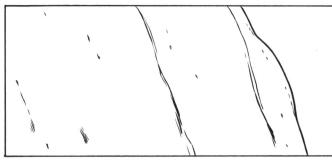

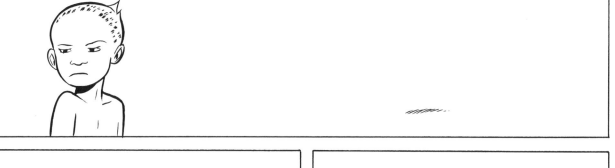

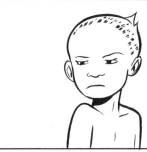

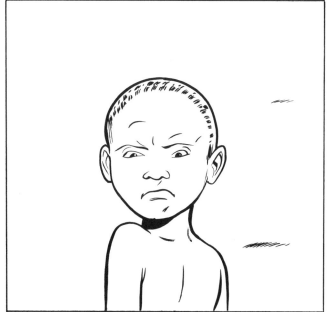

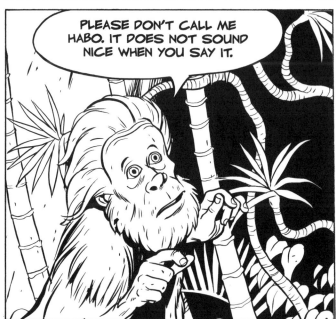

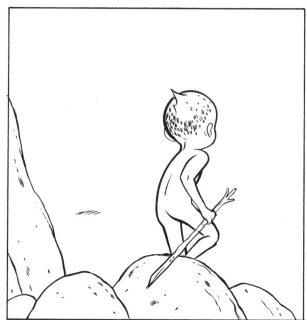

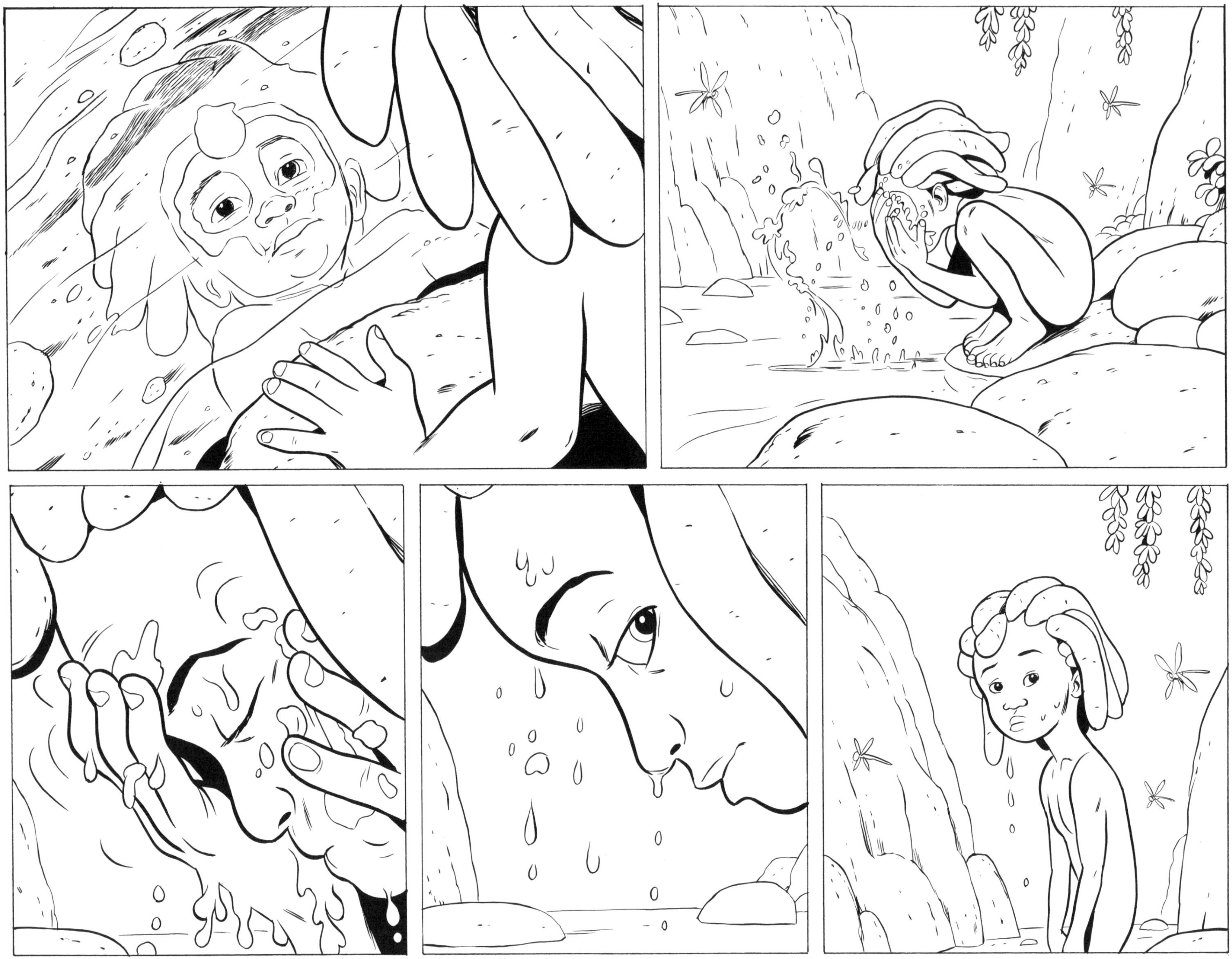

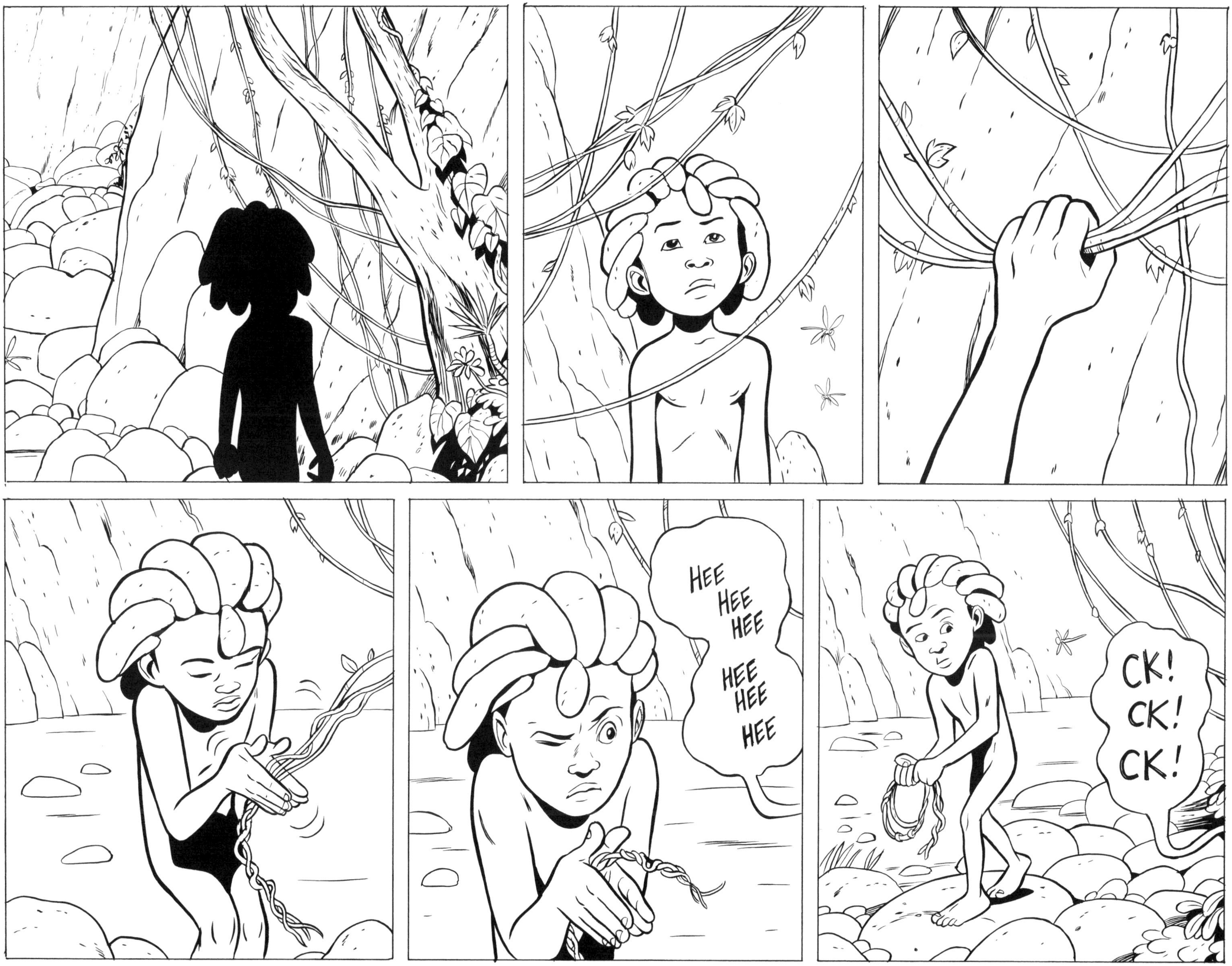
HEE HEE HEE
HEE HEE HEE
CK! CK! CK!

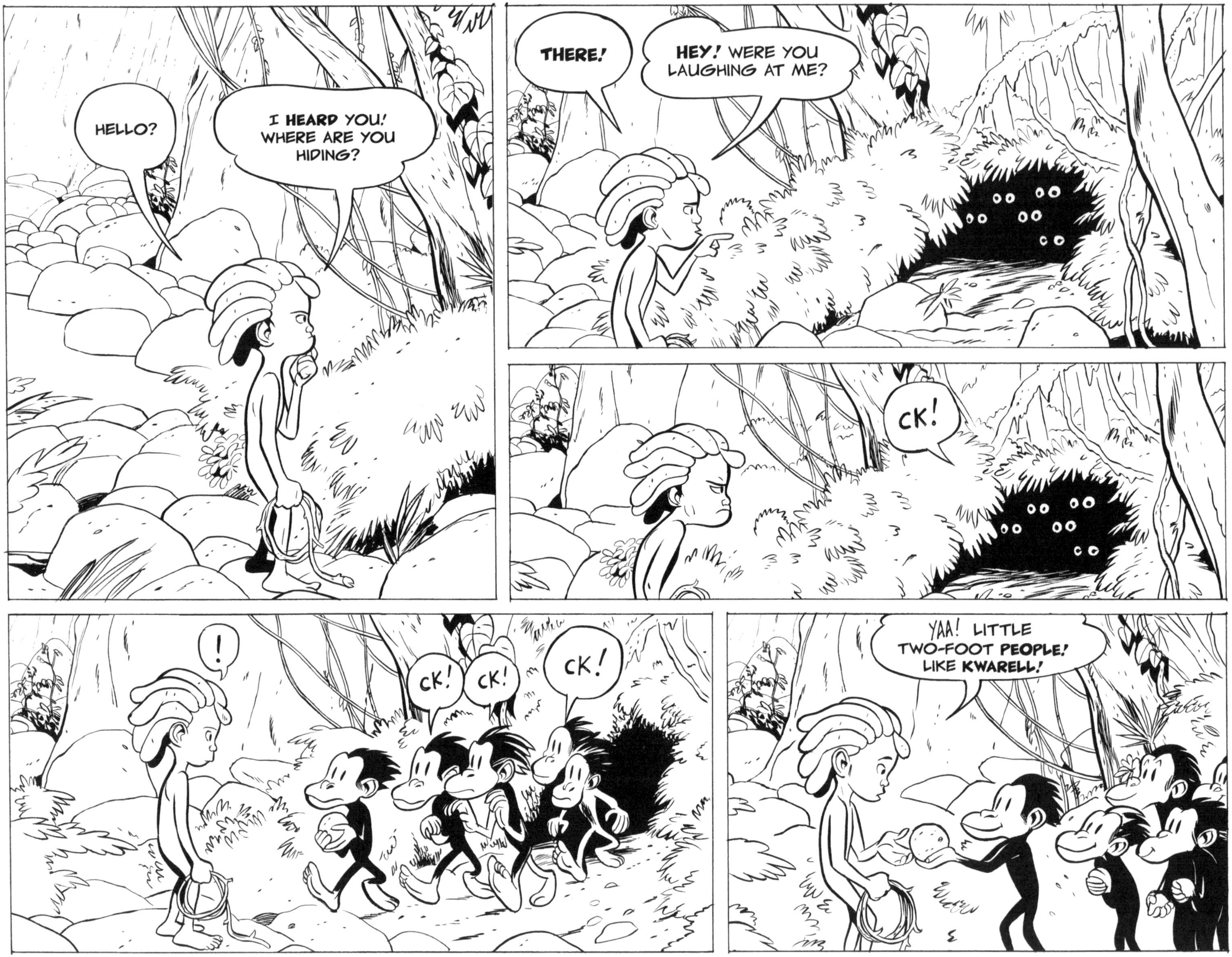
HELLO?
I HEARD YOU! WHERE ARE YOU HIDING?
THERE!
HEY! WERE YOU LAUGHING AT ME?
CK!
!
CK!
CK!
CK!
YAA! LITTLE TWO-FOOT PEOPLE! LIKE KWARELL!

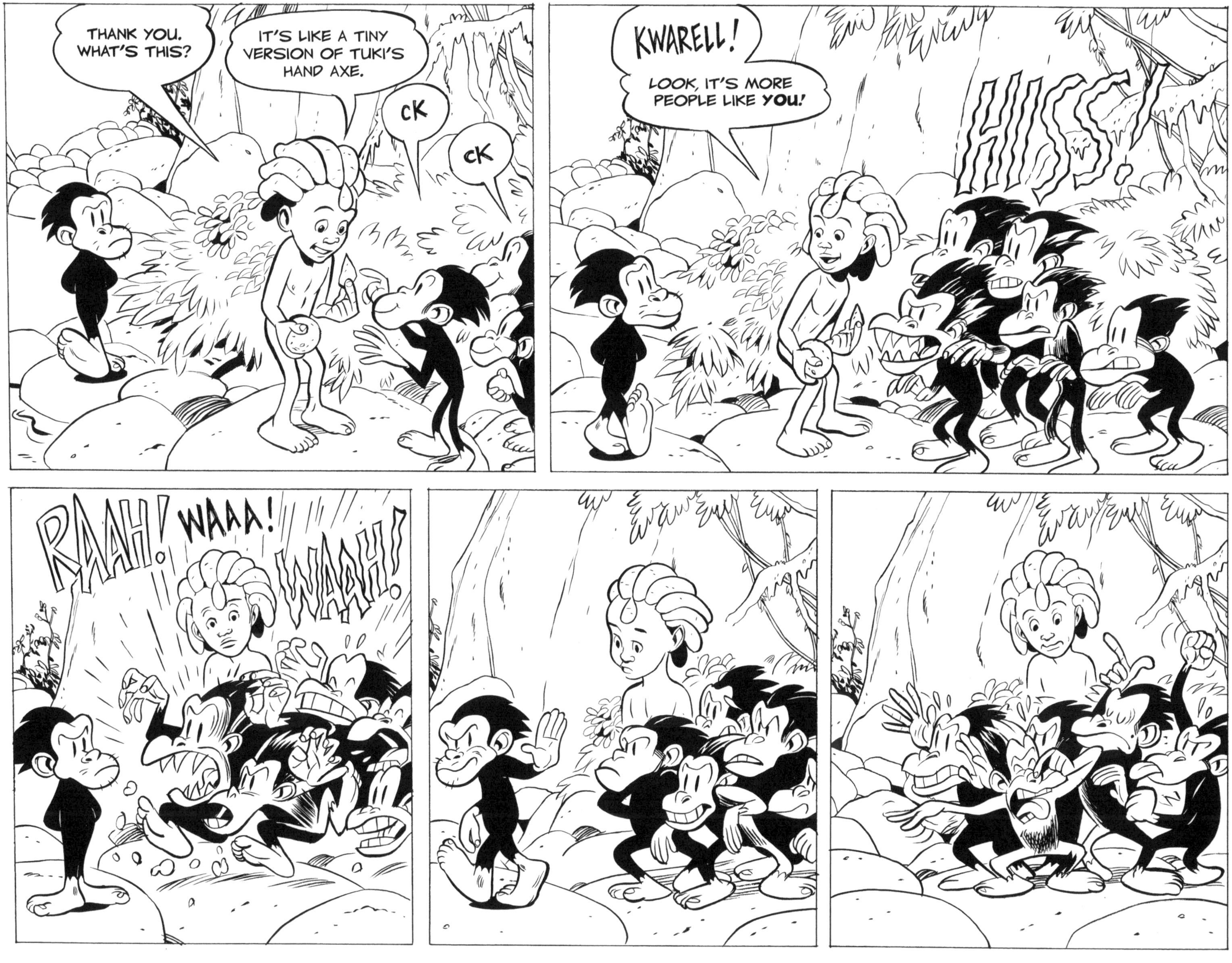
THANK YOU. WHAT'S THIS?
IT'S LIKE A TINY VERSION OF TUKI'S HAND AXE.
CK
CK
KWARELL!
LOOK, IT'S MORE PEOPLE LIKE YOU!
HISSS!
RAAH!
WAAA!
WAAH!

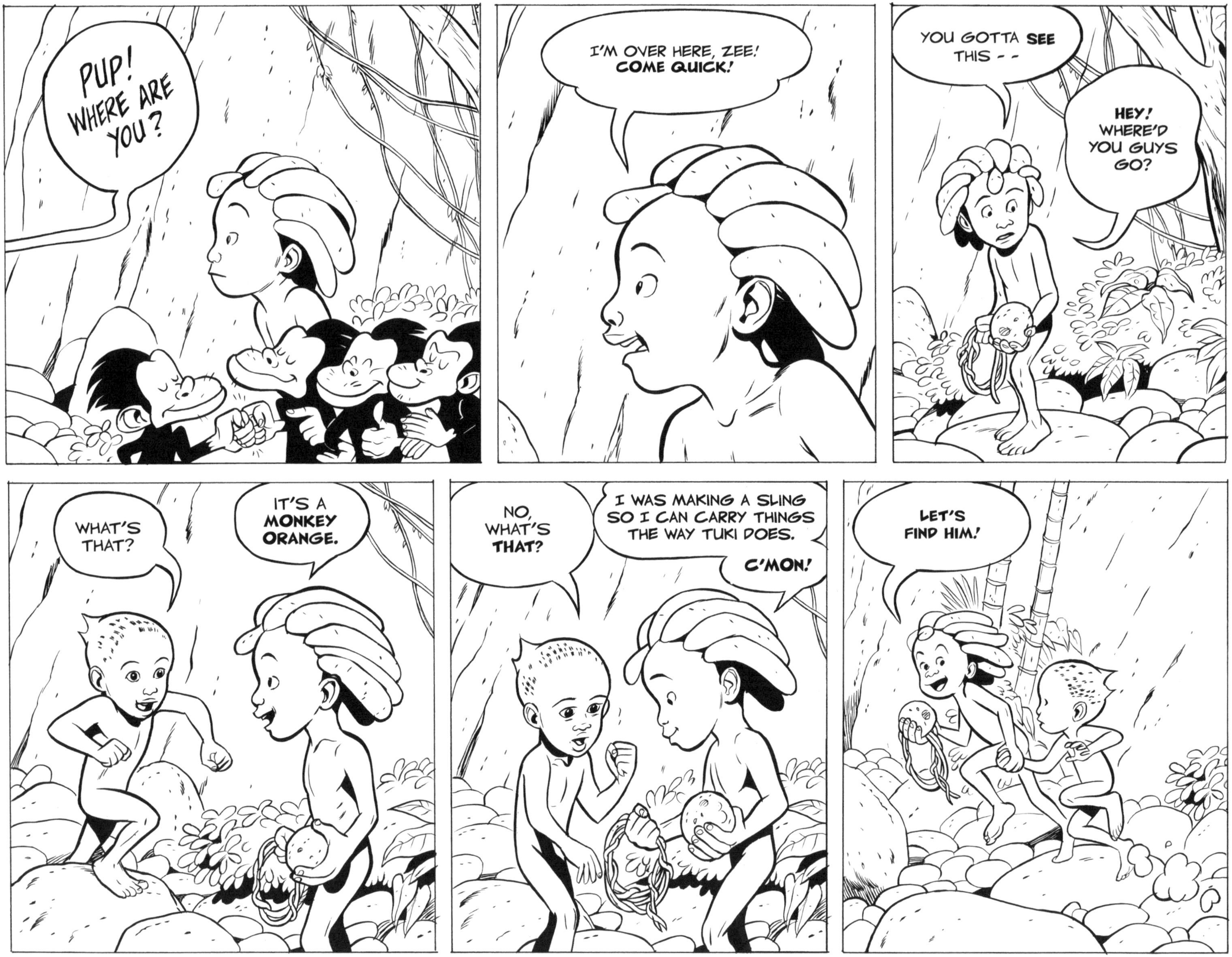
PUP! WHERE ARE YOU?
I'M OVER HERE, ZEE! COME QUICK!
YOU GOTTA SEE THIS --
HEY! WHERE'D YOU GUYS GO?
WHAT'S THAT?
IT'S A MONKEY ORANGE.
NO, WHAT'S THAT?
I WAS MAKING A SLING SO I CAN CARRY THINGS THE WAY TUKI DOES.
C'MON!
LET'S FIND HIM!

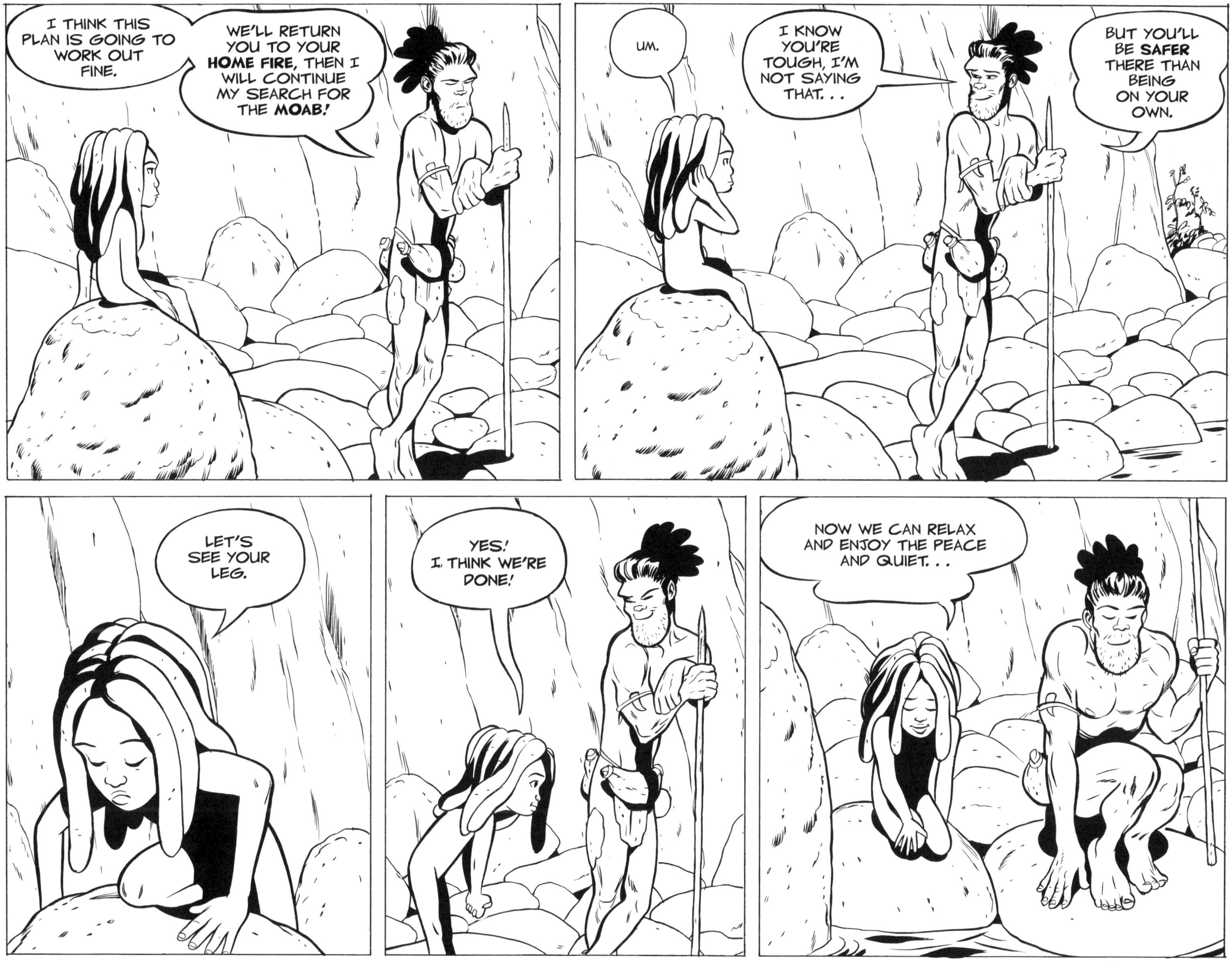
I THINK THIS PLAN IS GOING TO WORK OUT FINE.
WE'LL RETURN YOU TO YOUR **HOME FIRE**, THEN I WILL CONTINUE MY SEARCH FOR THE **MOAB**!
UM.
I KNOW YOU'RE TOUGH, I'M NOT SAYING THAT. . .
BUT YOU'LL BE **SAFER** THERE THAN BEING ON YOUR OWN.
LET'S SEE YOUR LEG.
YES! I THINK WE'RE DONE!
NOW WE CAN RELAX AND ENJOY THE PEACE AND QUIET. . .

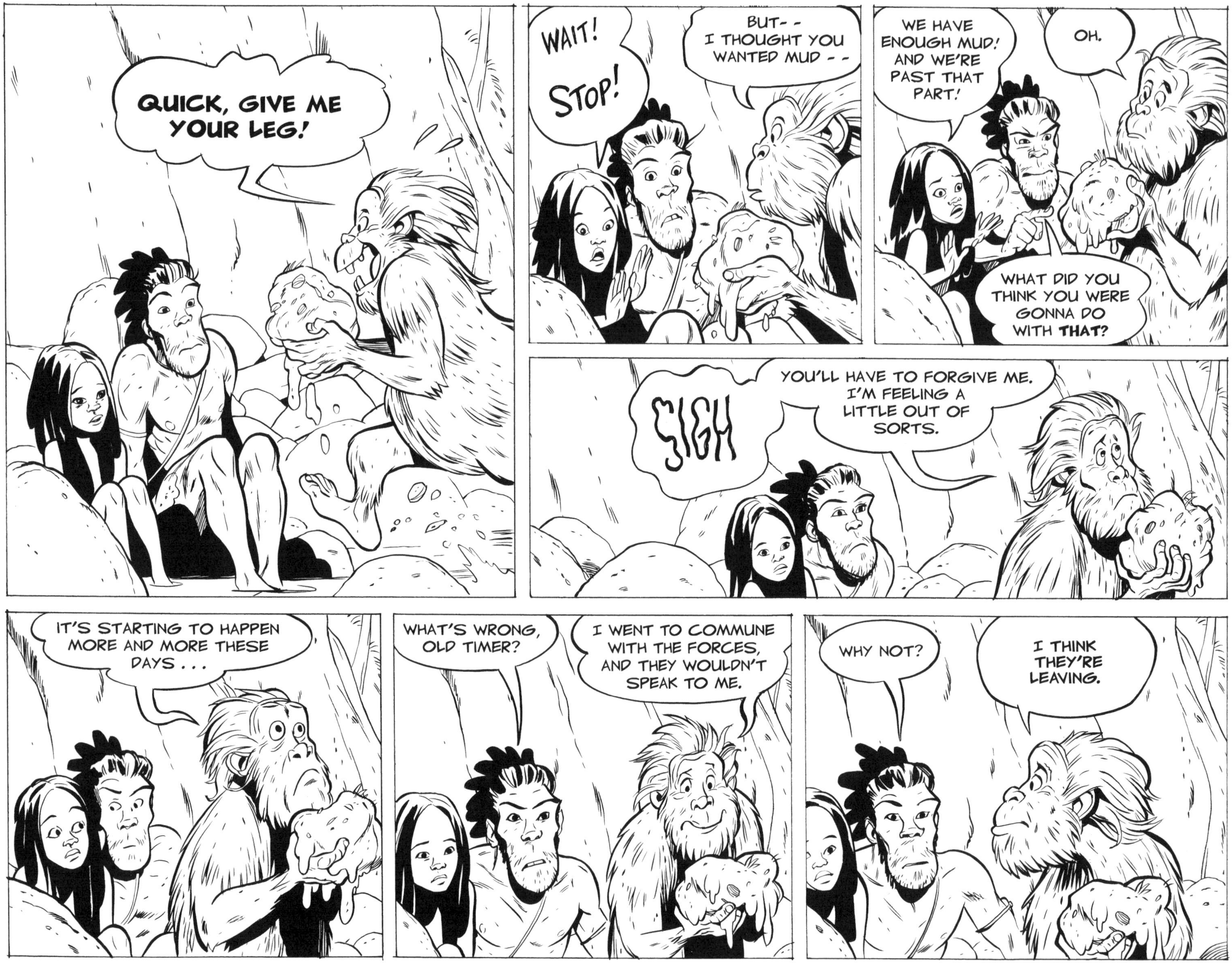
QUICK, GIVE ME YOUR LEG!
WAIT!
STOP!
BUT- - I THOUGHT YOU WANTED MUD - -
WE HAVE ENOUGH MUD! AND WE'RE PAST THAT PART!
OH.
WHAT DID YOU THINK YOU WERE GONNA DO WITH THAT?
SIGH
YOU'LL HAVE TO FORGIVE ME. I'M FEELING A LITTLE OUT OF SORTS.
IT'S STARTING TO HAPPEN MORE AND MORE THESE DAYS . . .
WHAT'S WRONG, OLD TIMER?
I WENT TO COMMUNE WITH THE FORCES, AND THEY WOULDN'T SPEAK TO ME.
WHY NOT?
I THINK THEY'RE LEAVING.

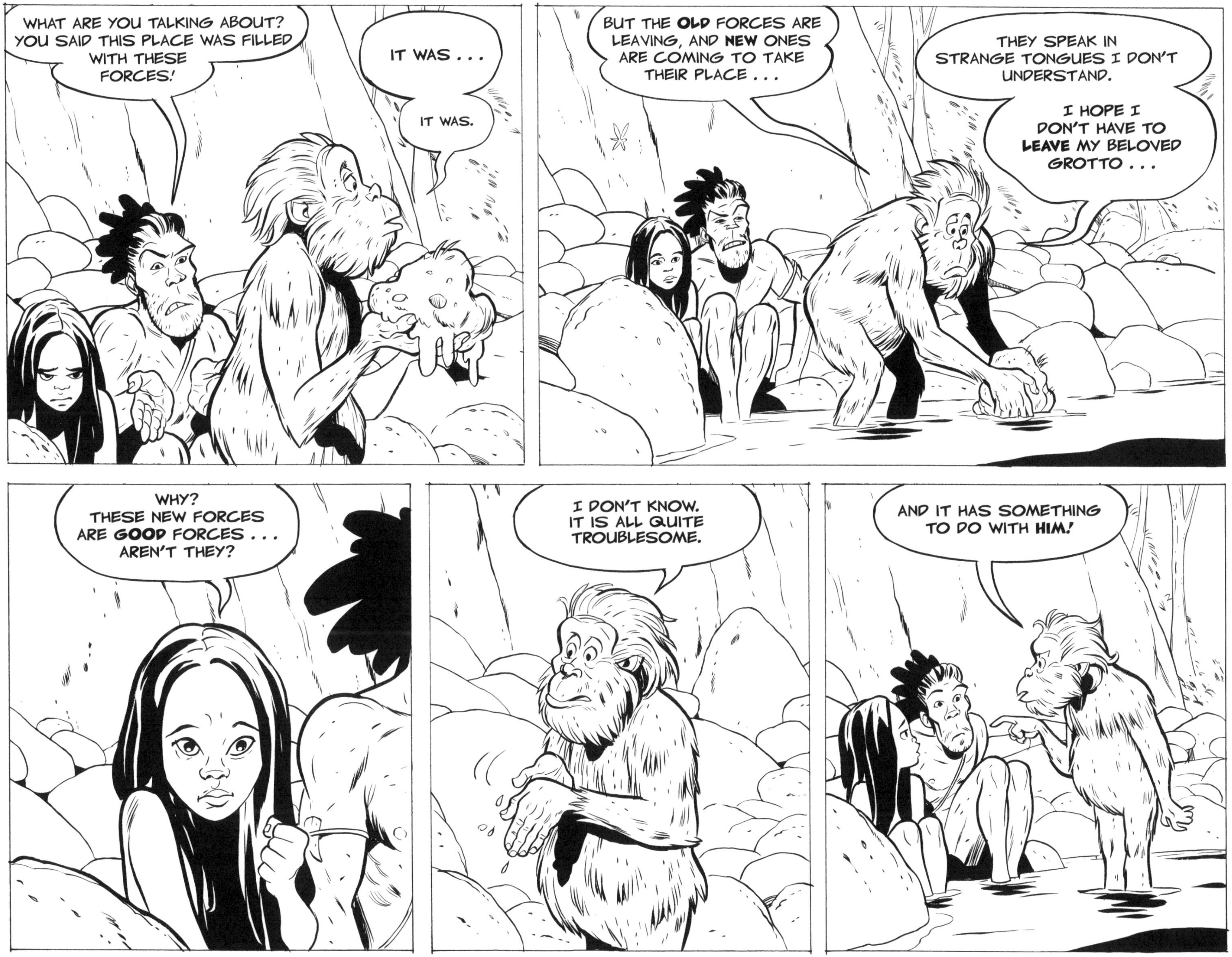
WHAT ARE YOU TALKING ABOUT? YOU SAID THIS PLACE WAS FILLED WITH THESE FORCES!
IT WAS . . .
IT WAS.
BUT THE OLD FORCES ARE LEAVING, AND NEW ONES ARE COMING TO TAKE THEIR PLACE . . .
THEY SPEAK IN STRANGE TONGUES I DON'T UNDERSTAND.
I HOPE I DON'T HAVE TO LEAVE MY BELOVED GROTTO . . .
WHY? THESE NEW FORCES ARE GOOD FORCES . . . AREN'T THEY?
I DON'T KNOW. IT IS ALL QUITE TROUBLESOME.
AND IT HAS SOMETHING TO DO WITH HIM!

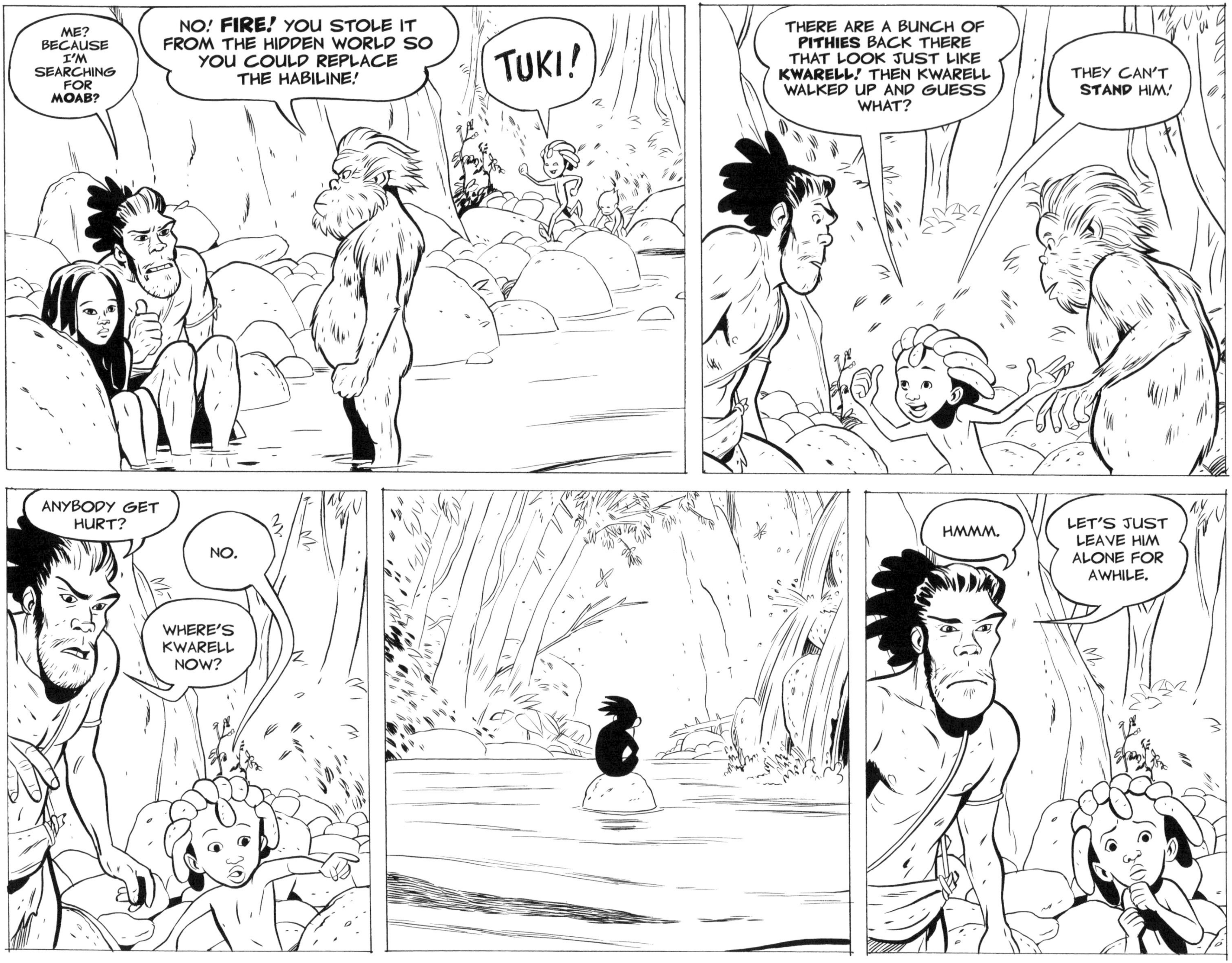
ME? BECAUSE I'M SEARCHING FOR MOAB?
NO! FIRE! YOU STOLE IT FROM THE HIDDEN WORLD SO YOU COULD REPLACE THE HABILINE!
TUKI!
THERE ARE A BUNCH OF PITHIES BACK THERE THAT LOOK JUST LIKE KWARELL! THEN KWARELL WALKED UP AND GUESS WHAT?
THEY CAN'T STAND HIM!
ANYBODY GET HURT?
NO.
WHERE'S KWARELL NOW?
HMMM.
LET'S JUST LEAVE HIM ALONE FOR AWHILE.

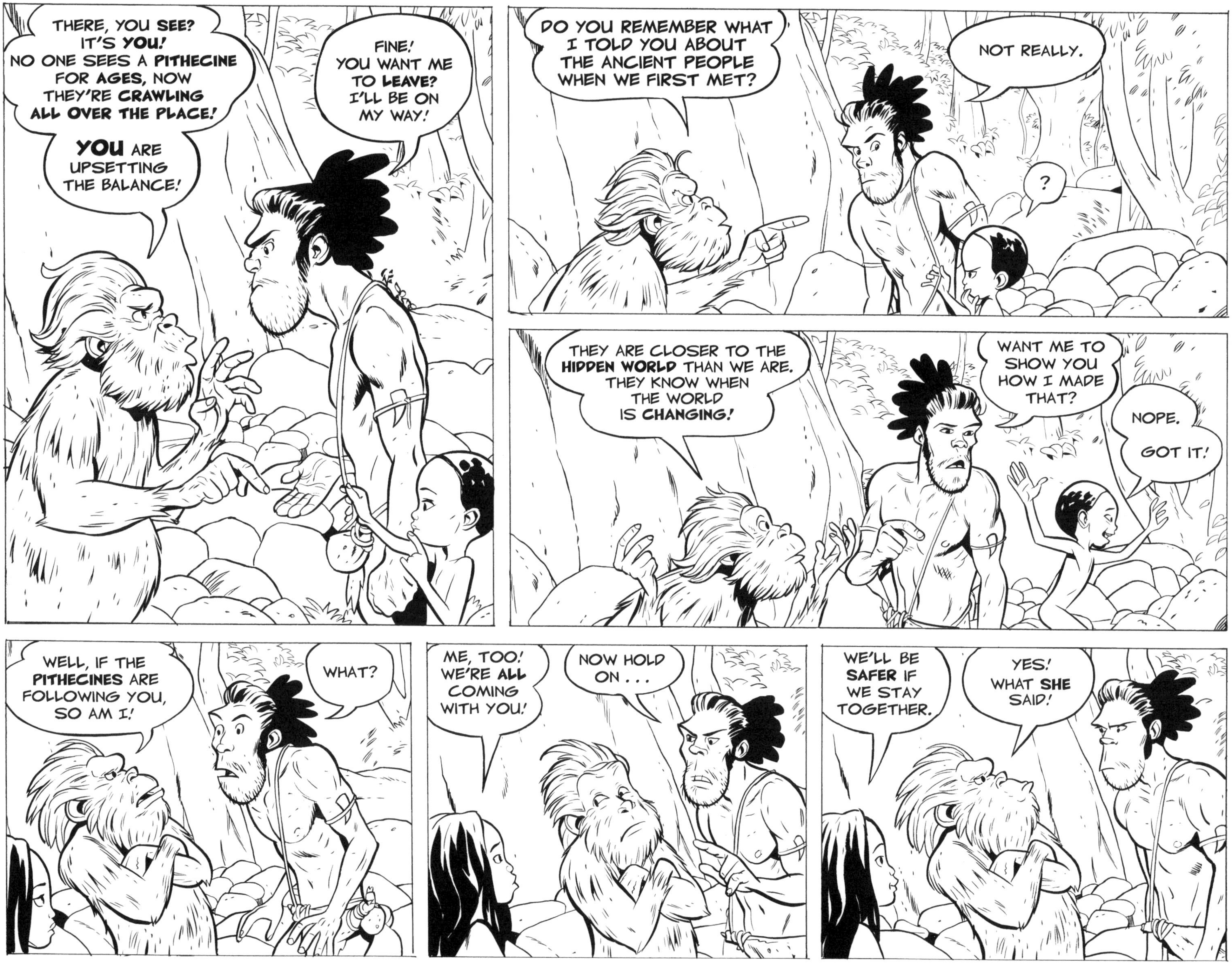
THERE, YOU SEE? IT'S YOU! NO ONE SEES A PITHECINE FOR AGES, NOW THEY'RE CRAWLING ALL OVER THE PLACE!
YOU ARE UPSETTING THE BALANCE!
FINE! YOU WANT ME TO LEAVE? I'LL BE ON MY WAY!
DO YOU REMEMBER WHAT I TOLD YOU ABOUT THE ANCIENT PEOPLE WHEN WE FIRST MET?
NOT REALLY.
?
THEY ARE CLOSER TO THE HIDDEN WORLD THAN WE ARE. THEY KNOW WHEN THE WORLD IS CHANGING!
WANT ME TO SHOW YOU HOW I MADE THAT?
NOPE.
GOT IT!
WELL, IF THE PITHECINES ARE FOLLOWING YOU, SO AM I!
WHAT?
ME, TOO! WE'RE ALL COMING WITH YOU!
NOW HOLD ON . . .
WE'LL BE SAFER IF WE STAY TOGETHER.
YES! WHAT SHE SAID!

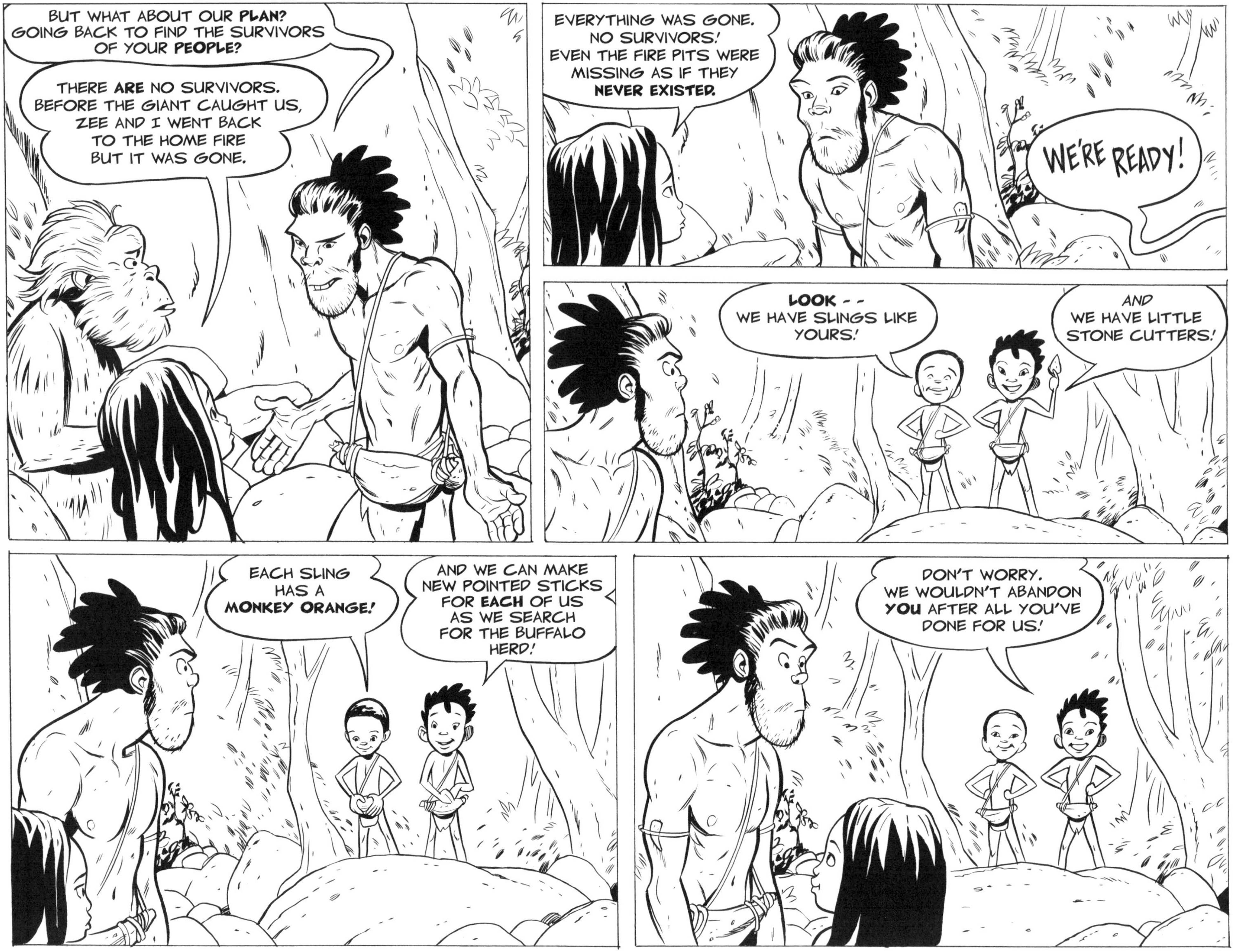

BUT WHAT ABOUT OUR PLAN? GOING BACK TO FIND THE SURVIVORS OF YOUR PEOPLE?
THERE ARE NO SURVIVORS. BEFORE THE GIANT CAUGHT US, ZEE AND I WENT BACK TO THE HOME FIRE BUT IT WAS GONE.
EVERYTHING WAS GONE. NO SURVIVORS! EVEN THE FIRE PITS WERE MISSING AS IF THEY NEVER EXISTED.
WE'RE READY!
LOOK -- WE HAVE SLINGS LIKE YOURS!
AND WE HAVE LITTLE STONE CUTTERS!
EACH SLING HAS A MONKEY ORANGE!
AND WE CAN MAKE NEW POINTED STICKS FOR EACH OF US AS WE SEARCH FOR THE BUFFALO HERD!
DON'T WORRY. WE WOULDN'T ABANDON YOU AFTER ALL YOU'VE DONE FOR US!

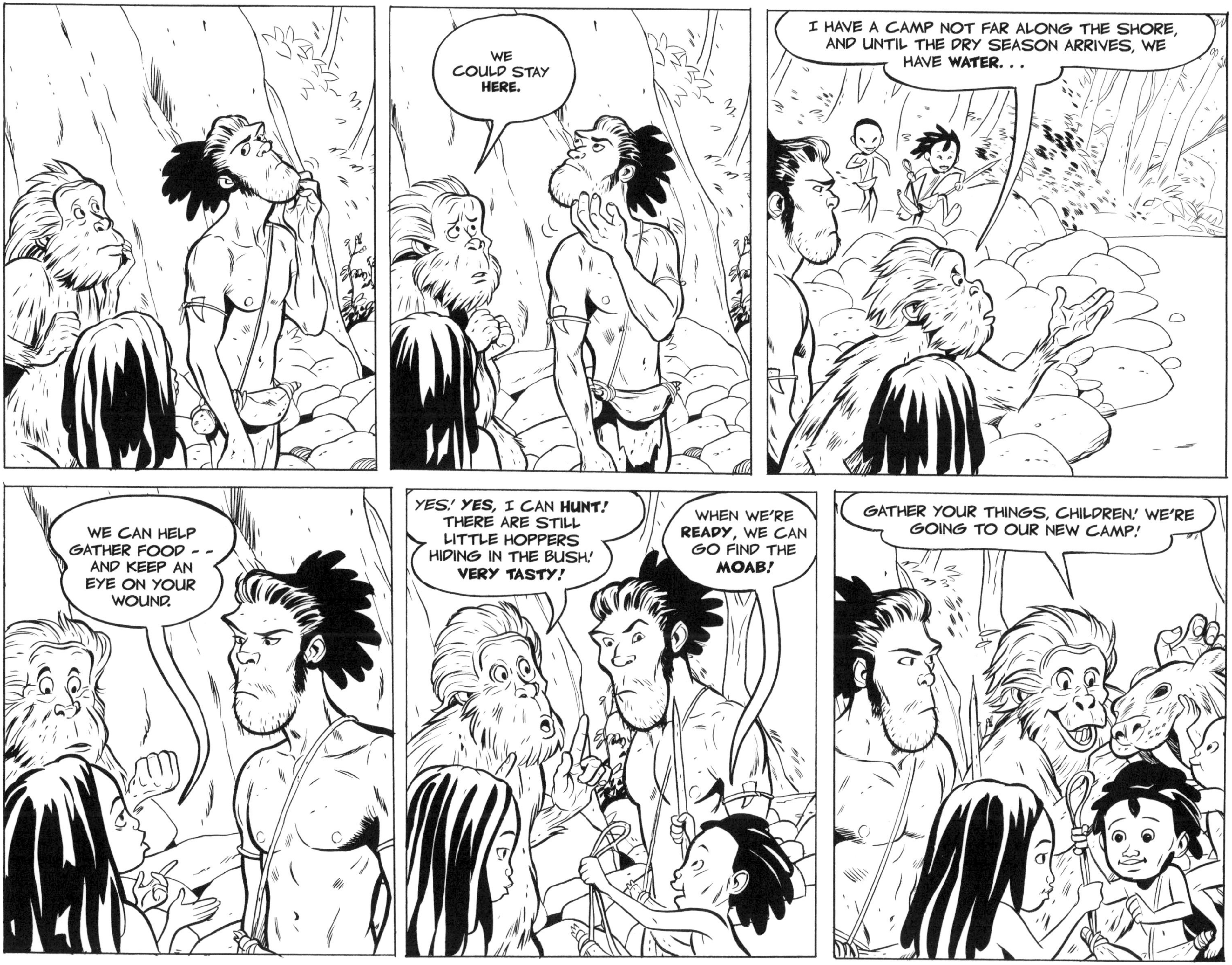
WE COULD STAY **HERE.**
I HAVE A CAMP NOT FAR ALONG THE SHORE, AND UNTIL THE DRY SEASON ARRIVES, WE HAVE **WATER. . .**
WE CAN HELP GATHER FOOD - - AND KEEP AN EYE ON YOUR WOUND.
YES! **YES,** I CAN **HUNT!** THERE ARE STILL LITTLE HOPPERS HIDING IN THE BUSH! **VERY TASTY!**
WHEN WE'RE **READY,** WE CAN GO FIND THE **MOAB!**
GATHER YOUR THINGS, CHILDREN! WE'RE GOING TO OUR NEW CAMP!

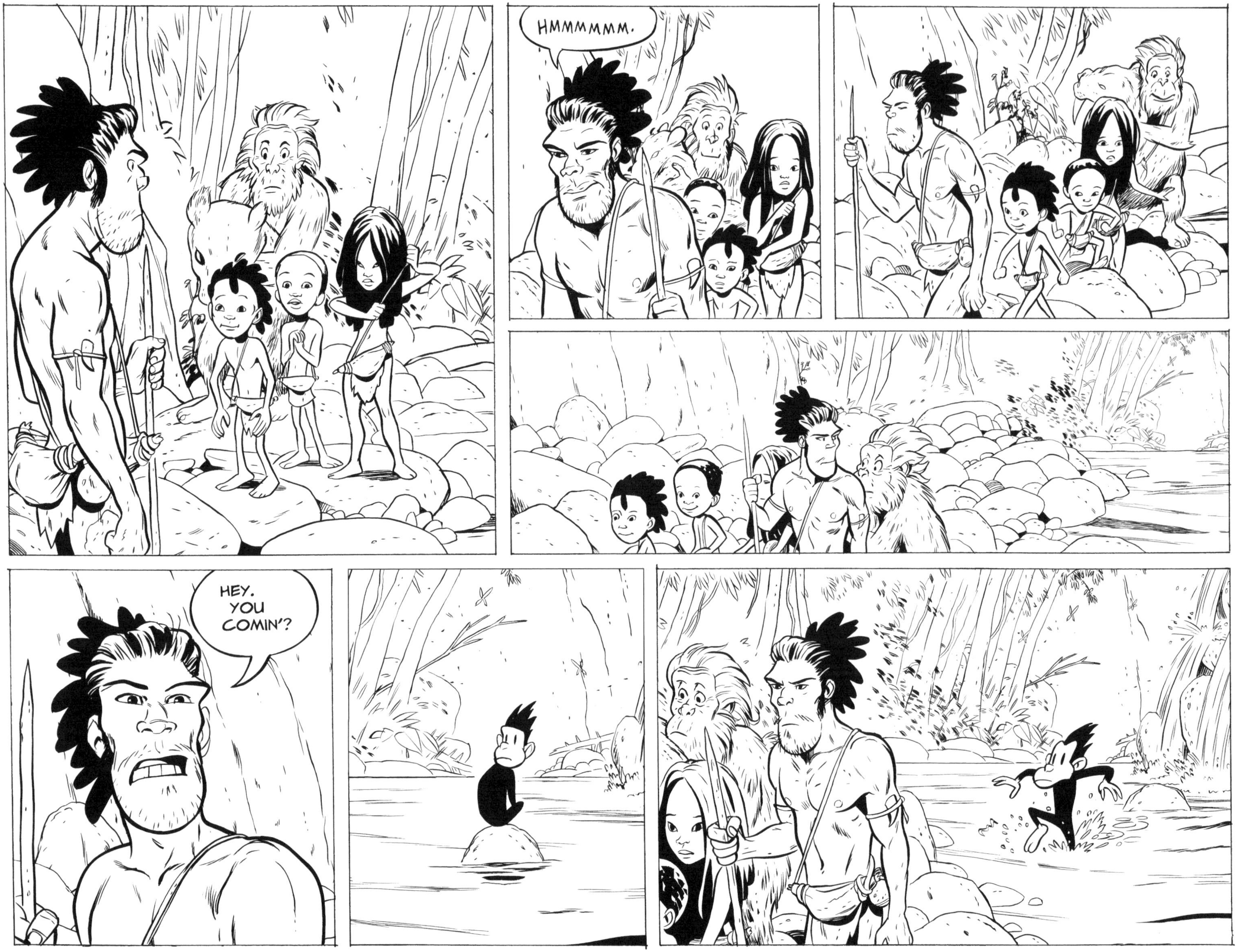
HMMMMMM.
HEY. YOU COMIN'?

Three

Hunting & Gathering

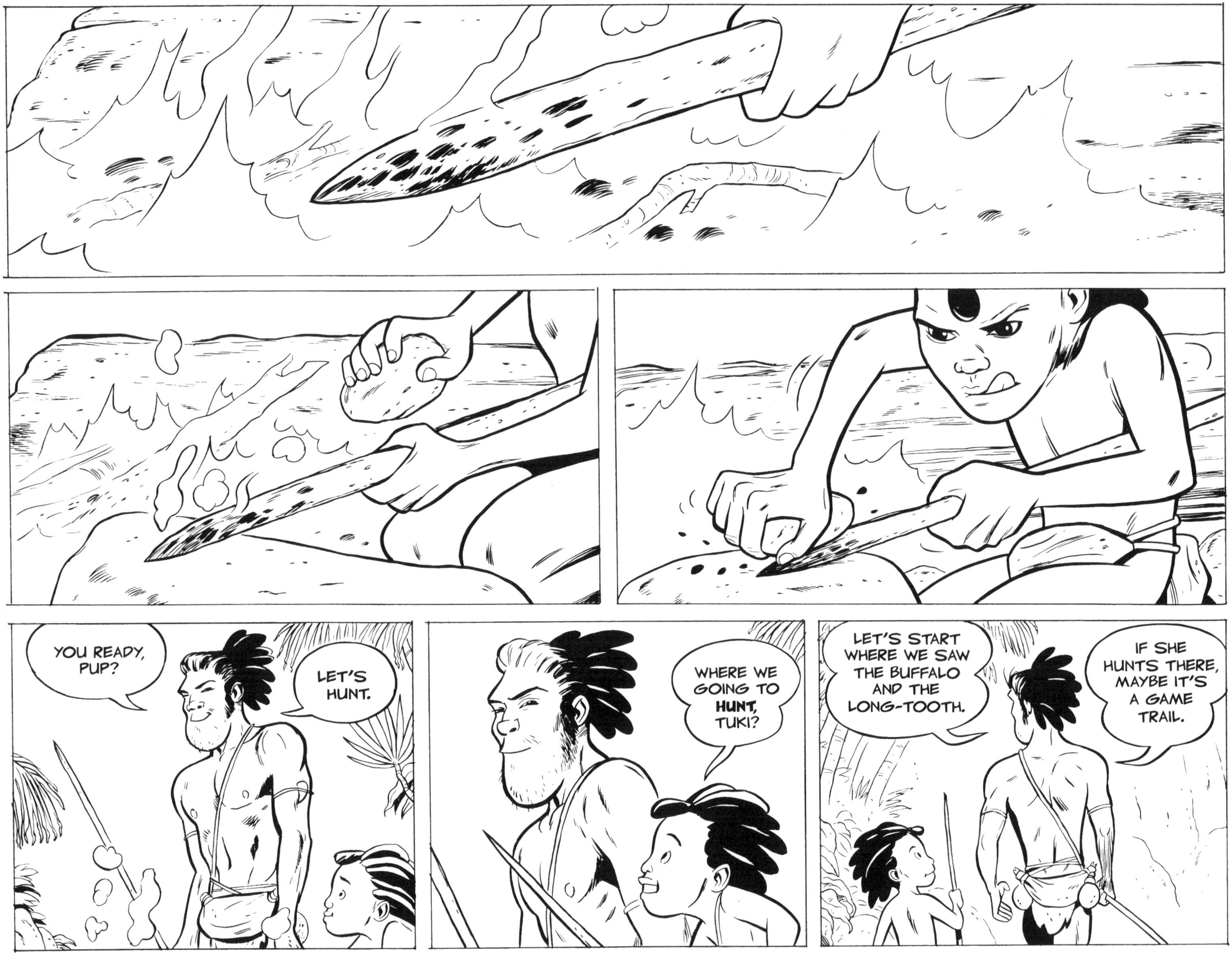
YOU READY, PUP?
LET'S HUNT.
WHERE WE GOING TO **HUNT,** TUKI?
LET'S START WHERE WE SAW THE BUFFALO AND THE LONG-TOOTH.
IF SHE HUNTS THERE, MAYBE IT'S A GAME TRAIL.

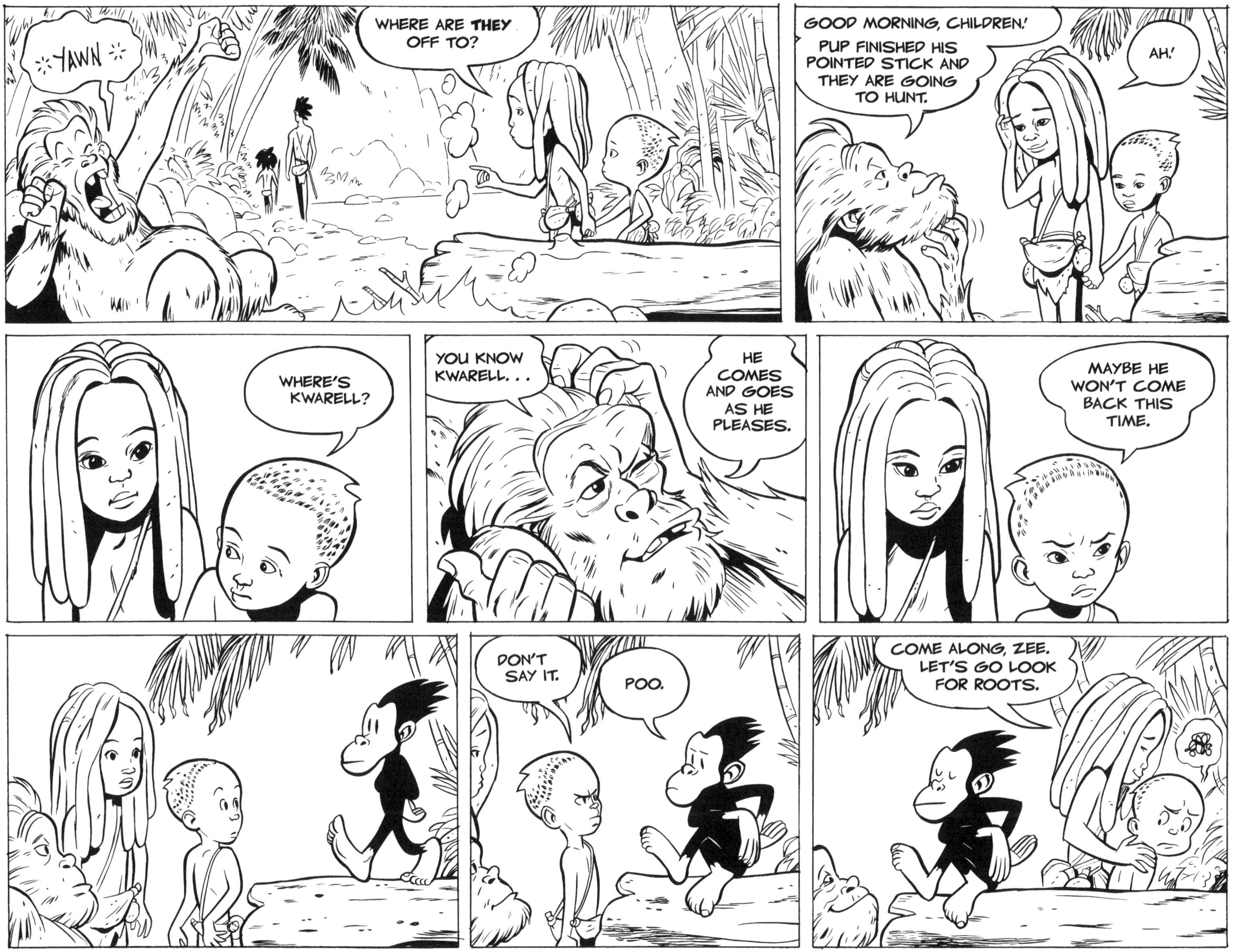
YAWN
WHERE ARE THEY OFF TO?
GOOD MORNING, CHILDREN!
PUP FINISHED HIS POINTED STICK AND THEY ARE GOING TO HUNT.
AH!
WHERE'S KWARELL?
YOU KNOW KWARELL. . .
HE COMES AND GOES AS HE PLEASES.
MAYBE HE WON'T COME BACK THIS TIME.
DON'T SAY IT.
POO.
COME ALONG, ZEE. LET'S GO LOOK FOR ROOTS.

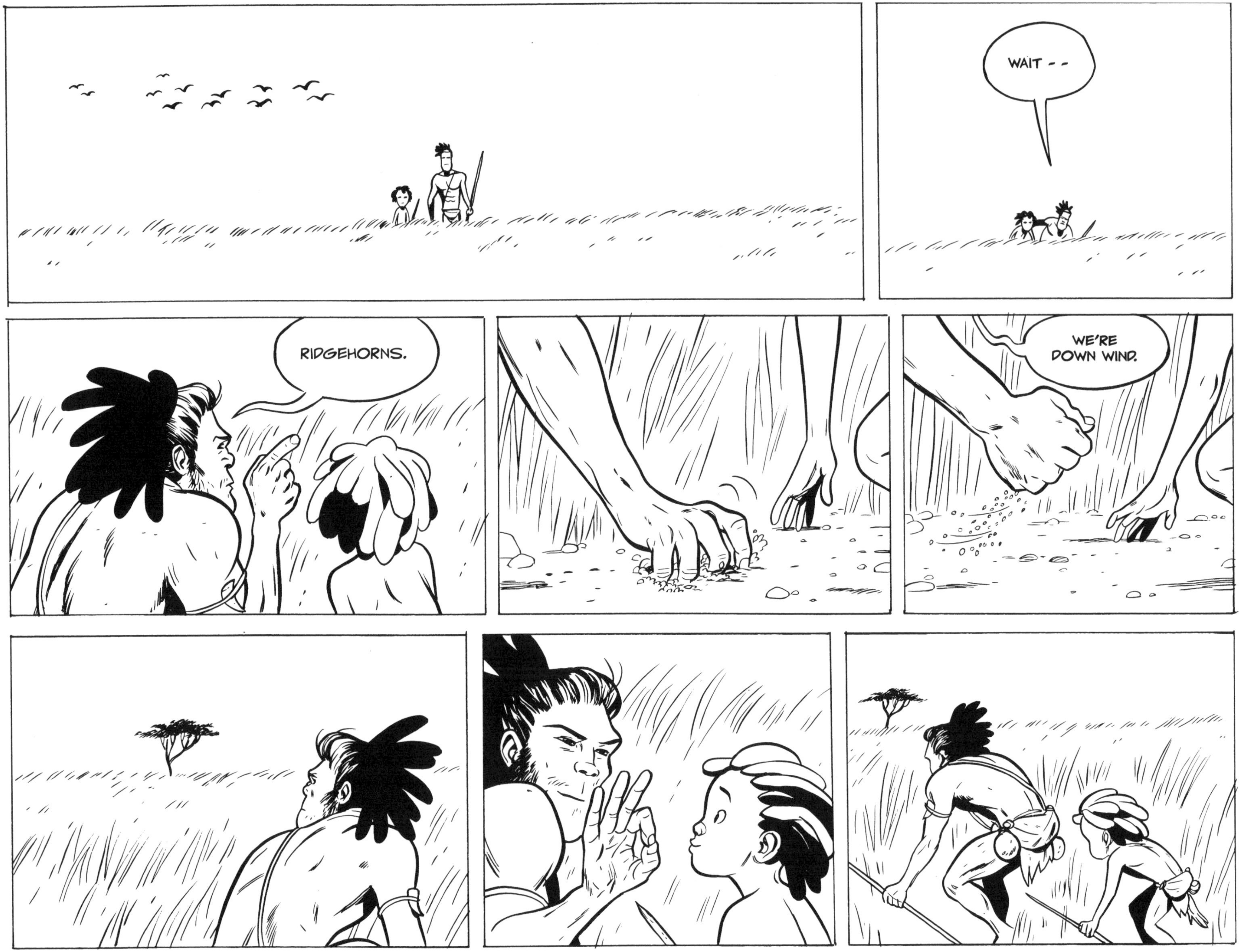
WAIT - -
RIDGEHORNS.
WE'RE DOWN WIND.

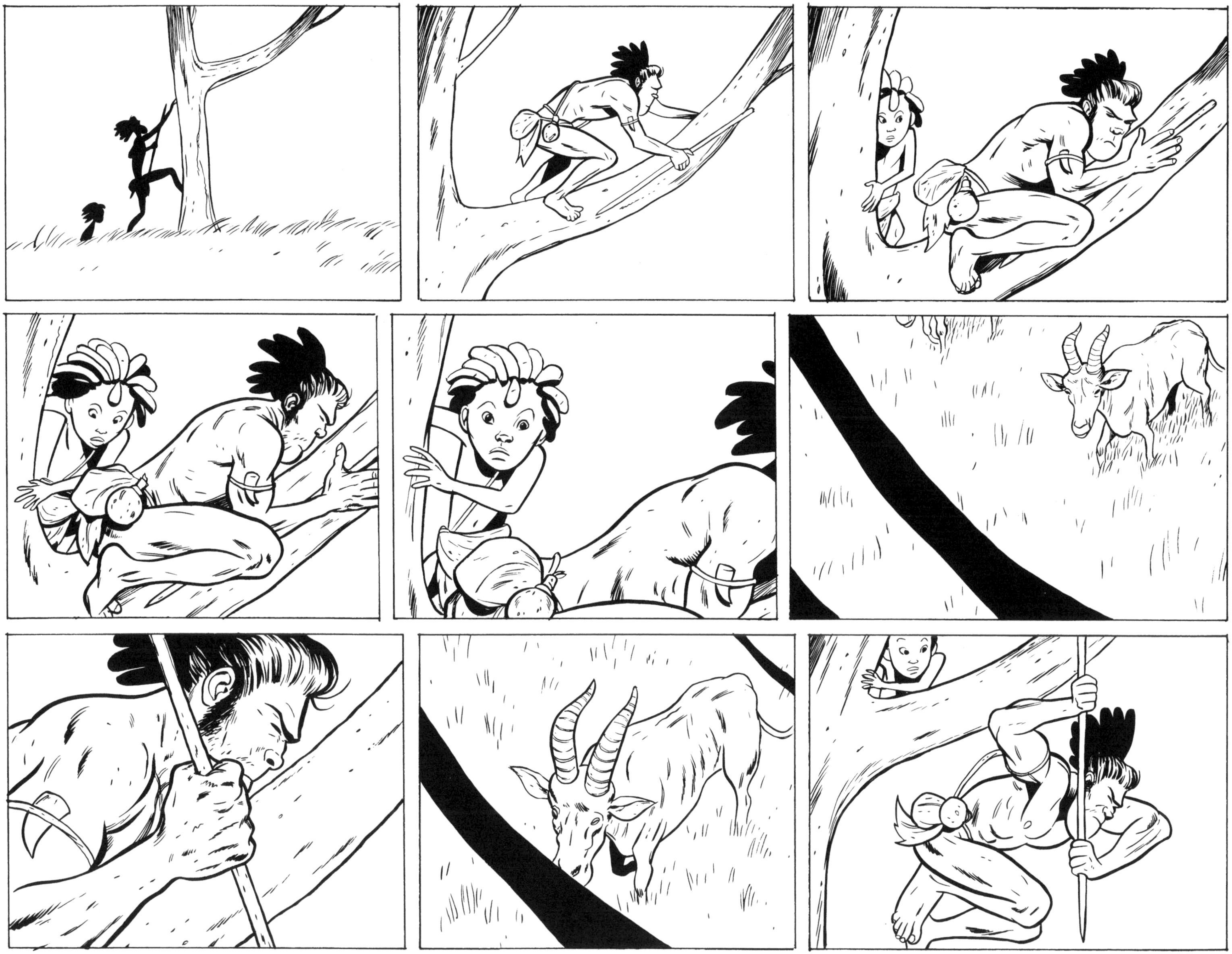

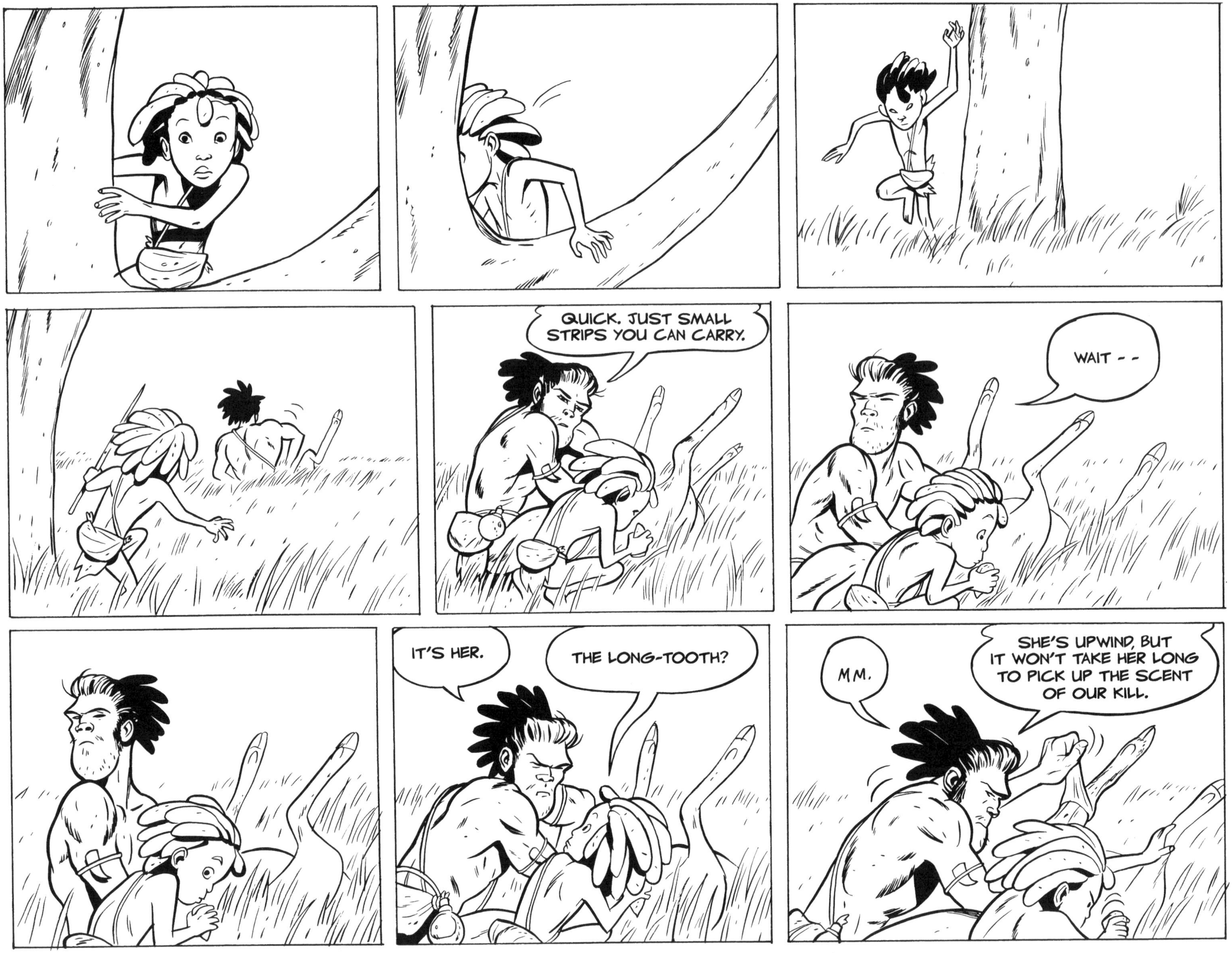
QUICK. JUST SMALL STRIPS YOU CAN CARRY.
WAIT - -
IT'S HER.
THE LONG-TOOTH?
MM.
SHE'S UPWIND, BUT IT WON'T TAKE HER LONG TO PICK UP THE SCENT OF OUR KILL.

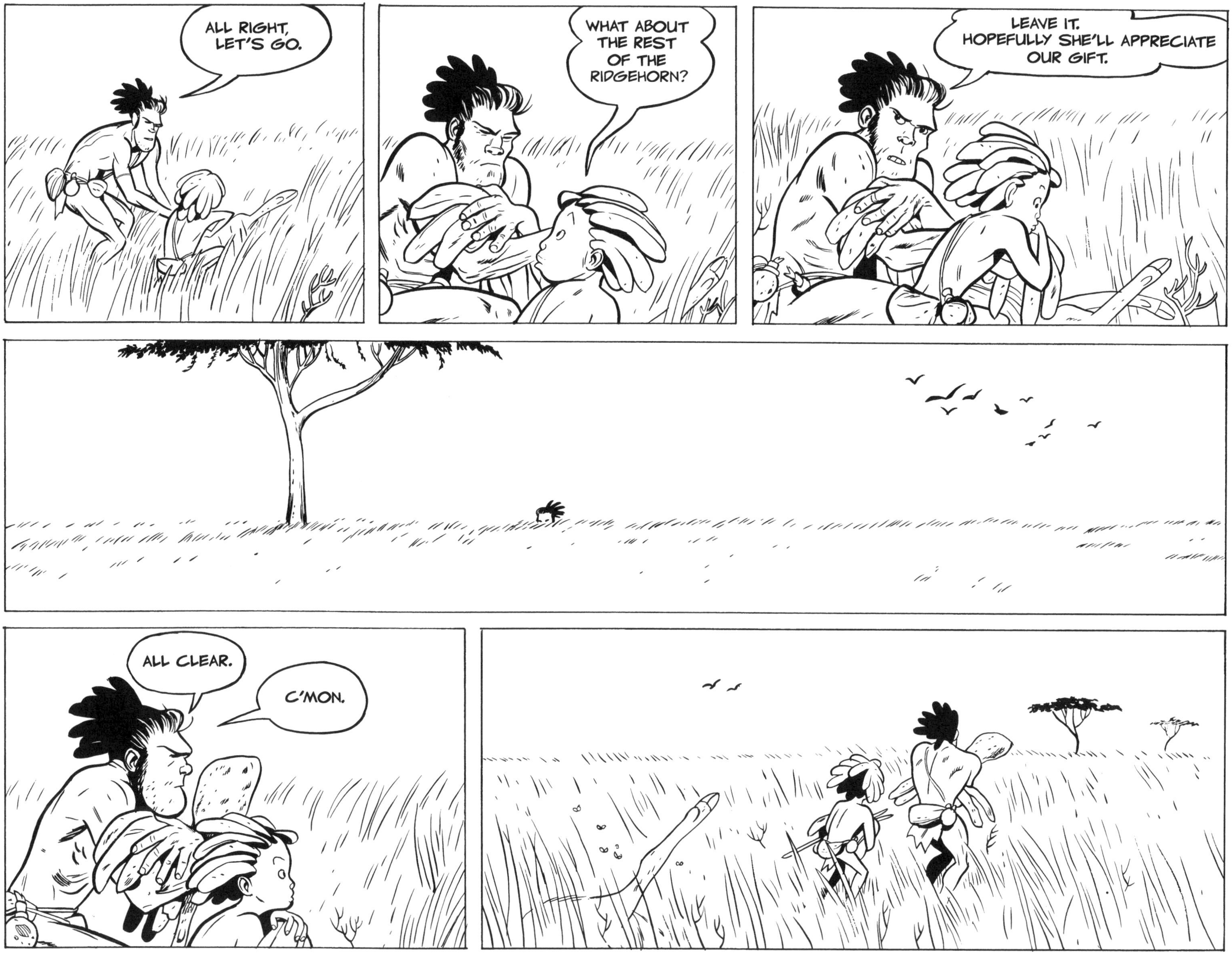
ALL RIGHT, LET'S GO.
WHAT ABOUT THE REST OF THE RIDGEHORN?
LEAVE IT. HOPEFULLY SHE'LL APPRECIATE OUR GIFT.
ALL CLEAR.
C'MON.

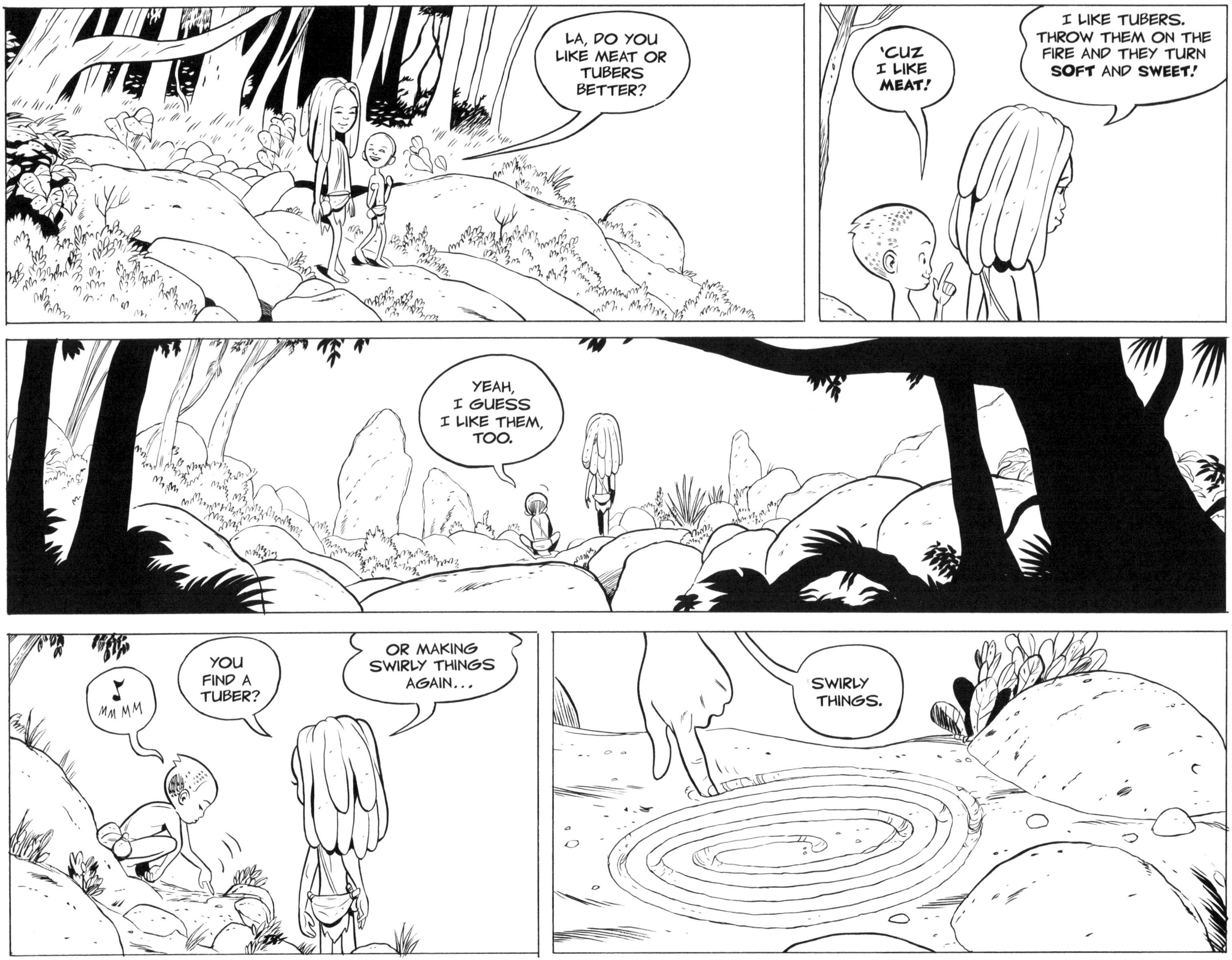
LA, DO YOU LIKE MEAT OR TUBERS BETTER?
'CUZ I LIKE **MEAT!**
I LIKE TUBERS. THROW THEM ON THE FIRE AND THEY TURN **SOFT** AND **SWEET!**
YEAH, I GUESS I LIKE THEM, TOO.
MMMM
YOU FIND A TUBER?
OR MAKING SWIRLY THINGS AGAIN...
SWIRLY THINGS.

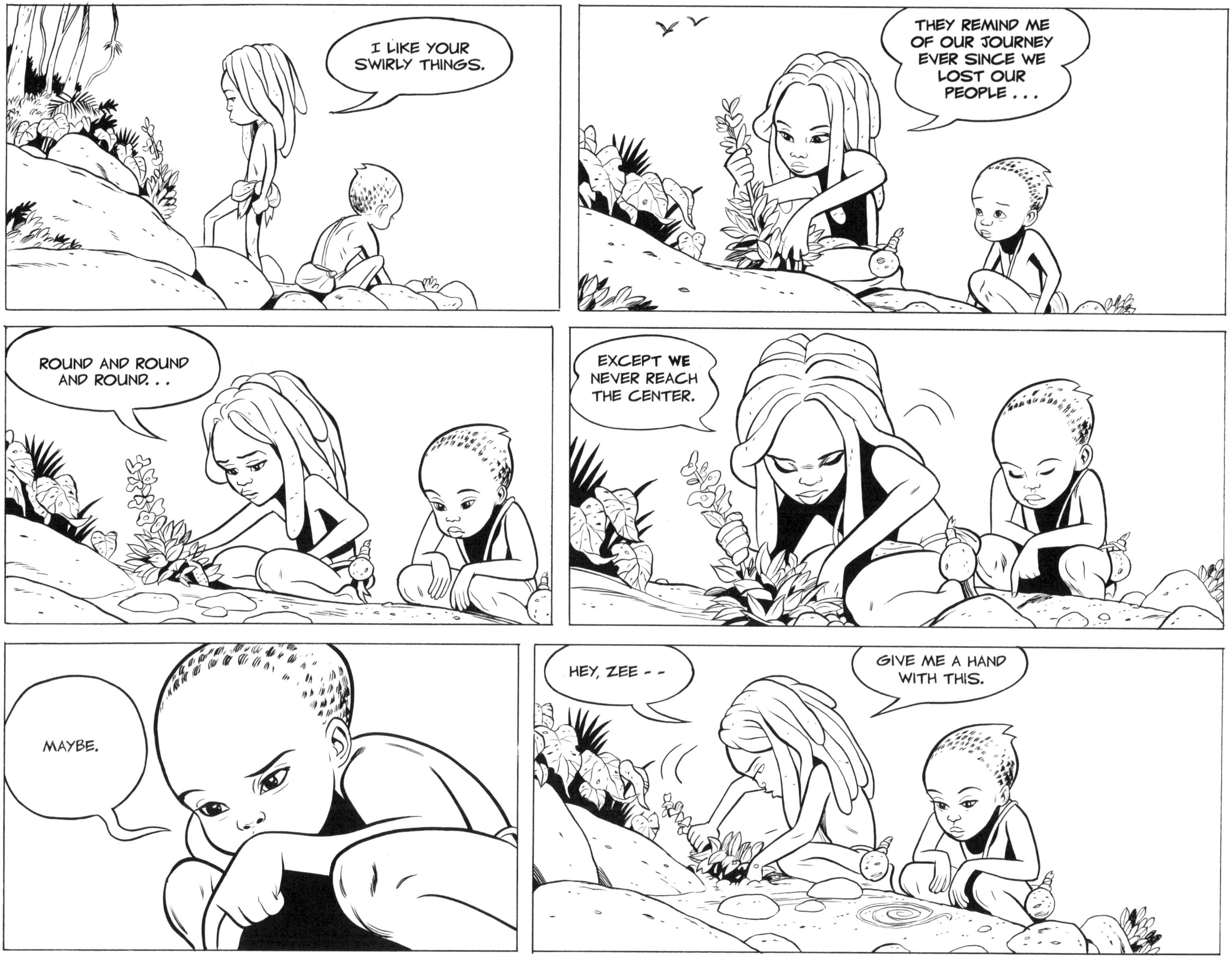
I LIKE YOUR SWIRLY THINGS.
THEY REMIND ME OF OUR JOURNEY EVER SINCE WE LOST OUR PEOPLE . . .
ROUND AND ROUND AND ROUND. . .
EXCEPT WE NEVER REACH THE CENTER.
MAYBE.
HEY, ZEE - -
GIVE ME A HAND WITH THIS.

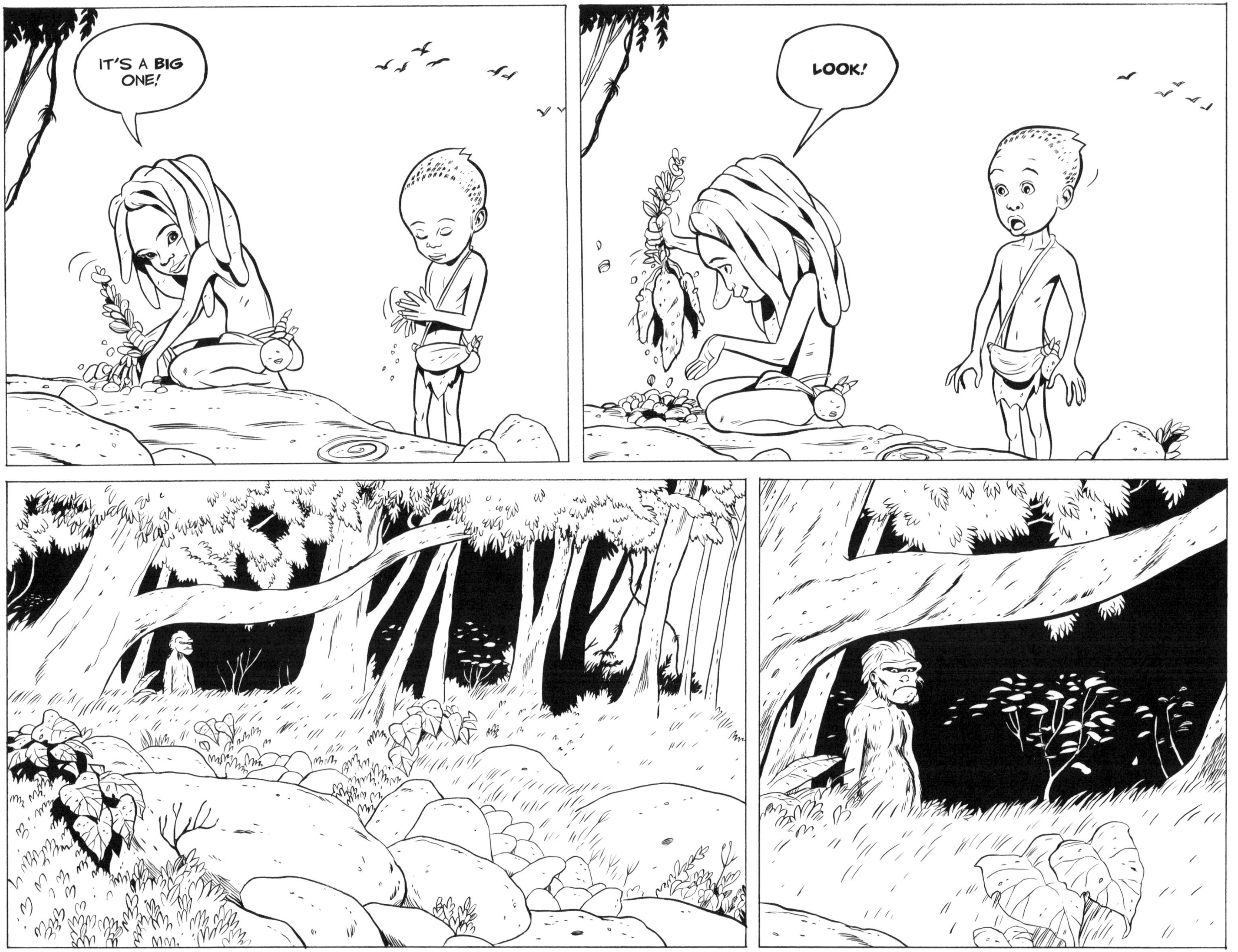
IT'S A BIG ONE!
LOOK!

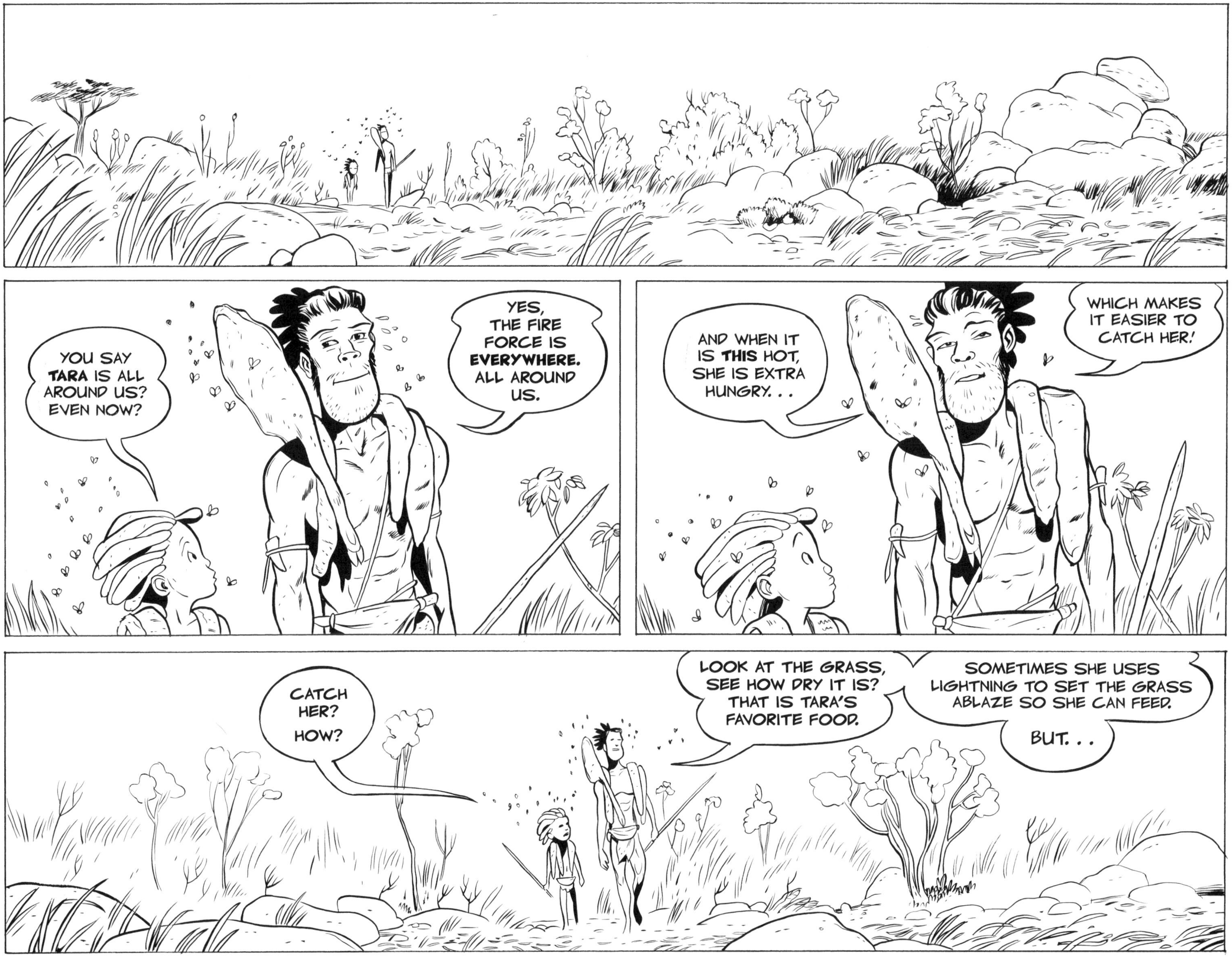

YOU SAY **TARA** IS ALL AROUND US? EVEN NOW?
YES, THE FIRE FORCE IS **EVERYWHERE.** ALL AROUND US.
AND WHEN IT IS **THIS** HOT, SHE IS EXTRA HUNGRY. . .
WHICH MAKES IT EASIER TO CATCH HER!
CATCH HER?
HOW?
LOOK AT THE GRASS, SEE HOW DRY IT IS? THAT IS TARA'S FAVORITE FOOD.
SOMETIMES SHE USES LIGHTNING TO SET THE GRASS ABLAZE SO SHE CAN FEED.
BUT. . .

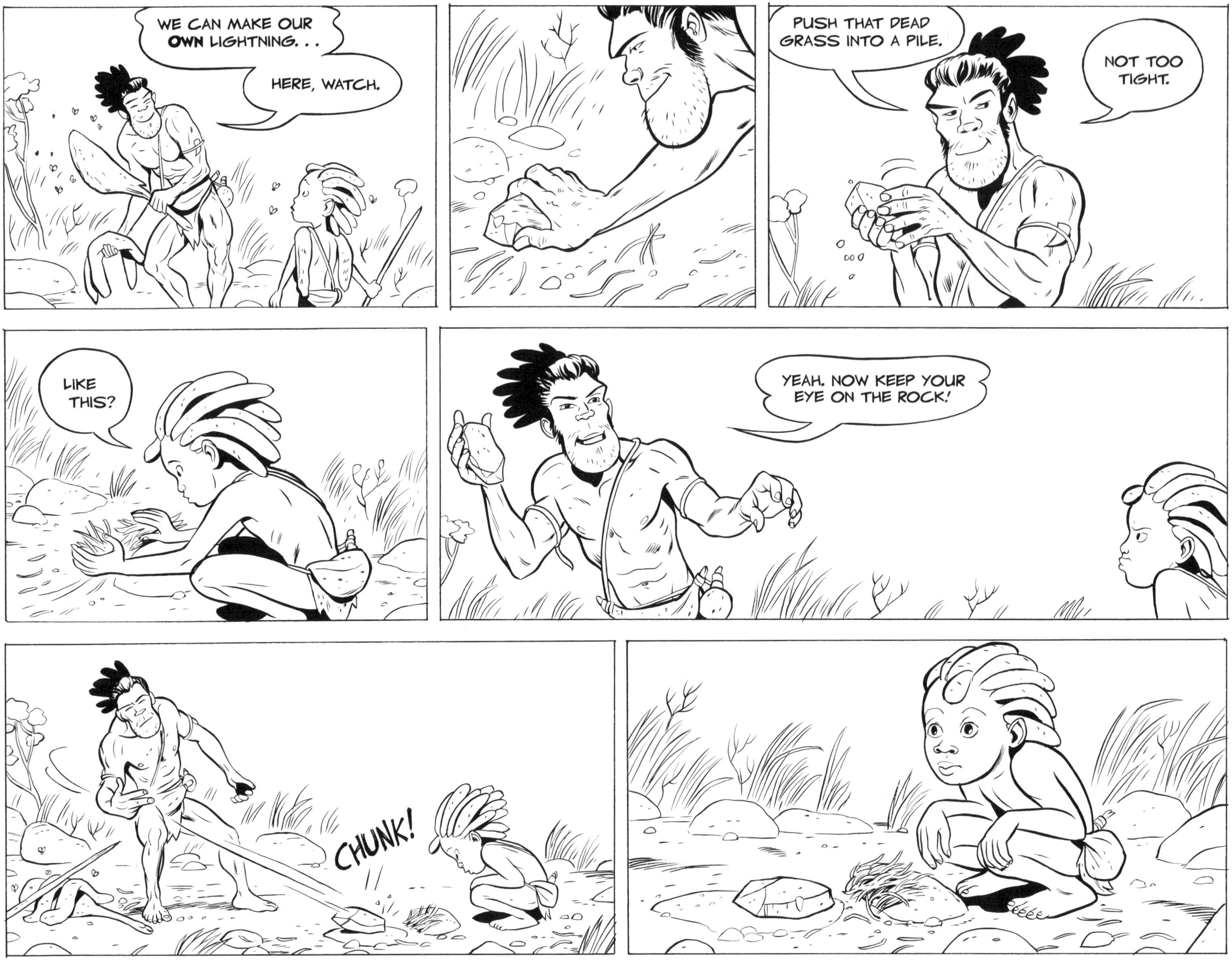

WE CAN MAKE OUR **OWN** LIGHTNING. . .
HERE, WATCH.
PUSH THAT DEAD GRASS INTO A PILE.
NOT TOO TIGHT.
LIKE THIS?
YEAH. NOW KEEP YOUR EYE ON THE ROCK!
CHUNK!

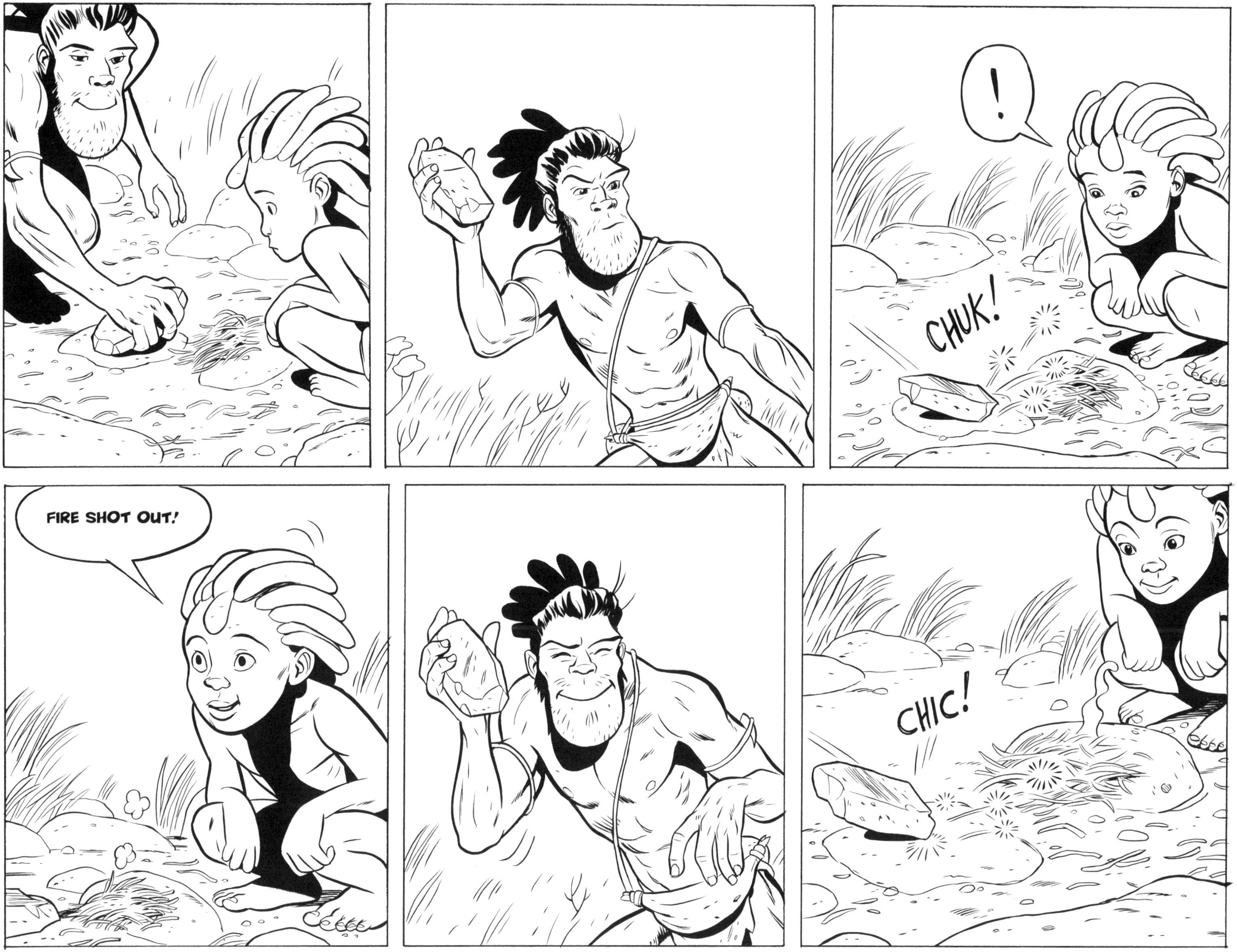
!
CHUK!
FIRE SHOT OUT!
CHIC!

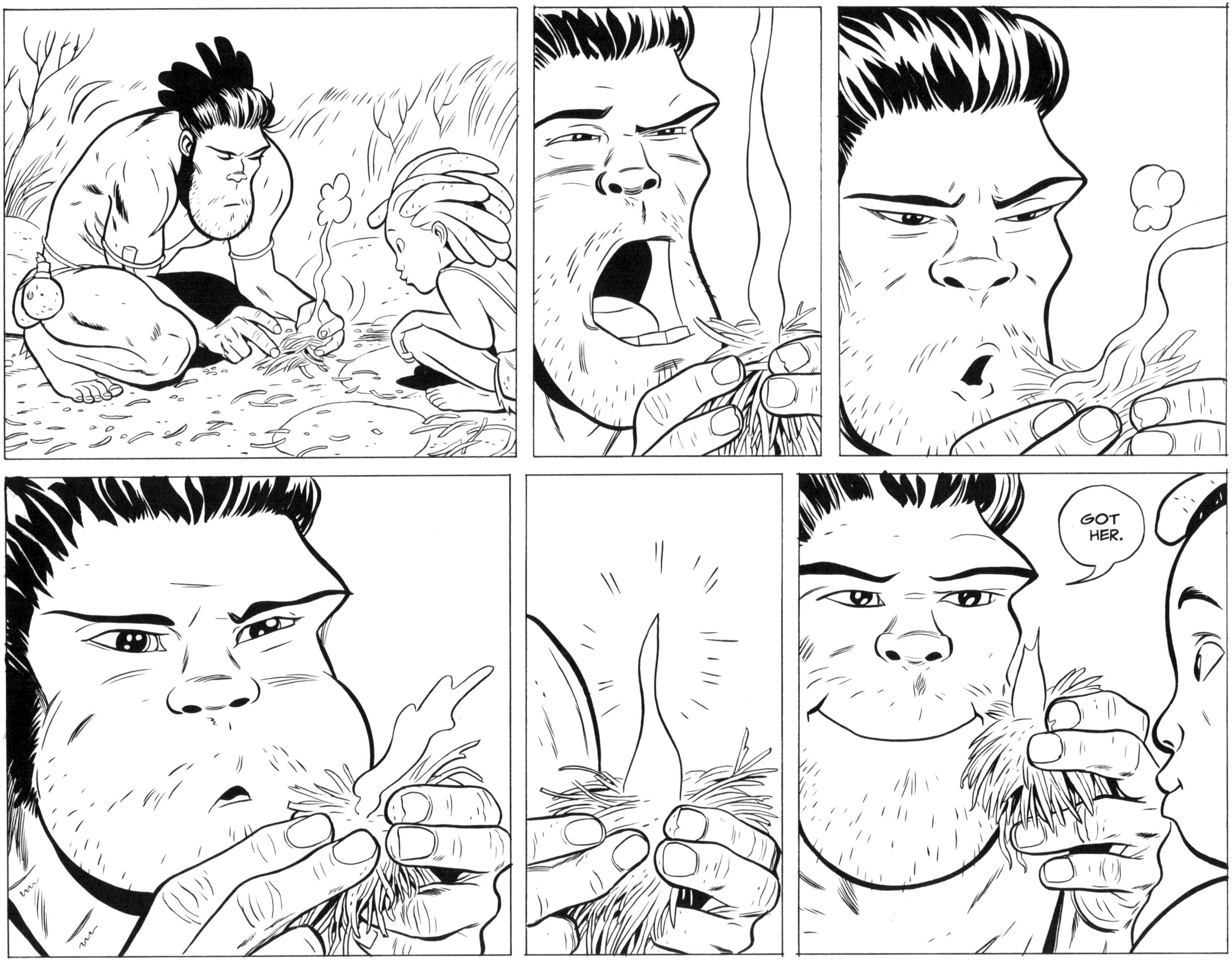
GOT HER.

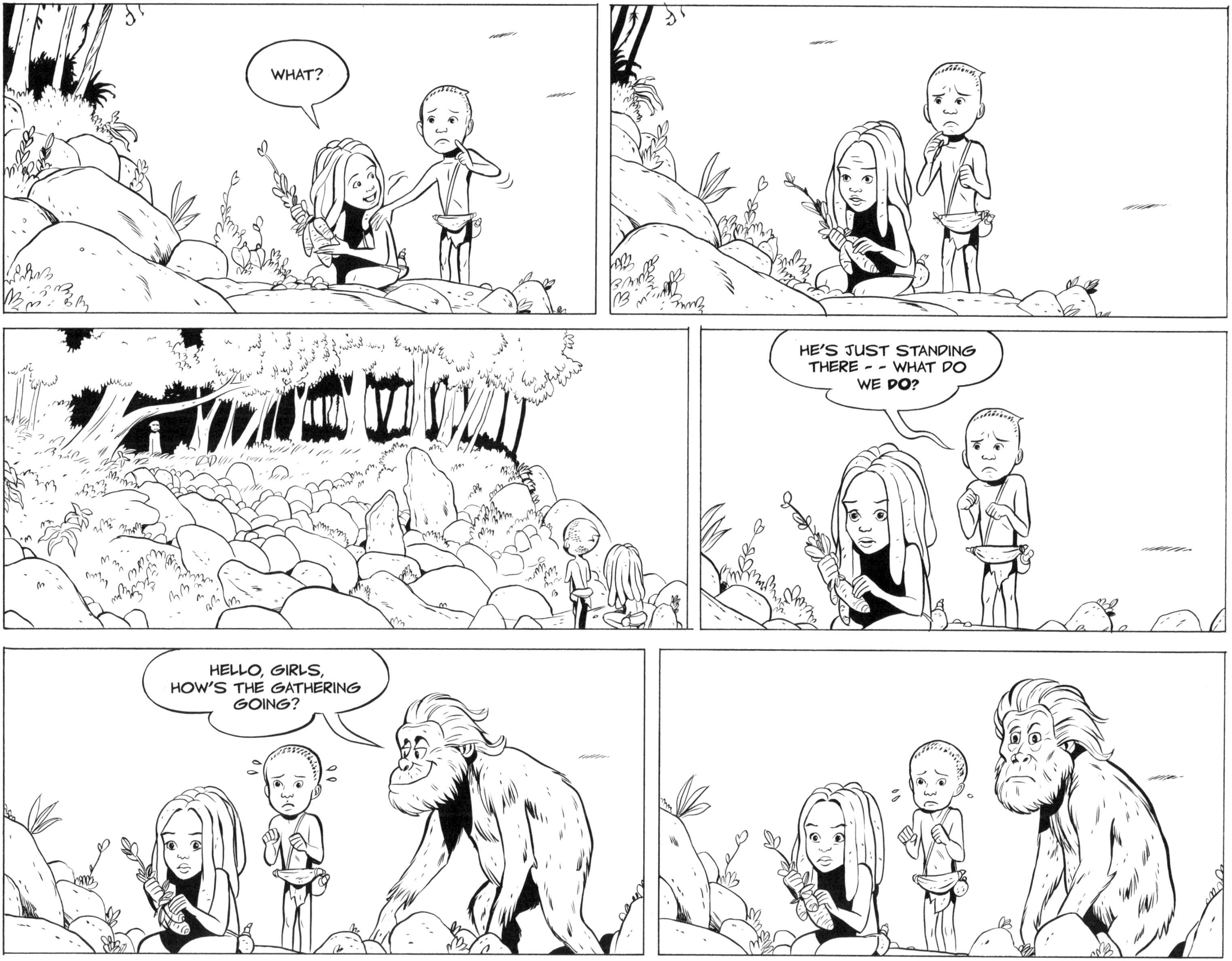
WHAT?
HE'S JUST STANDING THERE - - WHAT DO WE **DO**?
HELLO, GIRLS, HOW'S THE GATHERING GOING?

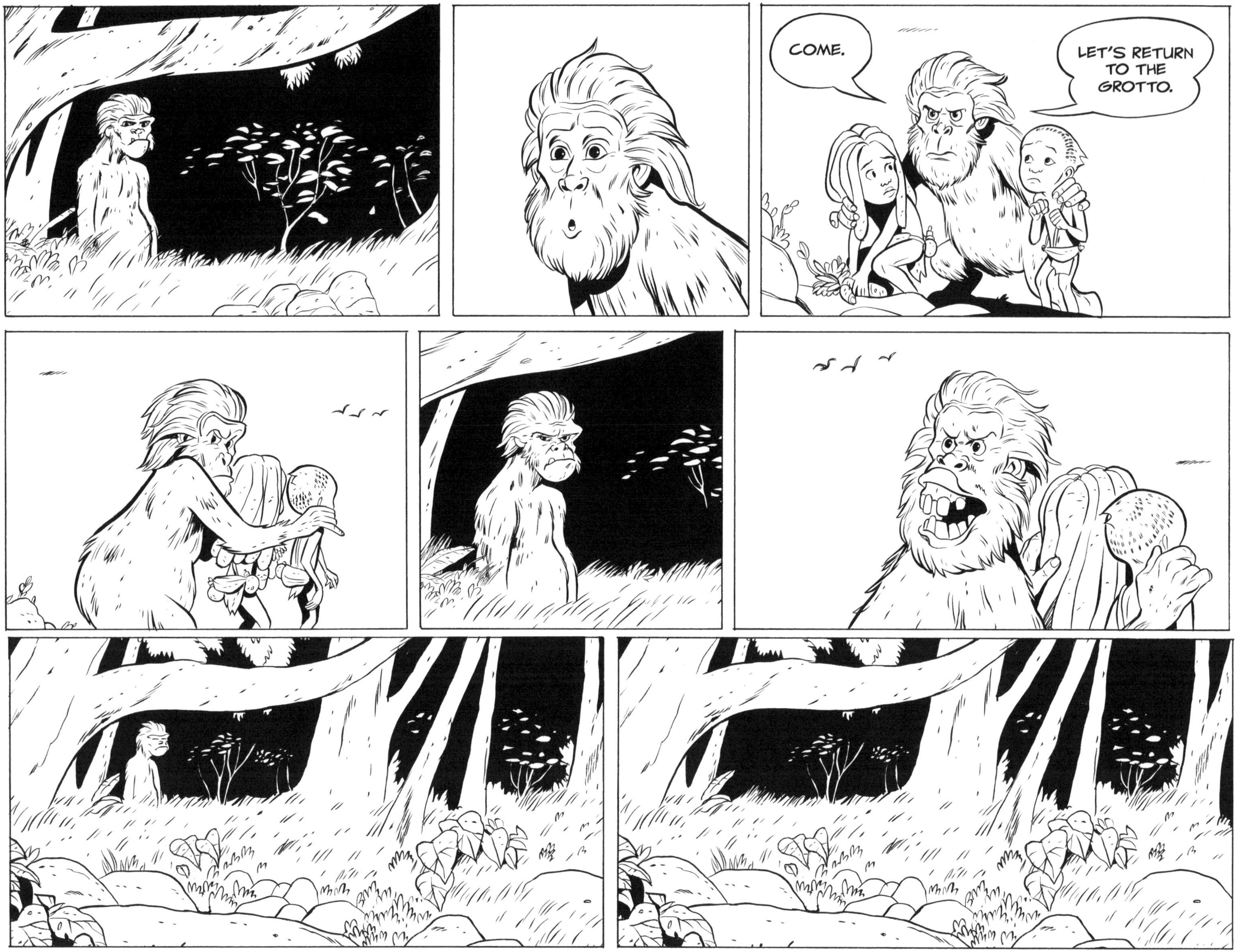
COME.
LET'S RETURN TO THE GROTTO.

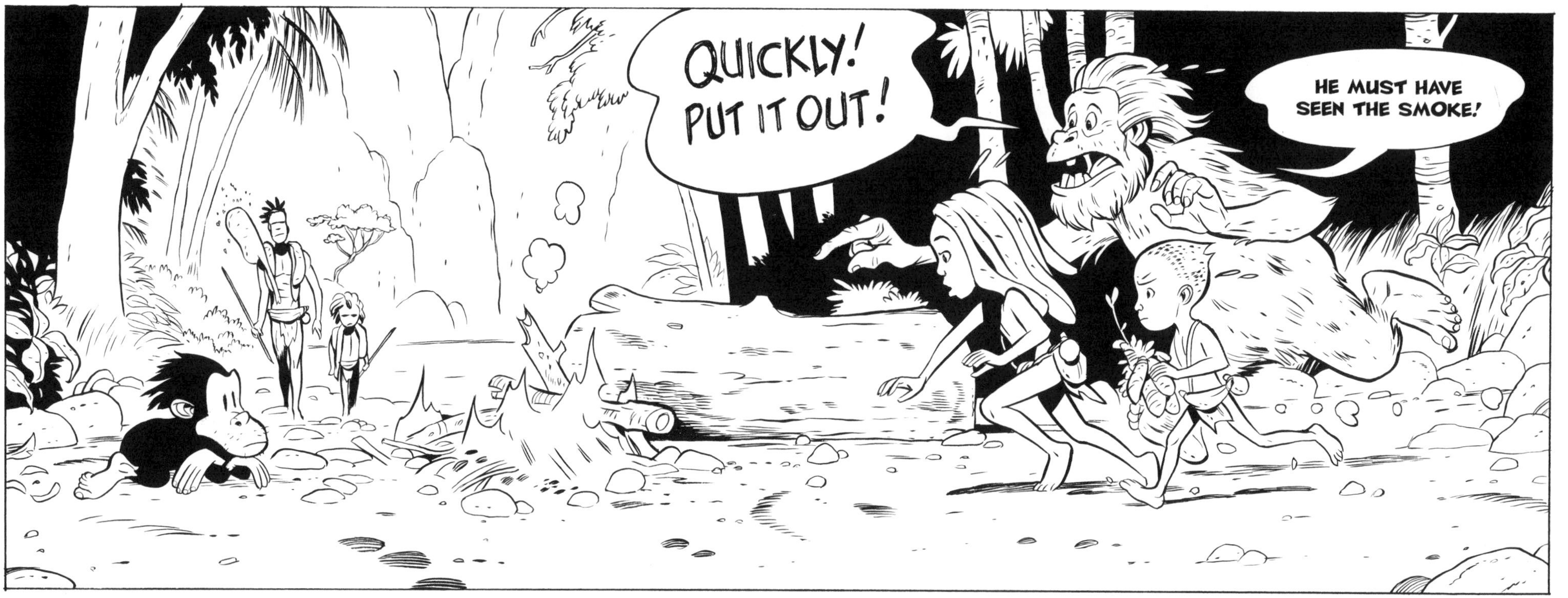
QUICKLY! PUT IT OUT!
HE MUST HAVE SEEN THE SMOKE!

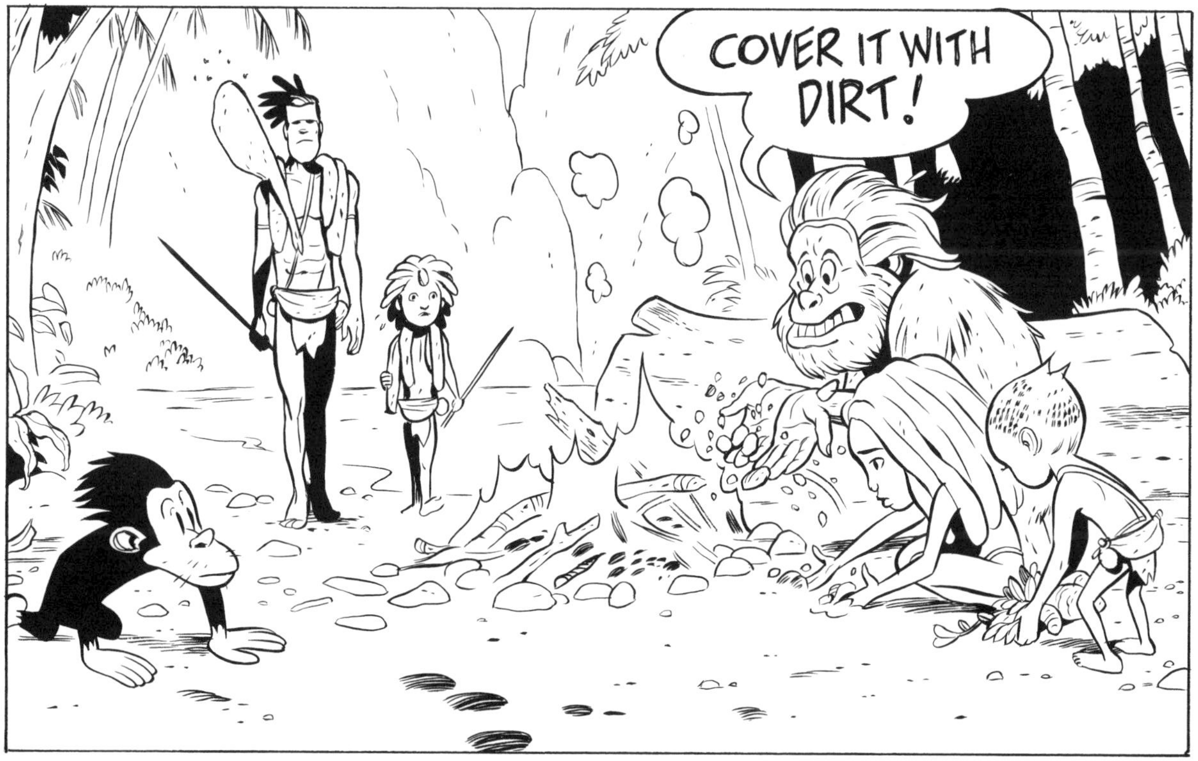
COVER IT WITH DIRT!

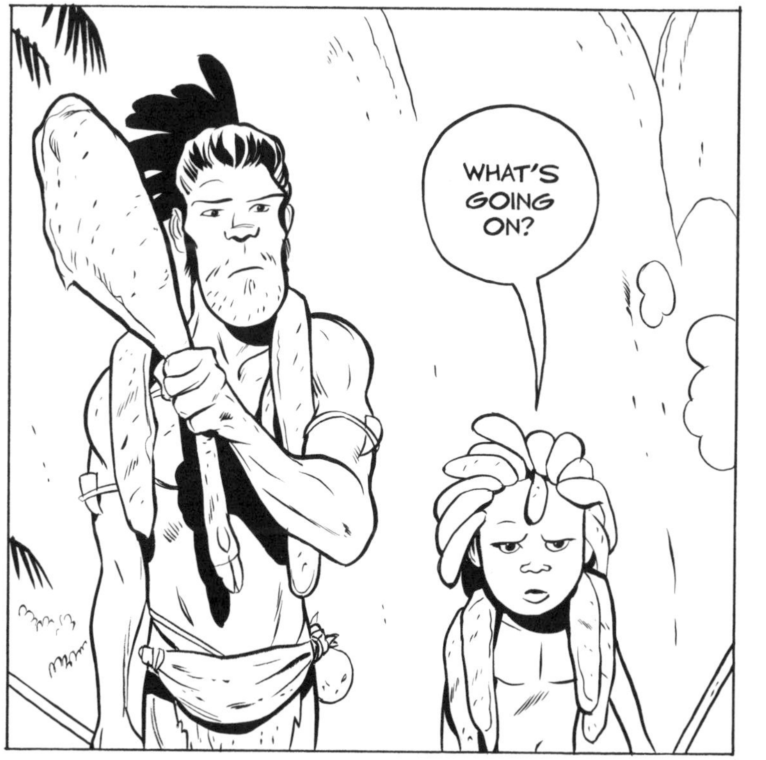
WHAT'S GOING ON?

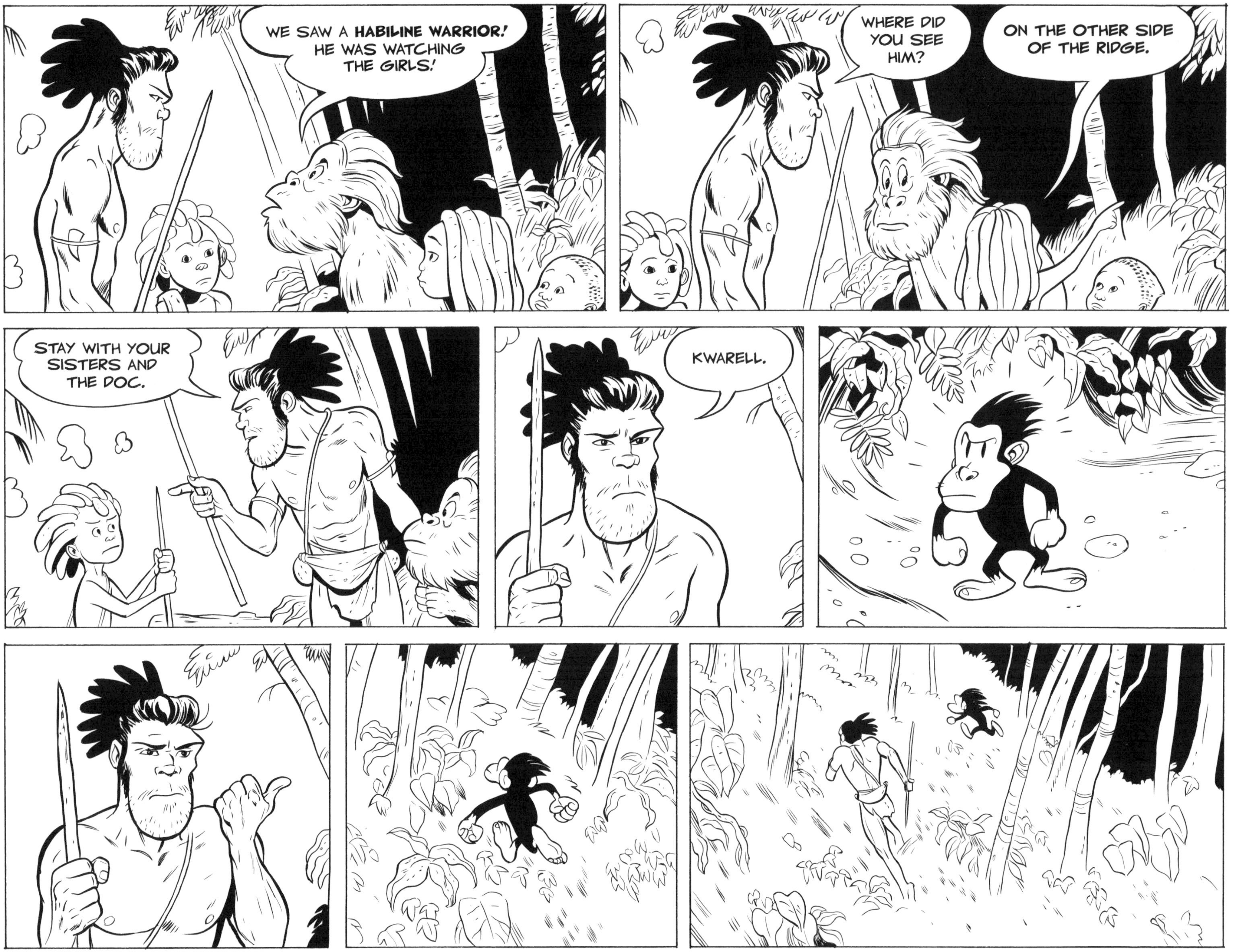
WE SAW A **HABILINE WARRIOR!** HE WAS WATCHING THE GIRLS!
WHERE DID YOU SEE HIM?
ON THE OTHER SIDE OF THE RIDGE.
STAY WITH YOUR SISTERS AND THE DOC.
KWARELL.

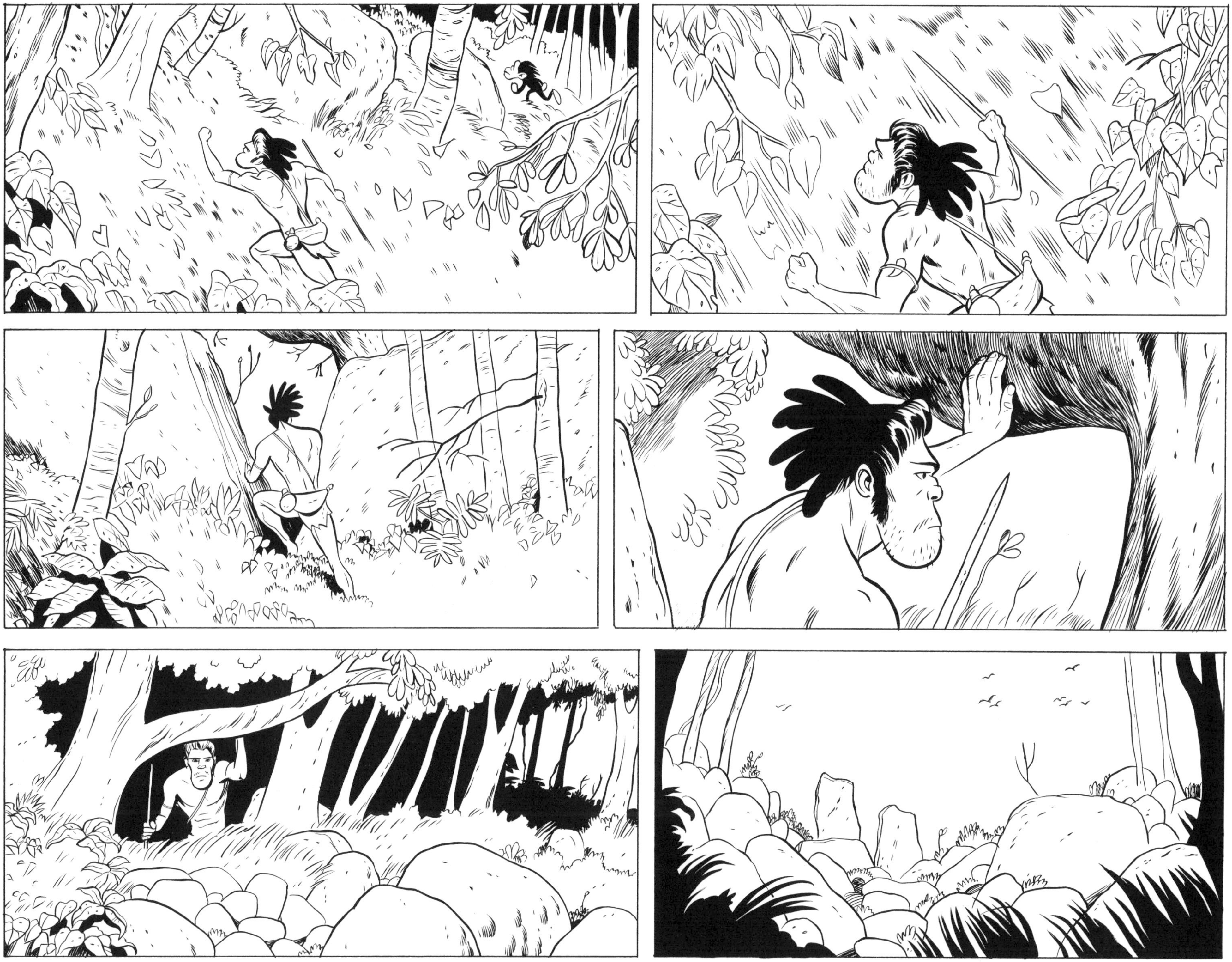

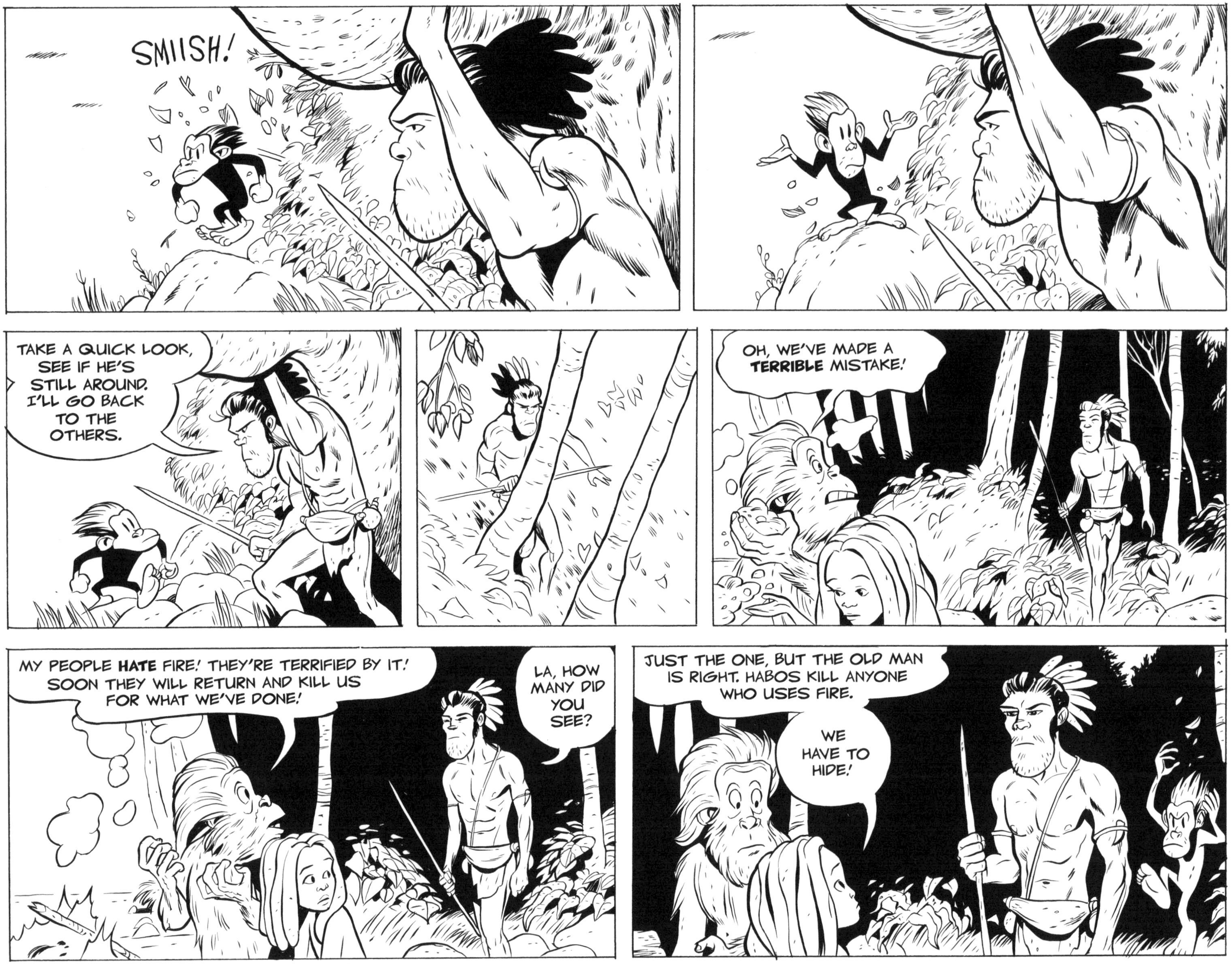
SMIISH!
TAKE A QUICK LOOK, SEE IF HE'S STILL AROUND. I'LL GO BACK TO THE OTHERS.
OH, WE'VE MADE A **TERRIBLE** MISTAKE!
MY PEOPLE **HATE** FIRE! THEY'RE TERRIFIED BY IT! SOON THEY WILL RETURN AND KILL US FOR WHAT WE'VE DONE!
LA, HOW MANY DID YOU SEE?
JUST THE ONE, BUT THE OLD MAN IS RIGHT. HABOS KILL ANYONE WHO USES FIRE.
WE HAVE TO HIDE!

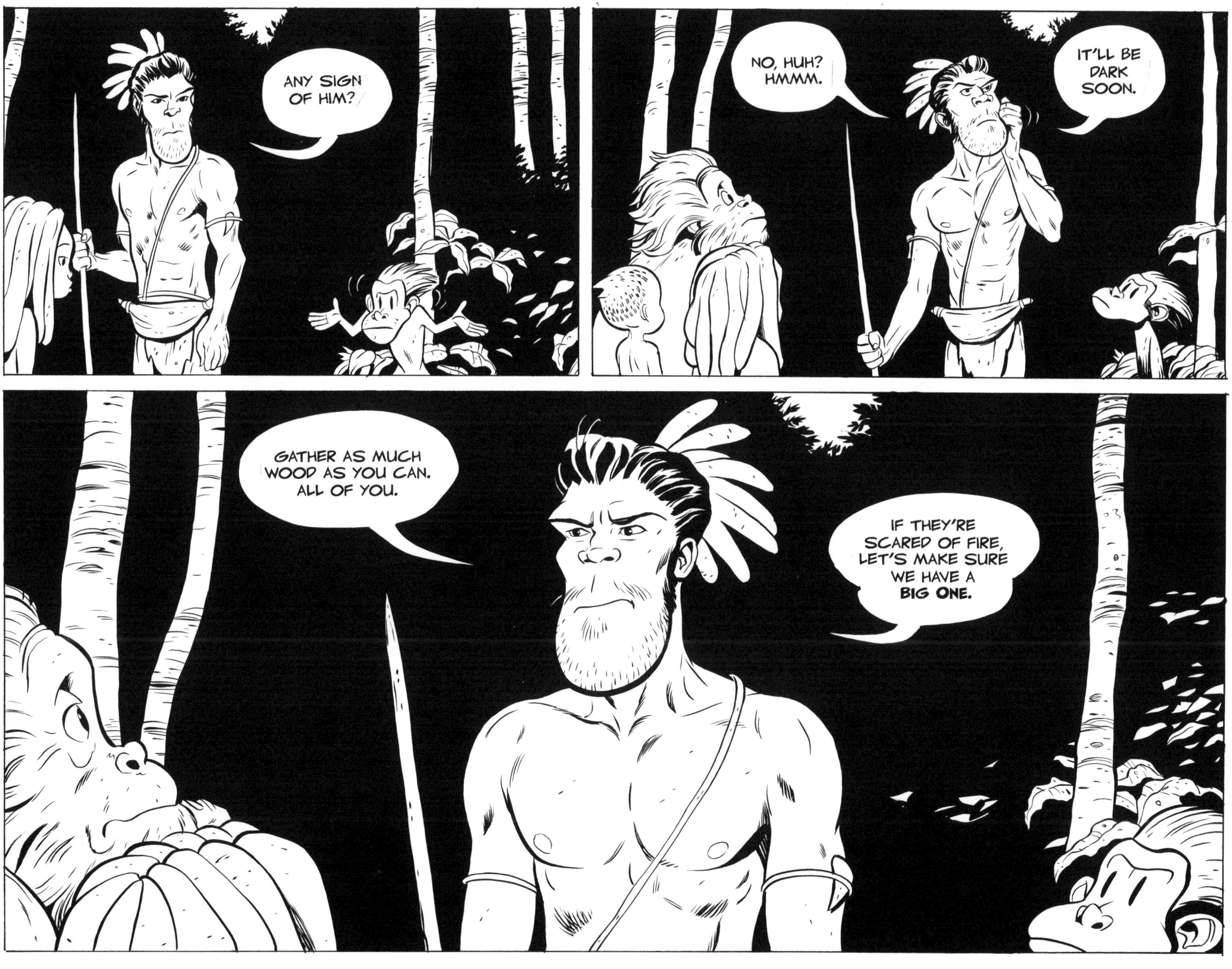
ANY SIGN OF HIM?
NO, HUH? HMMM.
IT'LL BE DARK SOON.
GATHER AS MUCH WOOD AS YOU CAN. ALL OF YOU.
IF THEY'RE SCARED OF FIRE, LET'S MAKE SURE WE HAVE A **BIG ONE.**

Four

Night Visitors

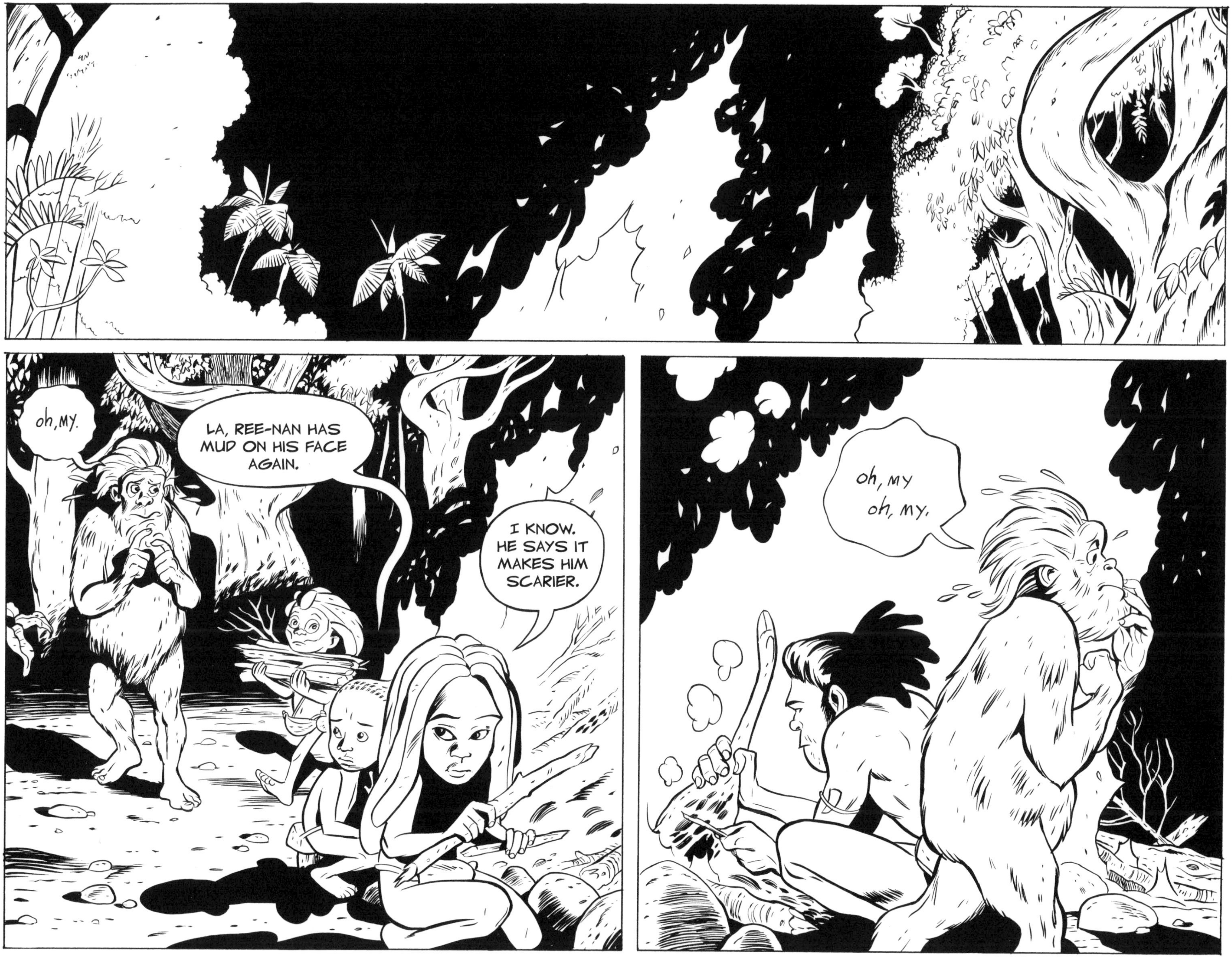
oh, my.
LA, REE-NAN HAS MUD ON HIS FACE AGAIN.
I KNOW. HE SAYS IT MAKES HIM SCARIER.
oh, my
oh, my.

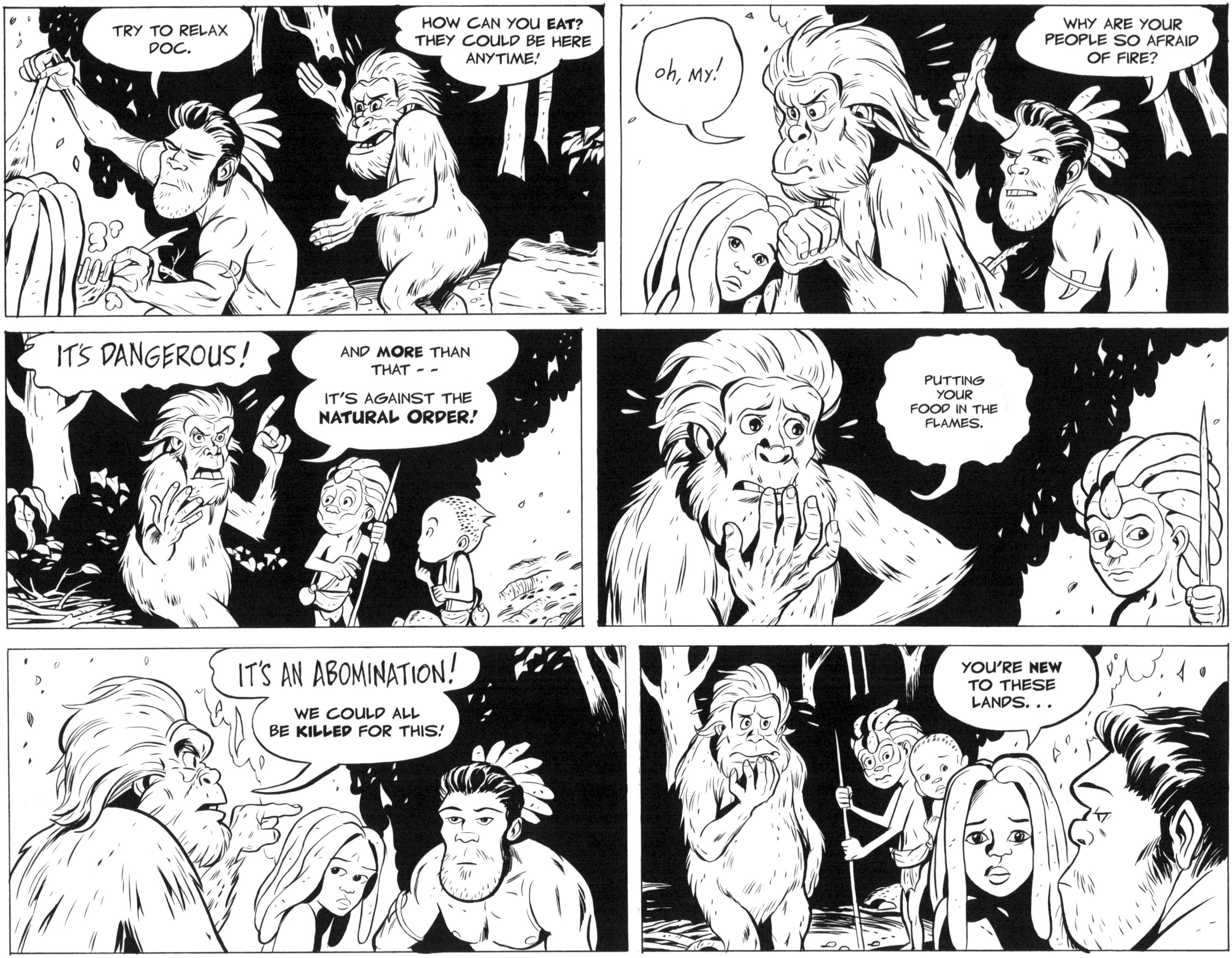
TRY TO RELAX DOC.
HOW CAN YOU EAT? THEY COULD BE HERE ANYTIME!
oh, MY!
WHY ARE YOUR PEOPLE SO AFRAID OF FIRE?
IT'S DANGEROUS!
AND MORE THAN THAT - -
IT'S AGAINST THE NATURAL ORDER!
PUTTING YOUR FOOD IN THE FLAMES.
IT'S AN ABOMINATION!
WE COULD ALL BE KILLED FOR THIS!
YOU'RE NEW TO THESE LANDS. . .

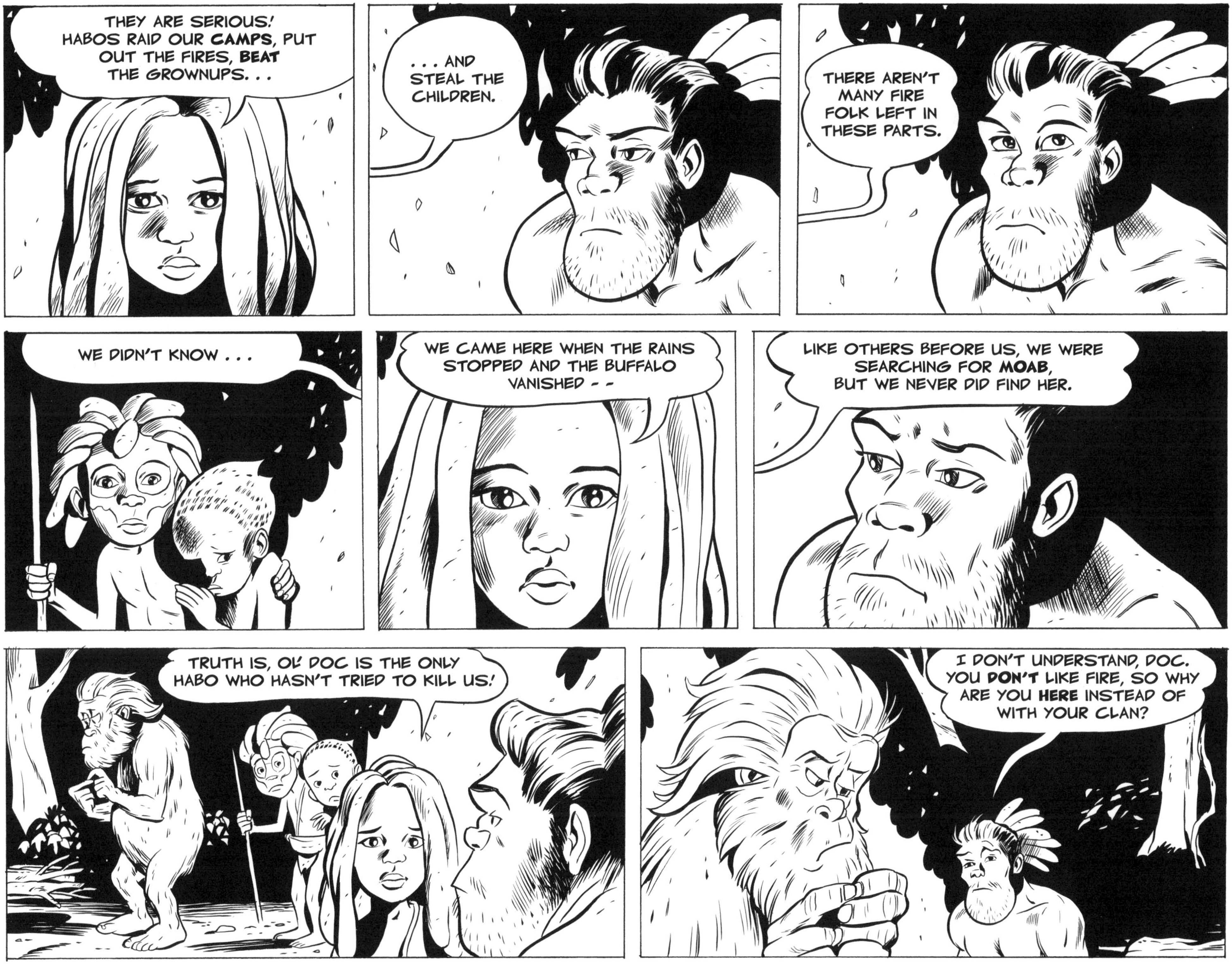
THEY ARE SERIOUS! HABOS RAID OUR **CAMPS**, PUT OUT THE FIRES, **BEAT** THE GROWNUPS. . .
. . . AND STEAL THE CHILDREN.
THERE AREN'T MANY FIRE FOLK LEFT IN THESE PARTS.
WE DIDN'T KNOW . . .
WE CAME HERE WHEN THE RAINS STOPPED AND THE BUFFALO VANISHED - -
LIKE OTHERS BEFORE US, WE WERE SEARCHING FOR **MOAB**, BUT WE NEVER DID FIND HER.
TRUTH IS, OL' DOC IS THE ONLY HABO WHO HASN'T TRIED TO KILL US!
I DON'T UNDERSTAND, DOC. YOU **DON'T** LIKE FIRE, SO WHY ARE YOU **HERE** INSTEAD OF WITH YOUR CLAN?

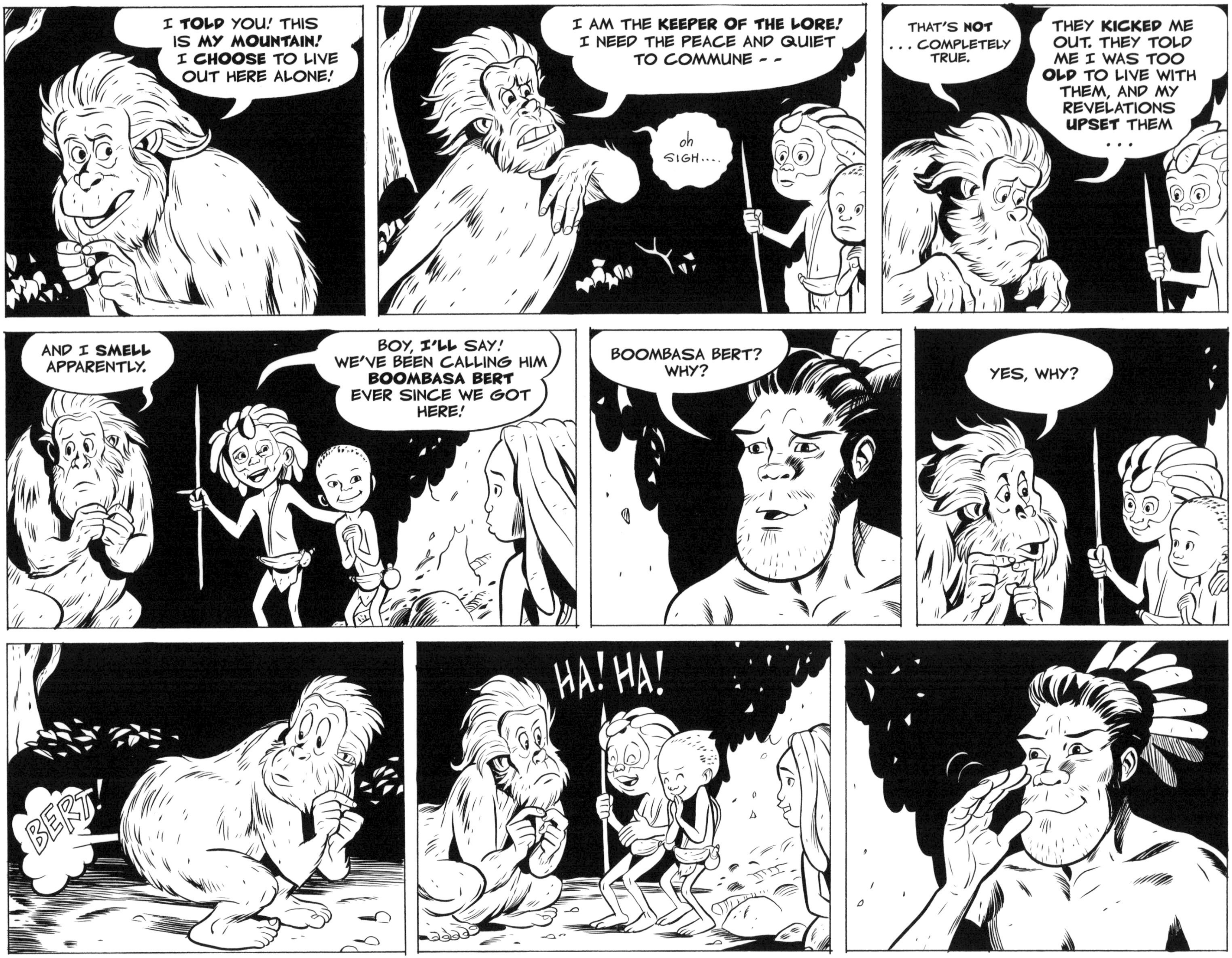
I TOLD YOU! THIS IS MY MOUNTAIN! I CHOOSE TO LIVE OUT HERE ALONE!
I AM THE KEEPER OF THE LORE! I NEED THE PEACE AND QUIET TO COMMUNE --
oh SIGH....
THAT'S NOT ...COMPLETELY TRUE.
THEY KICKED ME OUT. THEY TOLD ME I WAS TOO OLD TO LIVE WITH THEM, AND MY REVELATIONS UPSET THEM ...
AND I SMELL APPARENTLY.
BOY, I'LL SAY! WE'VE BEEN CALLING HIM BOOMBASA BERT EVER SINCE WE GOT HERE!
BOOMBASA BERT? WHY?
YES, WHY?
BERT!
HA! HA!

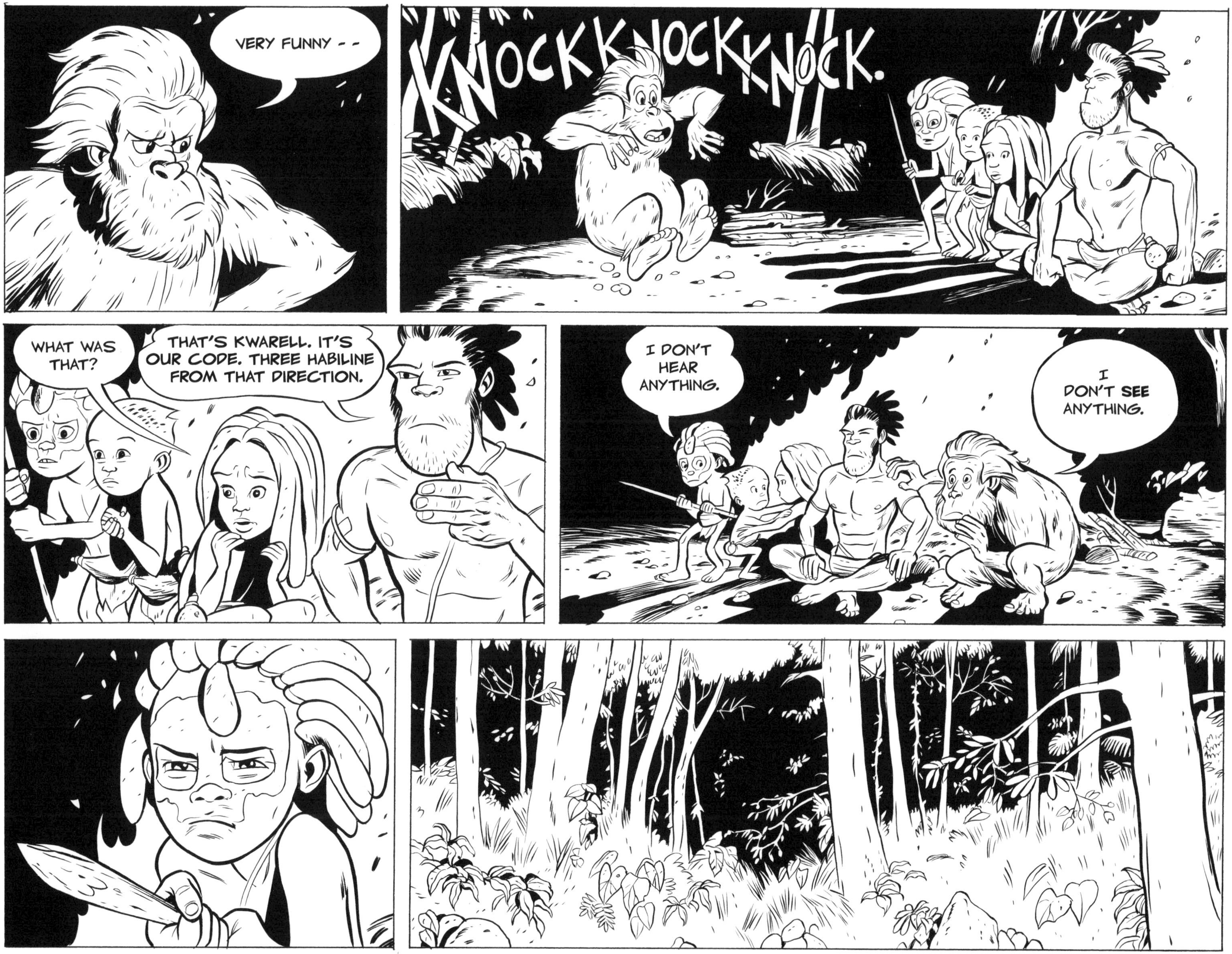
VERY FUNNY - -
KNOCK KNOCK KNOCK.
WHAT WAS THAT?
THAT'S KWARELL. IT'S OUR CODE. THREE HABILINE FROM THAT DIRECTION.
I DON'T HEAR ANYTHING.
I DON'T SEE ANYTHING.

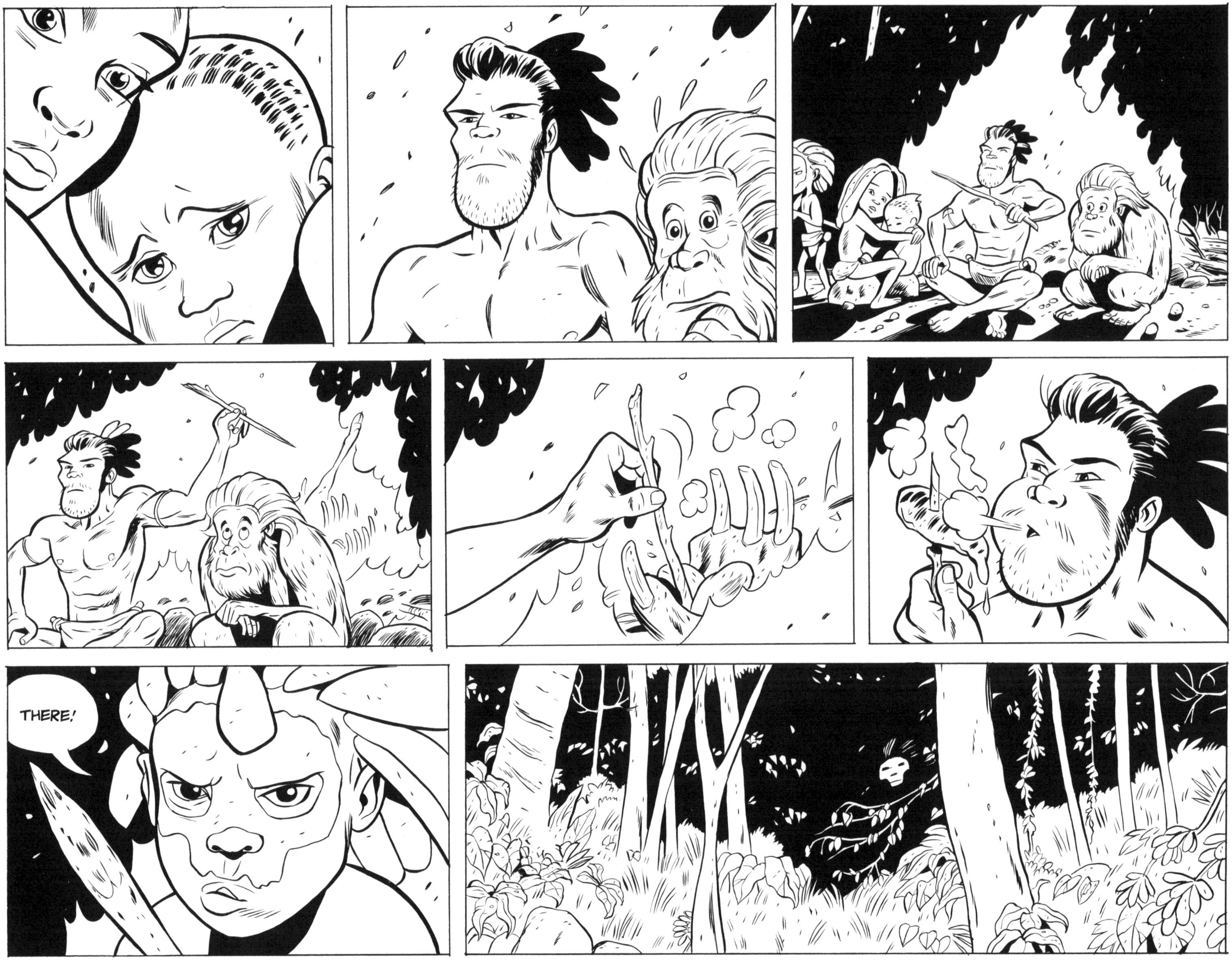
THERE!

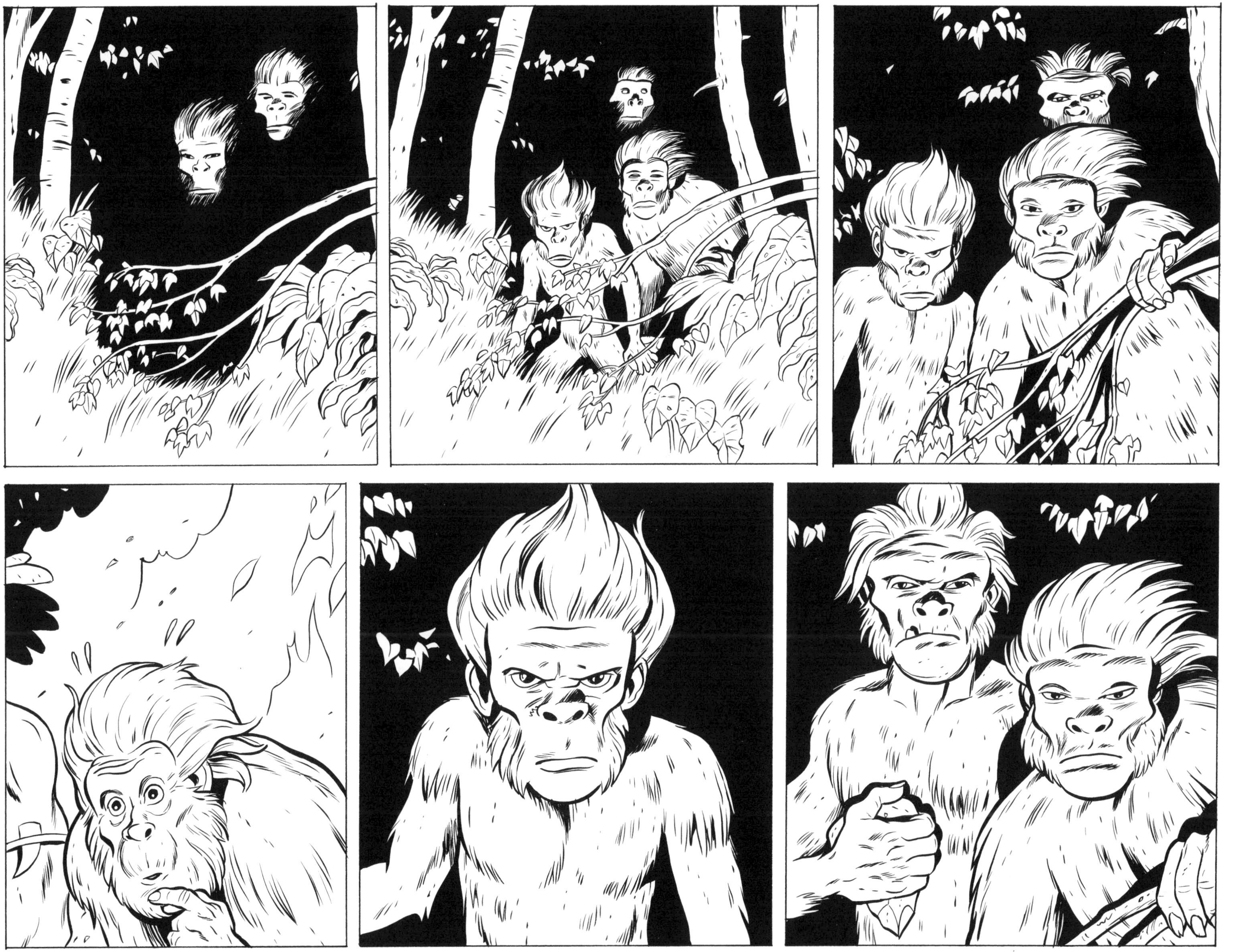

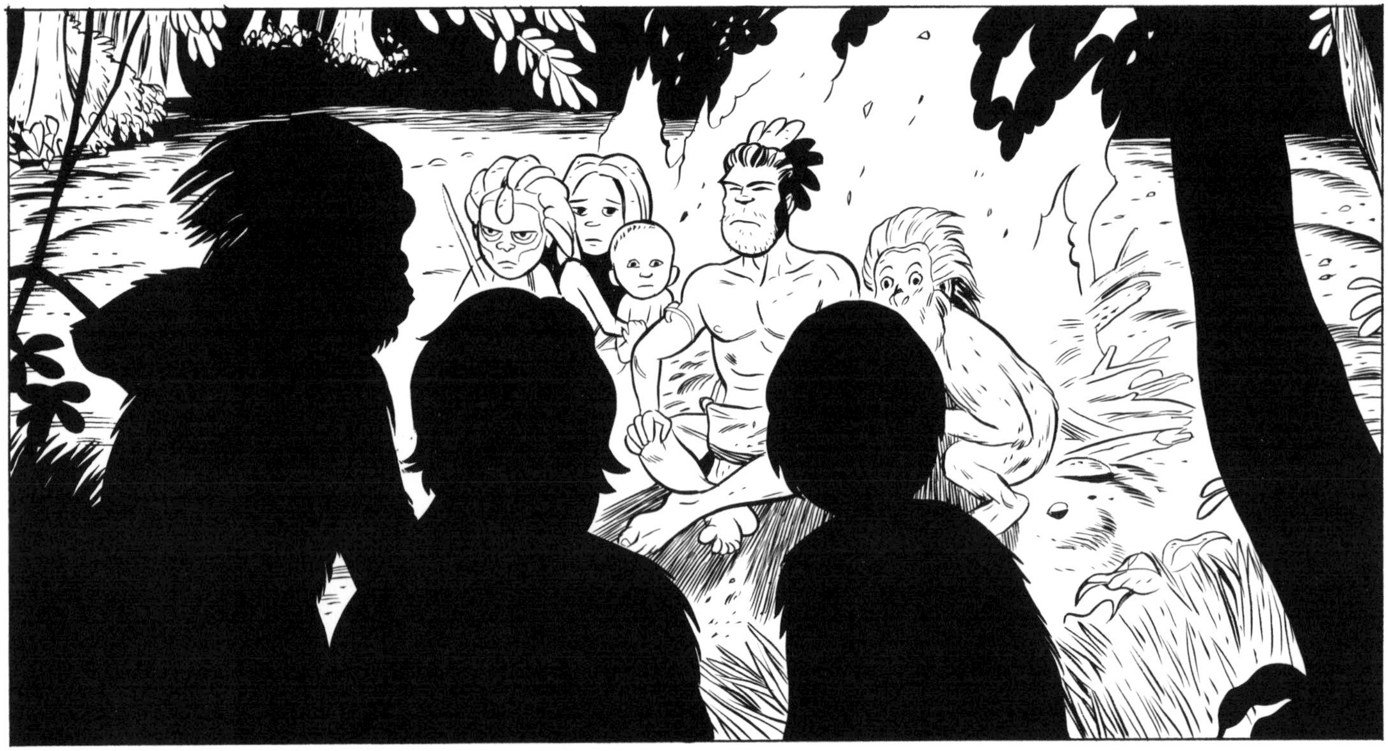
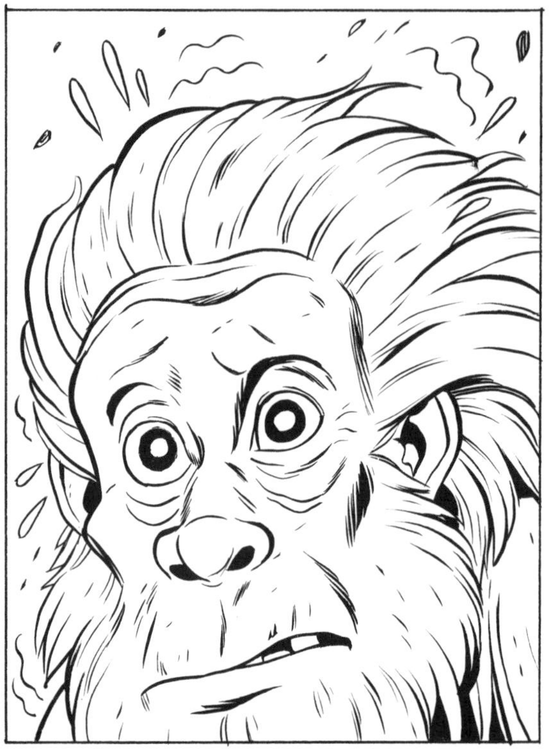
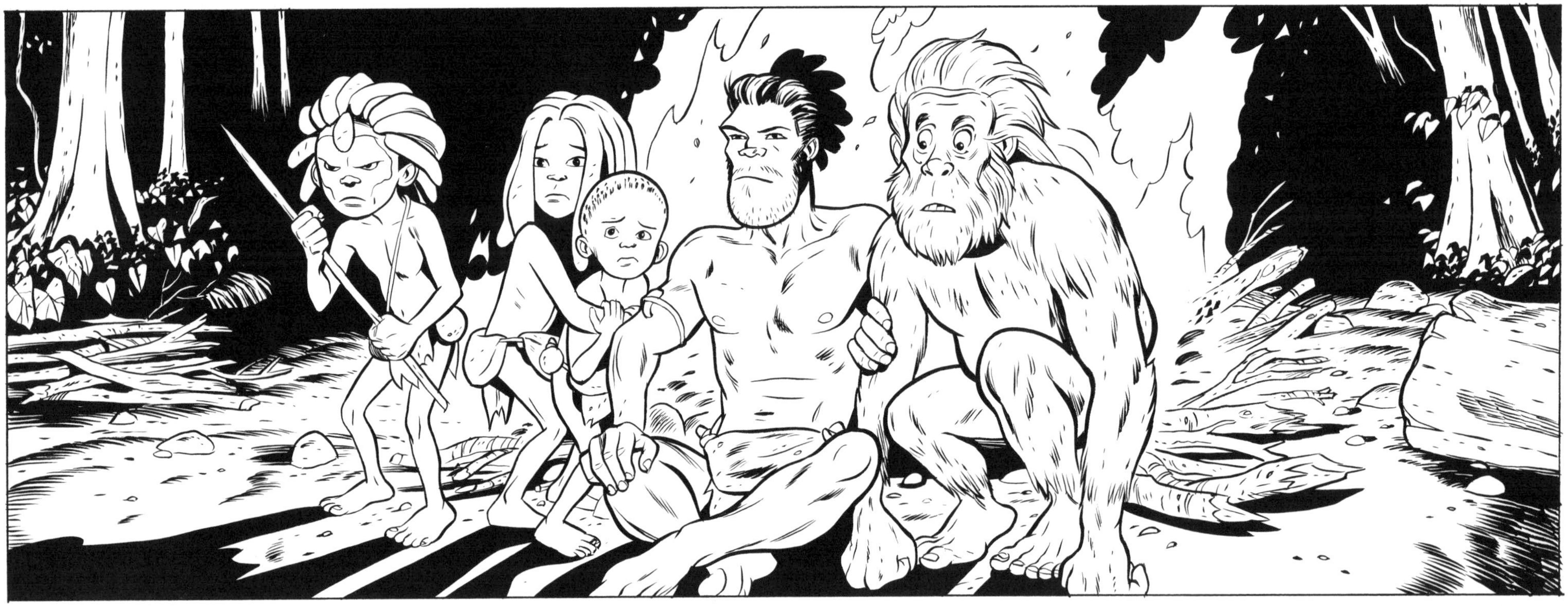

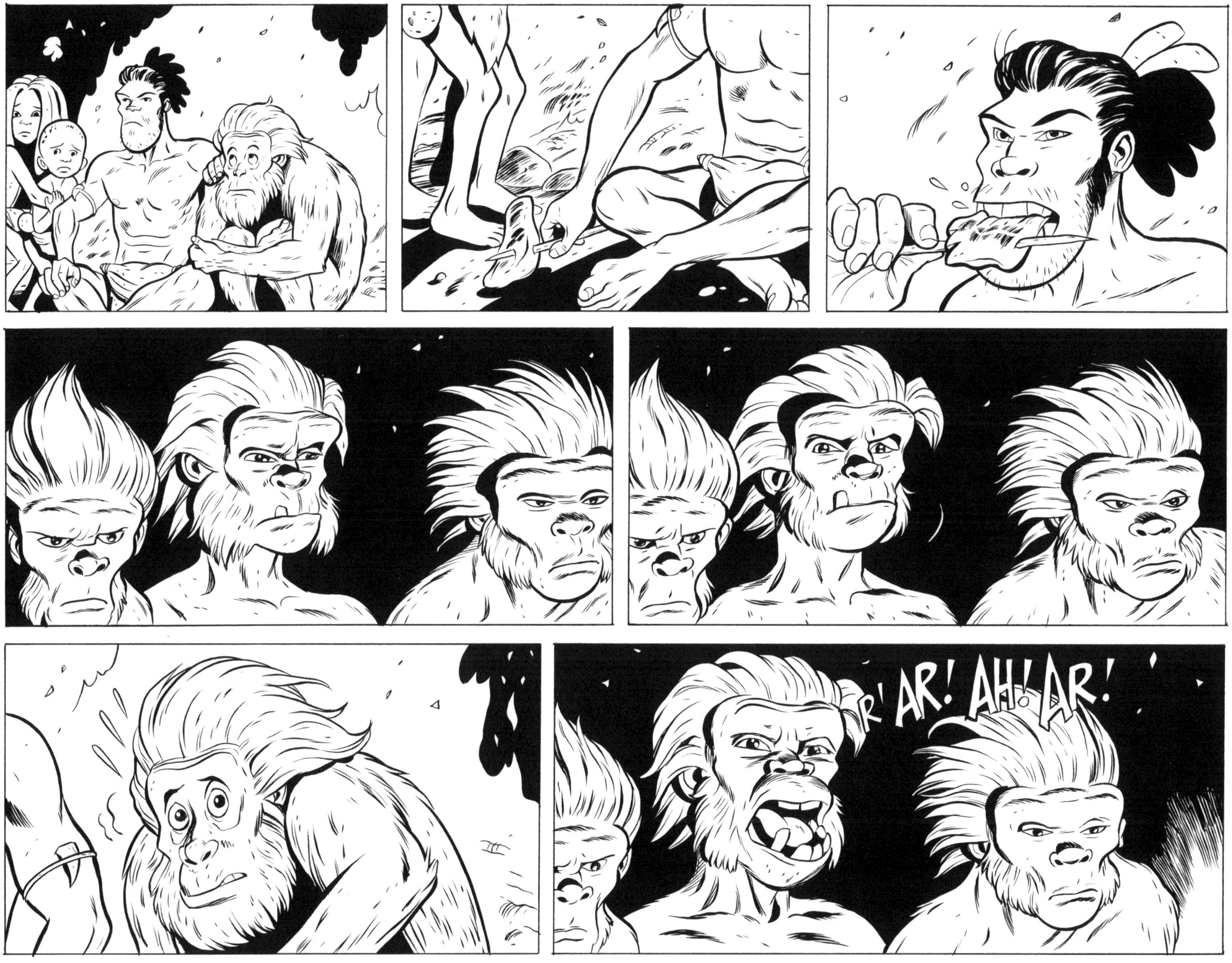
R' AR! AH! AR!

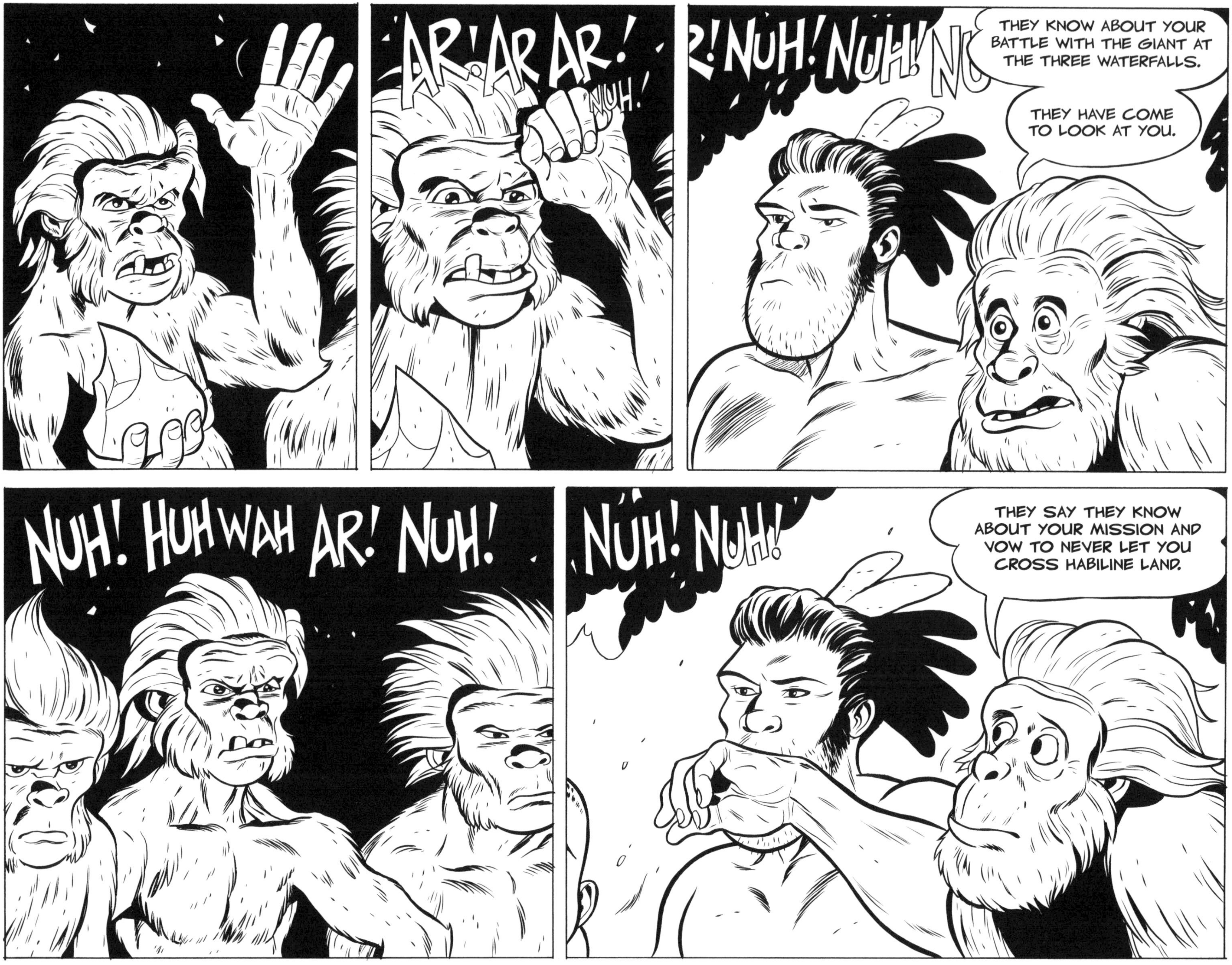
AR! AR AR!
NUH!
R! NUH! NUH! NU
THEY KNOW ABOUT YOUR BATTLE WITH THE GIANT AT THE THREE WATERFALLS.
THEY HAVE COME TO LOOK AT YOU.
NUH! HUH WAH AR! NUH!
NUH! NUH!
THEY SAY THEY KNOW ABOUT YOUR MISSION AND VOW TO NEVER LET YOU CROSS HABILINE LAND.

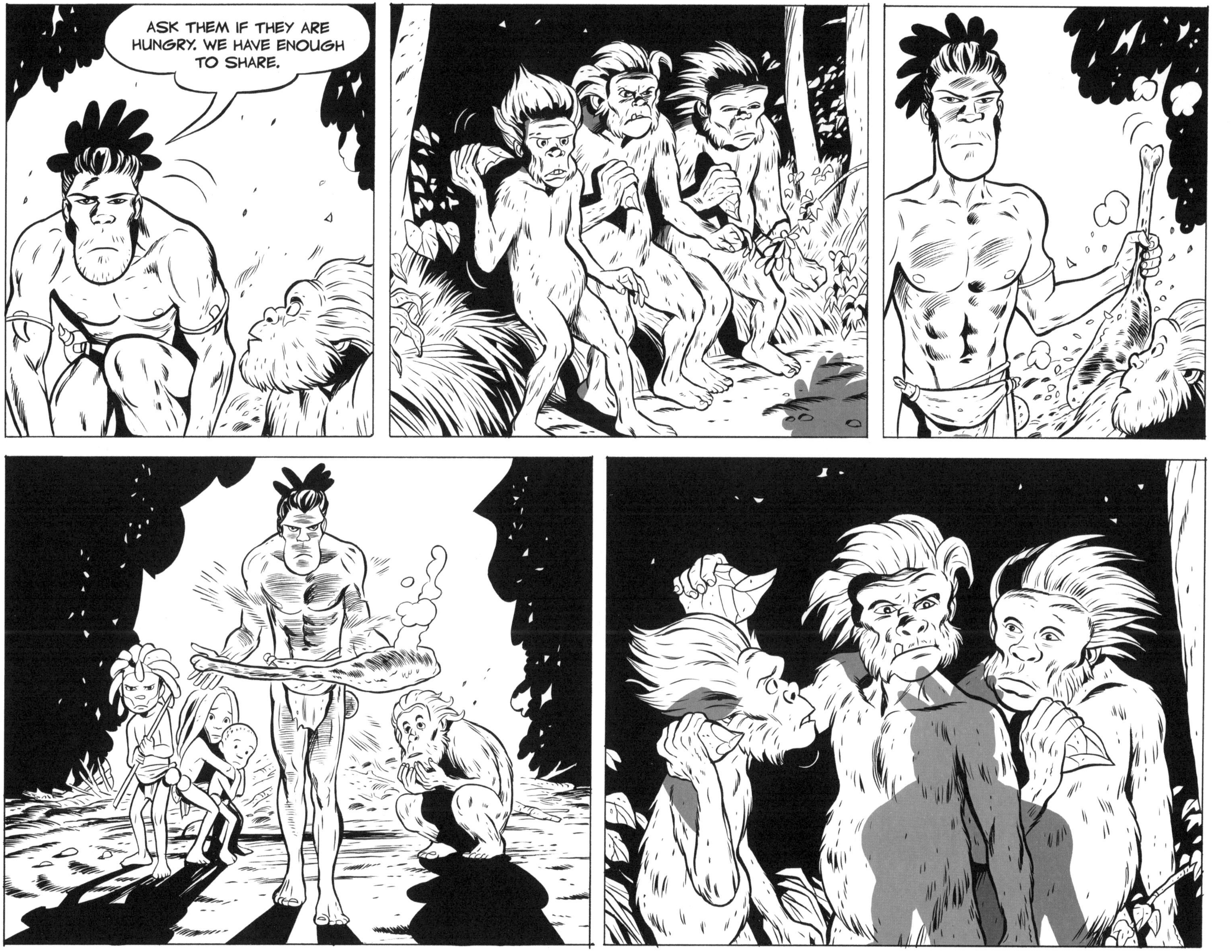
ASK THEM IF THEY ARE HUNGRY. WE HAVE ENOUGH TO SHARE.

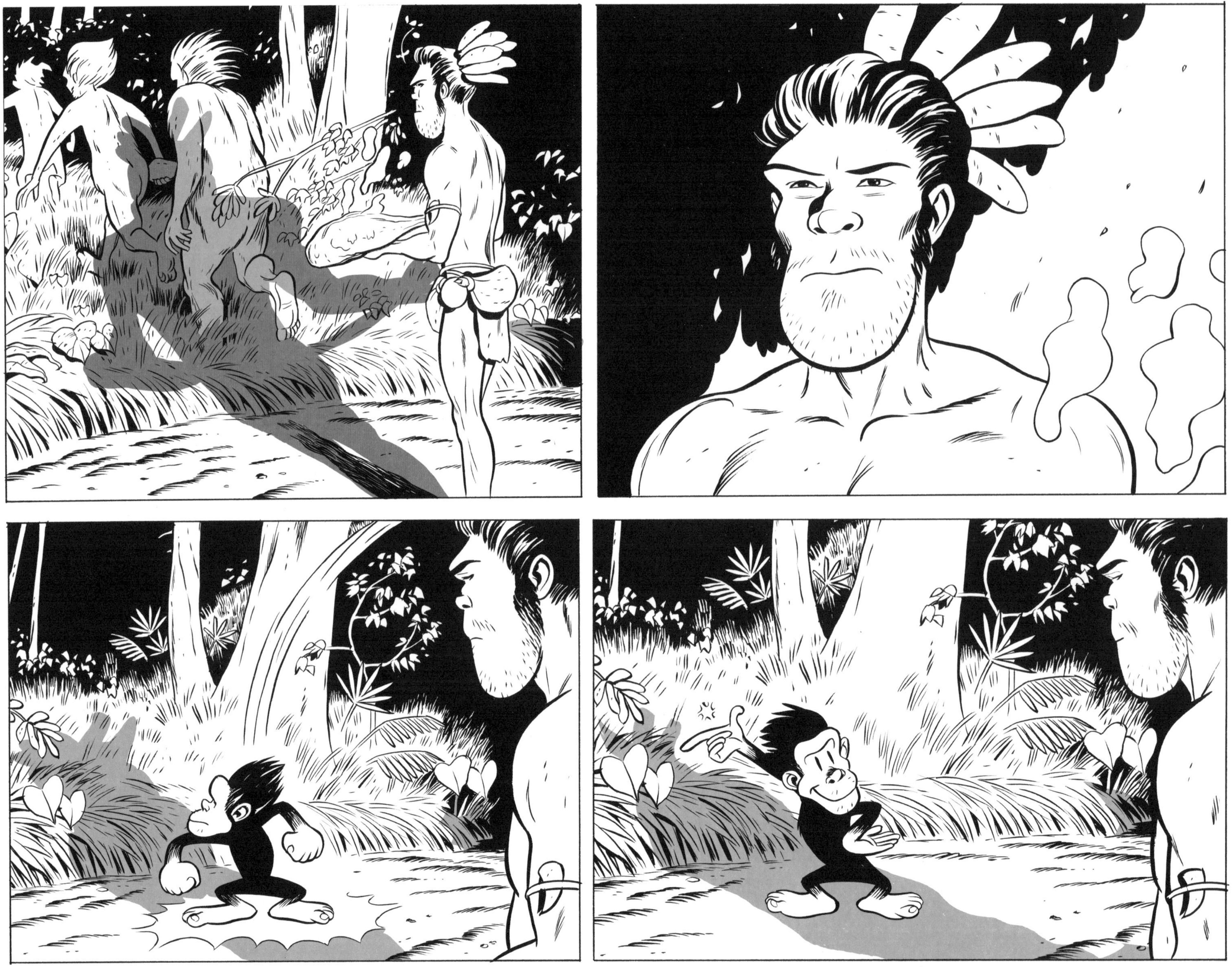

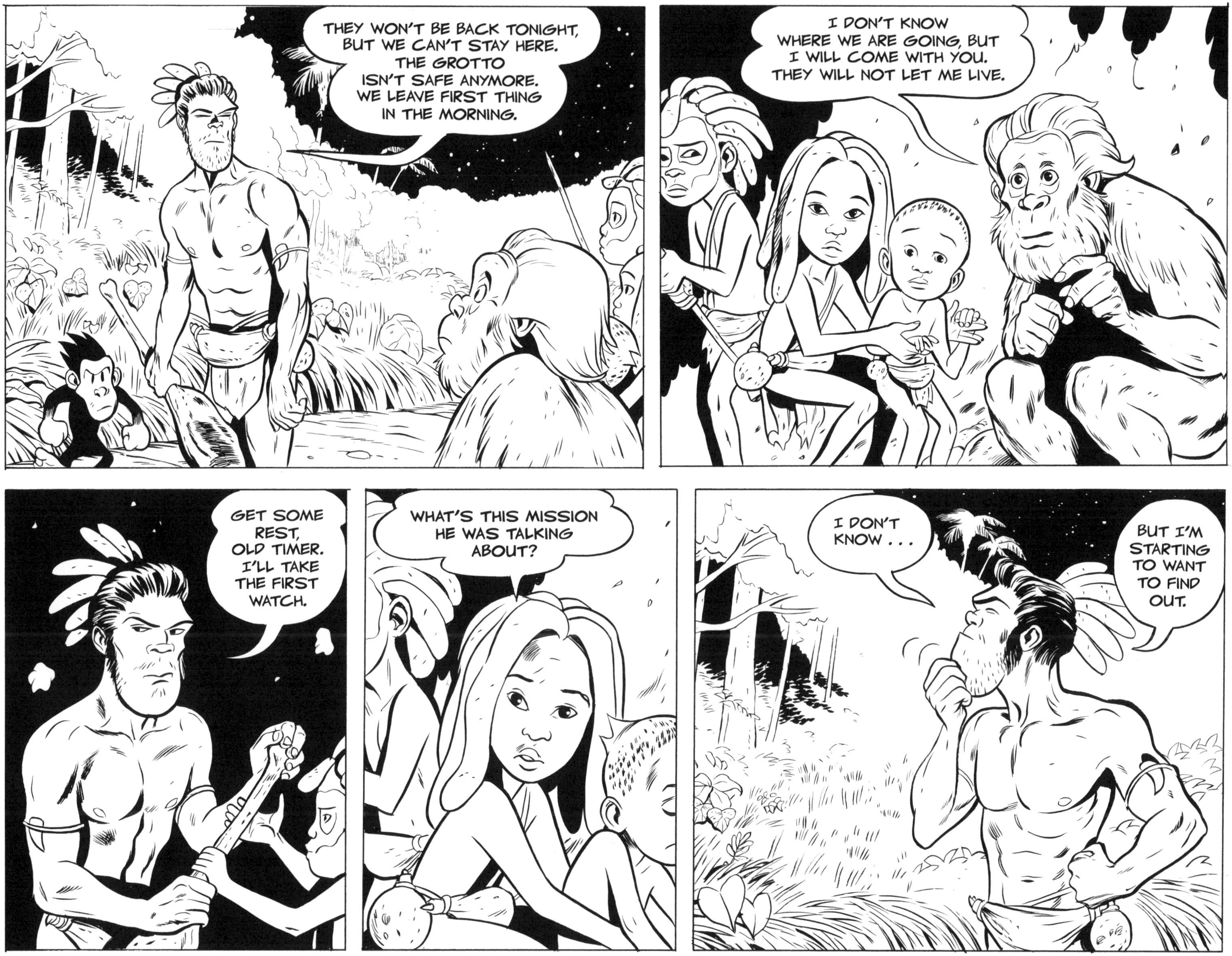
THEY WON'T BE BACK TONIGHT, BUT WE CAN'T STAY HERE. THE GROTTO ISN'T SAFE ANYMORE. WE LEAVE FIRST THING IN THE MORNING.
I DON'T KNOW WHERE WE ARE GOING, BUT I WILL COME WITH YOU. THEY WILL NOT LET ME LIVE.
GET SOME REST, OLD TIMER. I'LL TAKE THE FIRST WATCH.
WHAT'S THIS MISSION HE WAS TALKING ABOUT?
I DON'T KNOW . . .
BUT I'M STARTING TO WANT TO FIND OUT.

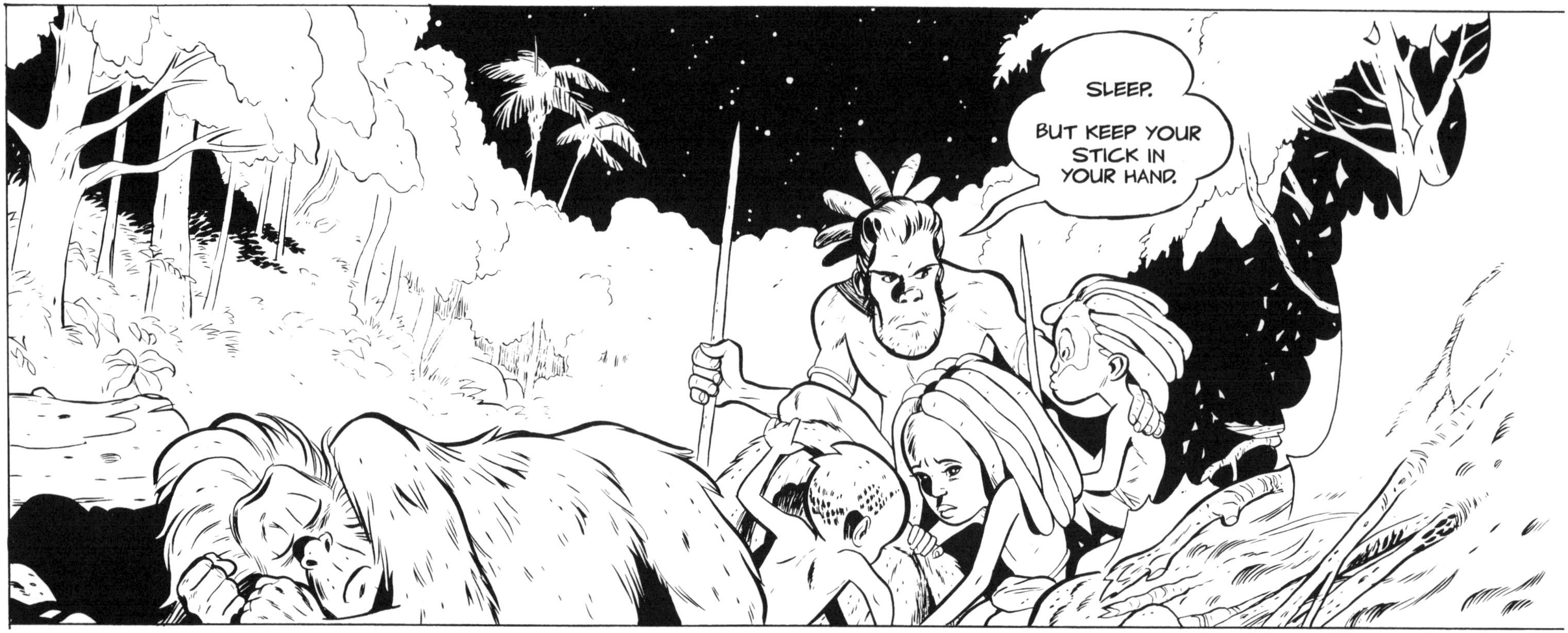
SLEEP.
BUT KEEP YOUR STICK IN YOUR HAND.

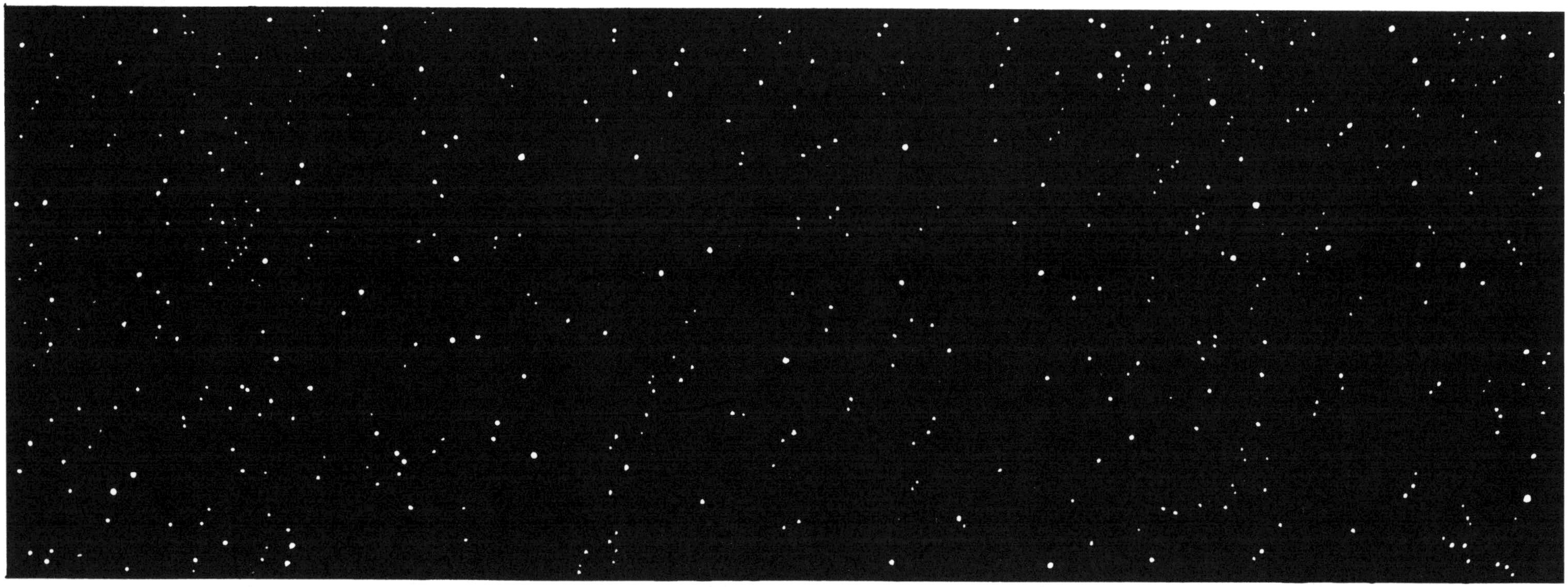

Five

The Second Miracle

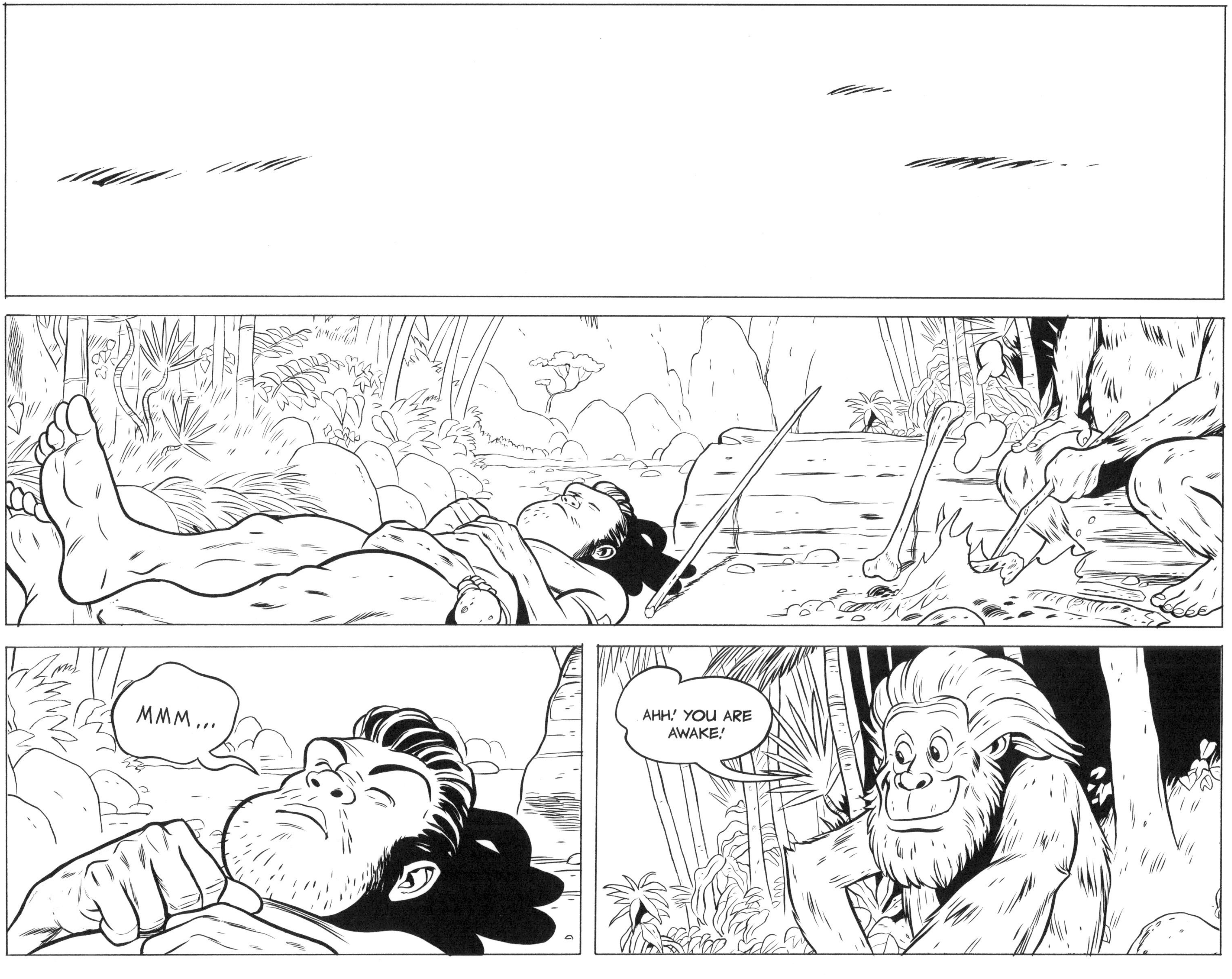
MMM...
AHH! YOU ARE AWAKE!

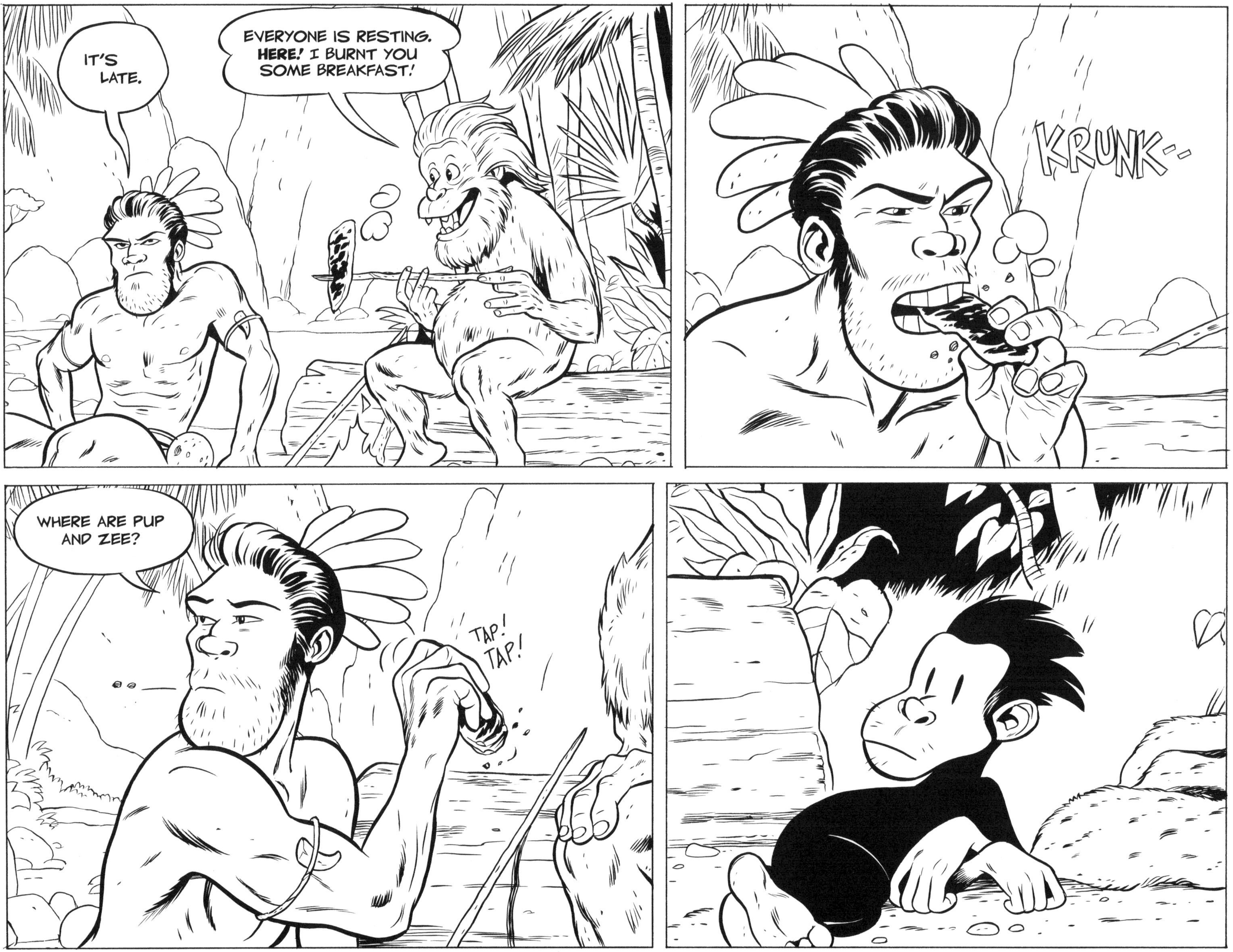
IT'S LATE.
EVERYONE IS RESTING. **HERE!** I BURNT YOU SOME BREAKFAST!
KRUNK--
WHERE ARE PUP AND ZEE?
TAP! TAP!

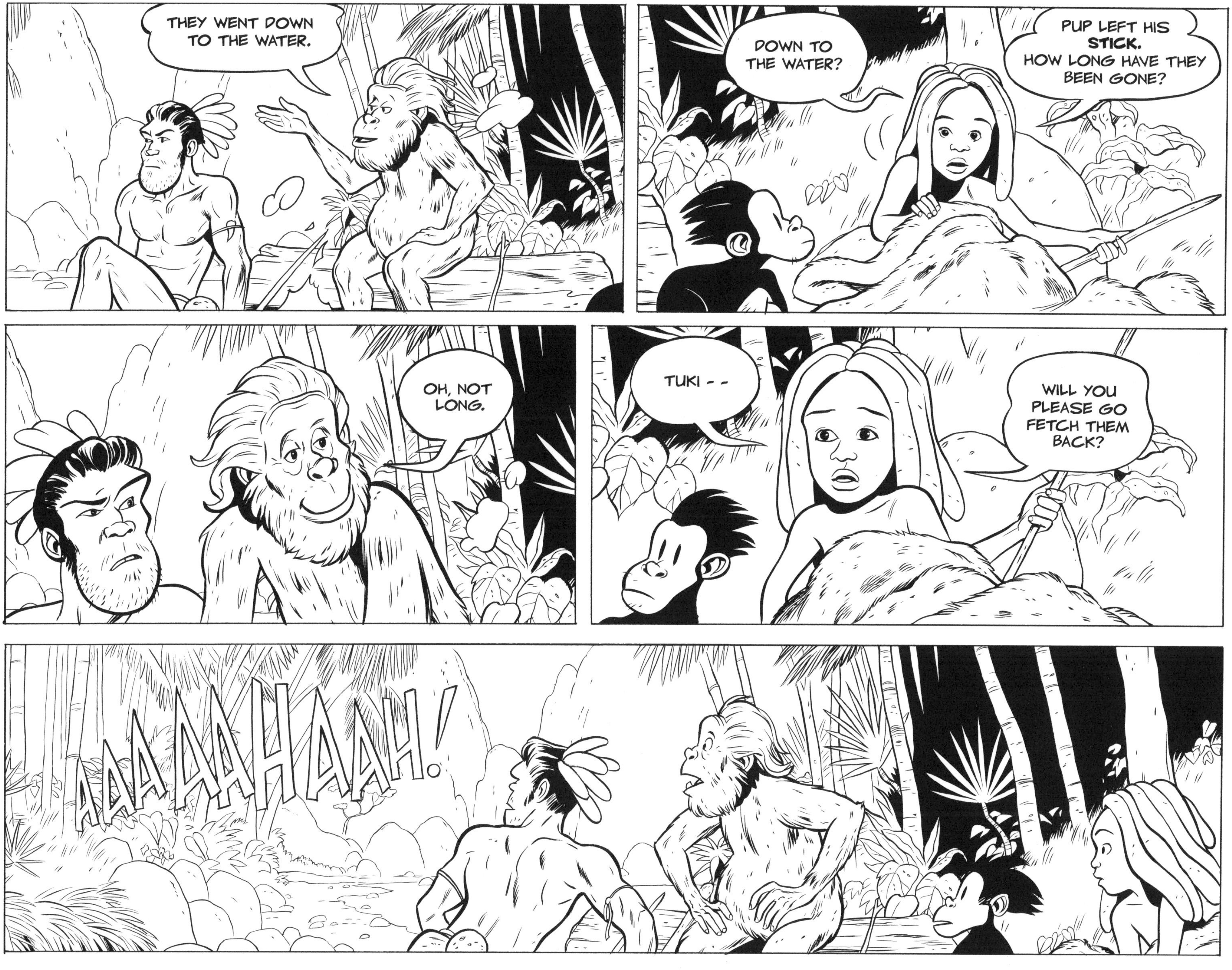
THEY WENT DOWN TO THE WATER.
DOWN TO THE WATER?
PUP LEFT HIS **STICK.** HOW LONG HAVE THEY BEEN GONE?
OH, NOT LONG.
TUKI - -
WILL YOU PLEASE GO FETCH THEM BACK?
AAAAAHAAAH!

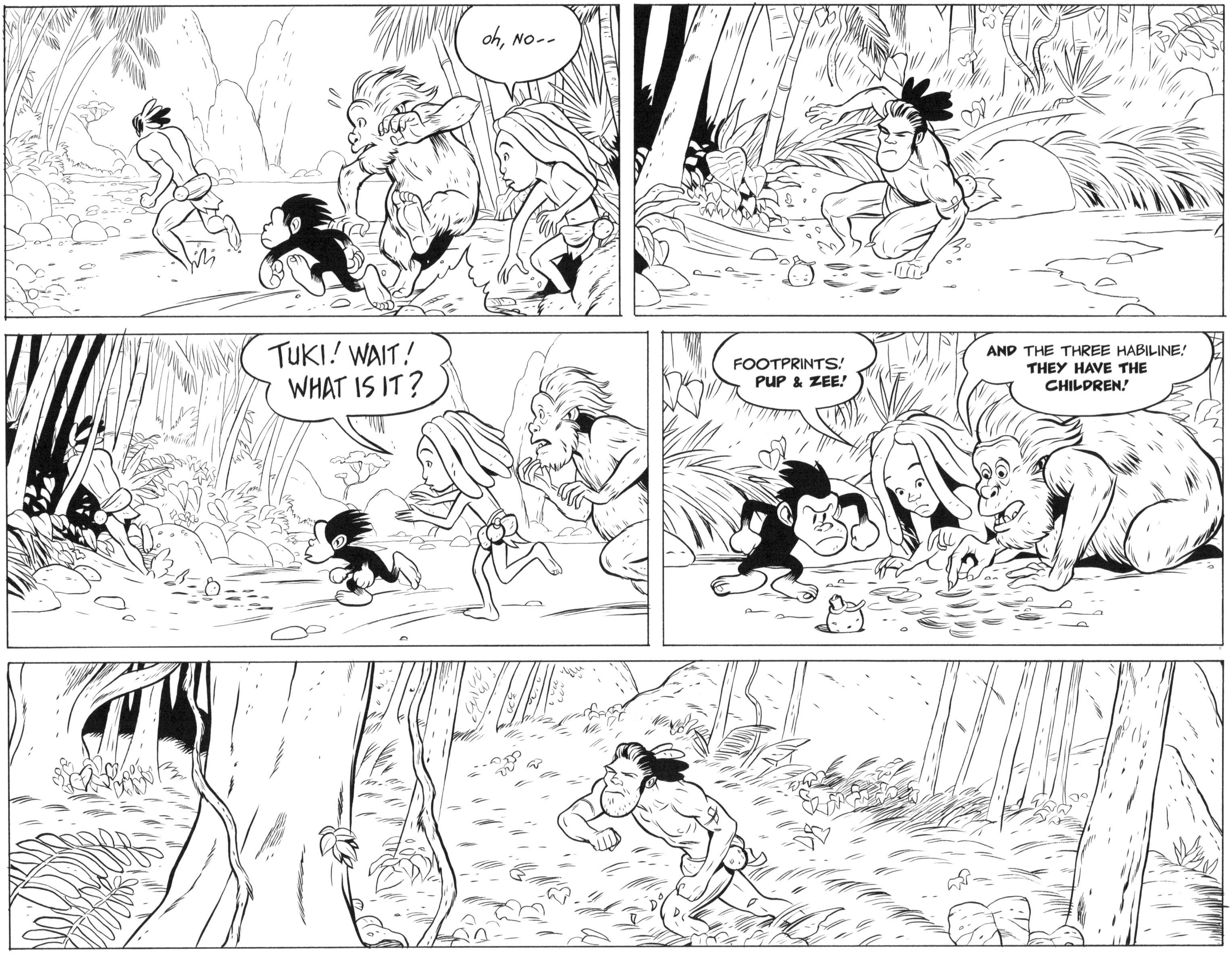
oh, NO--
TUKI! WAIT! WHAT IS IT?
FOOTPRINTS! PUP & ZEE!
AND THE THREE HABILINE! THEY HAVE THE CHILDREN!

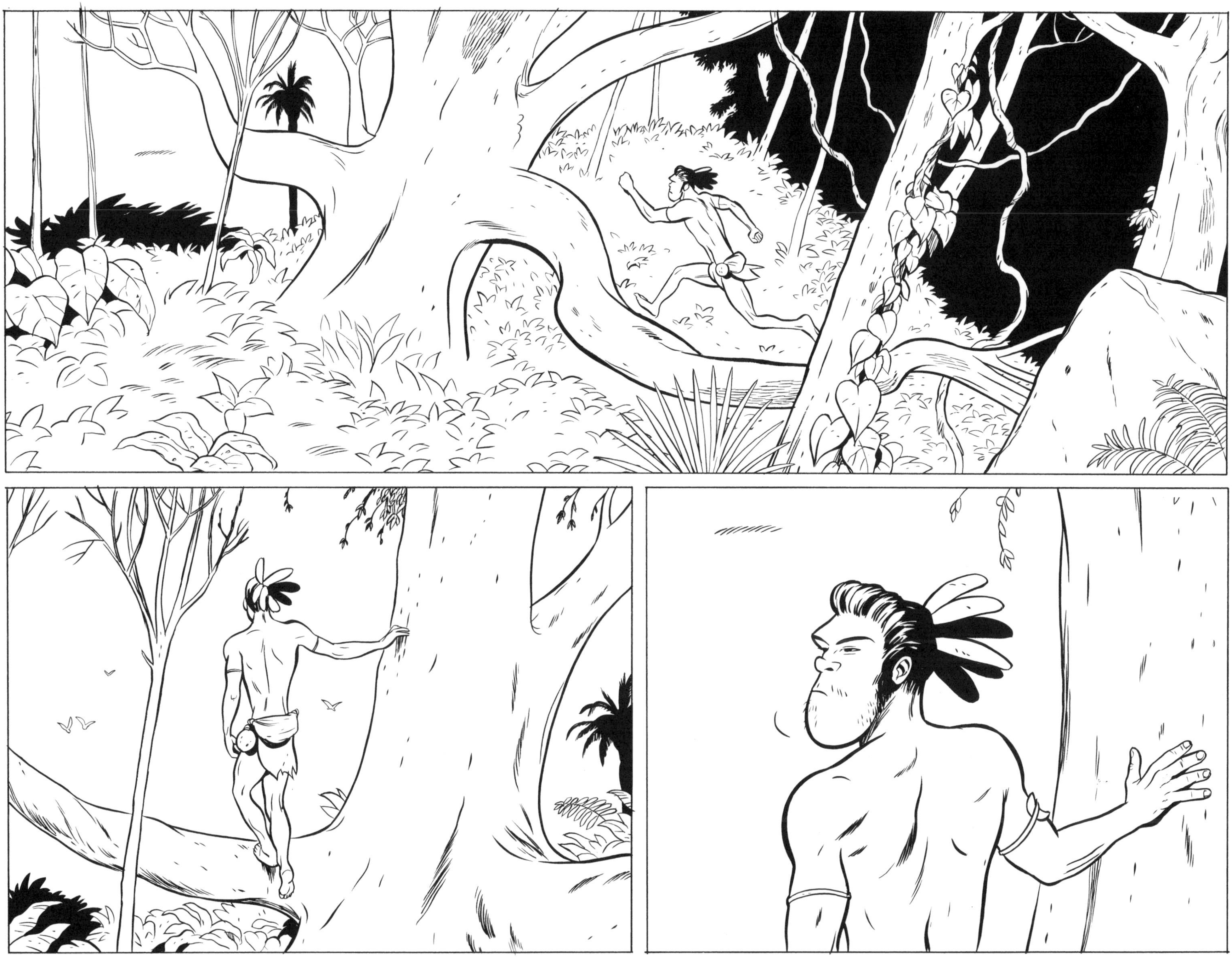

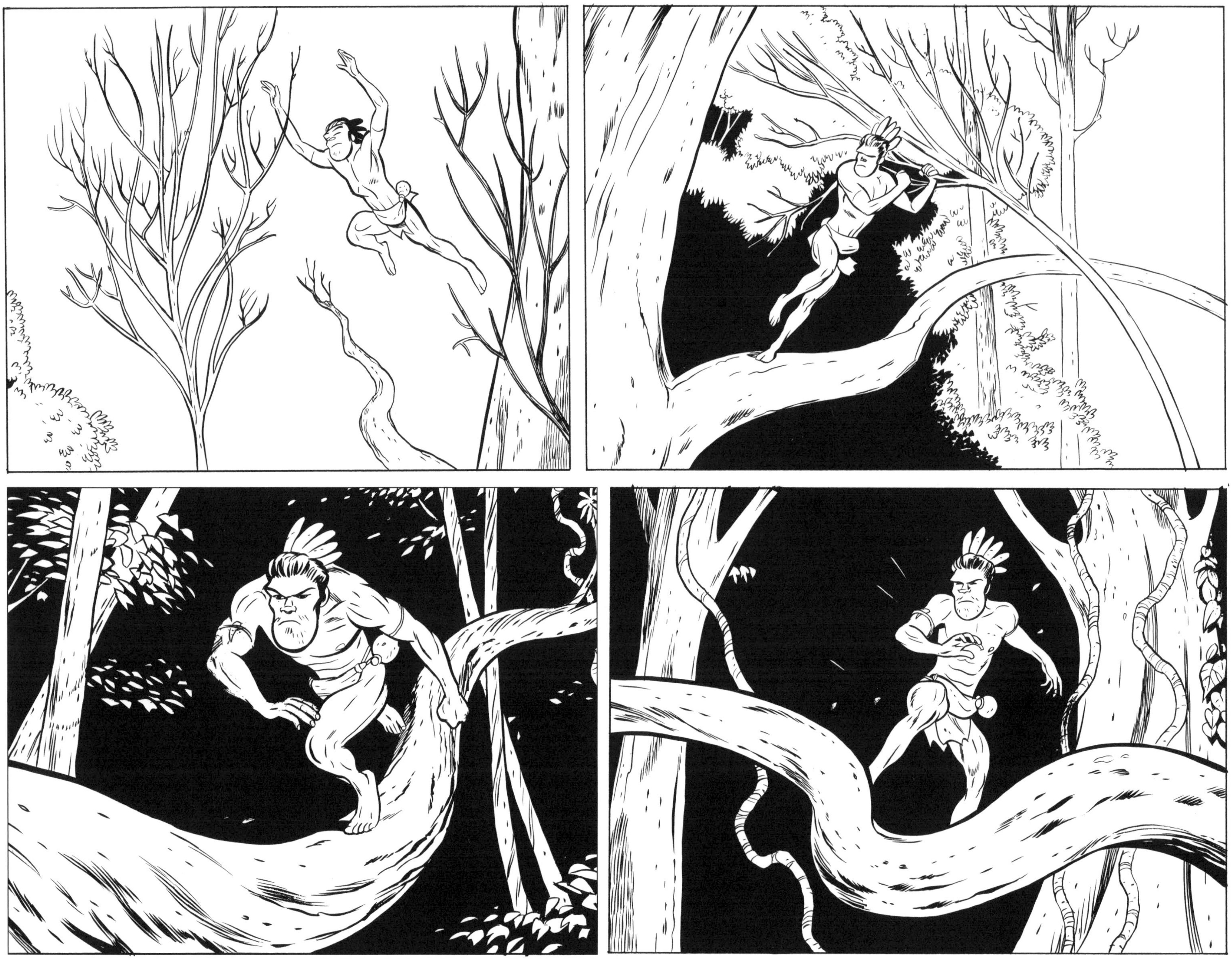

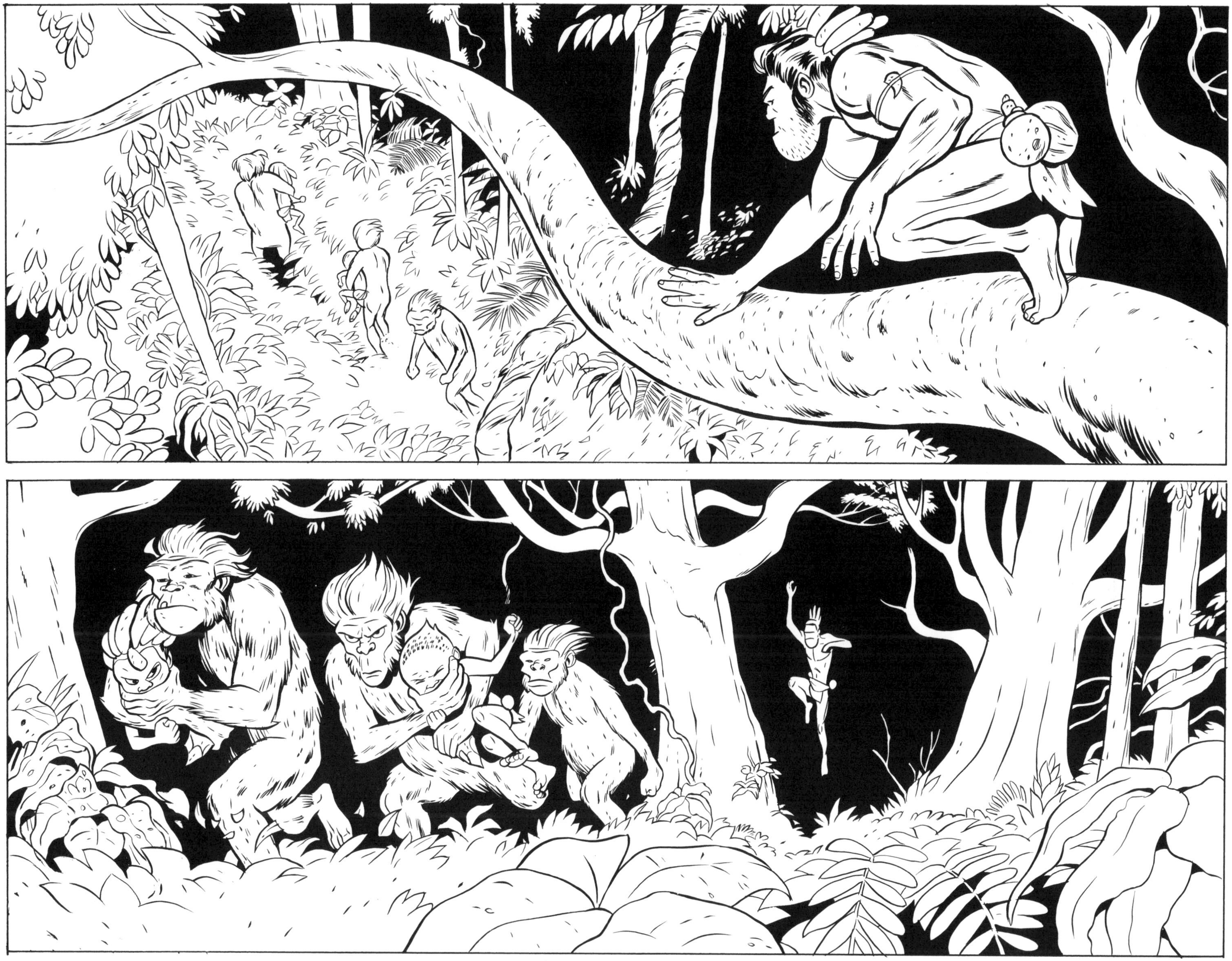

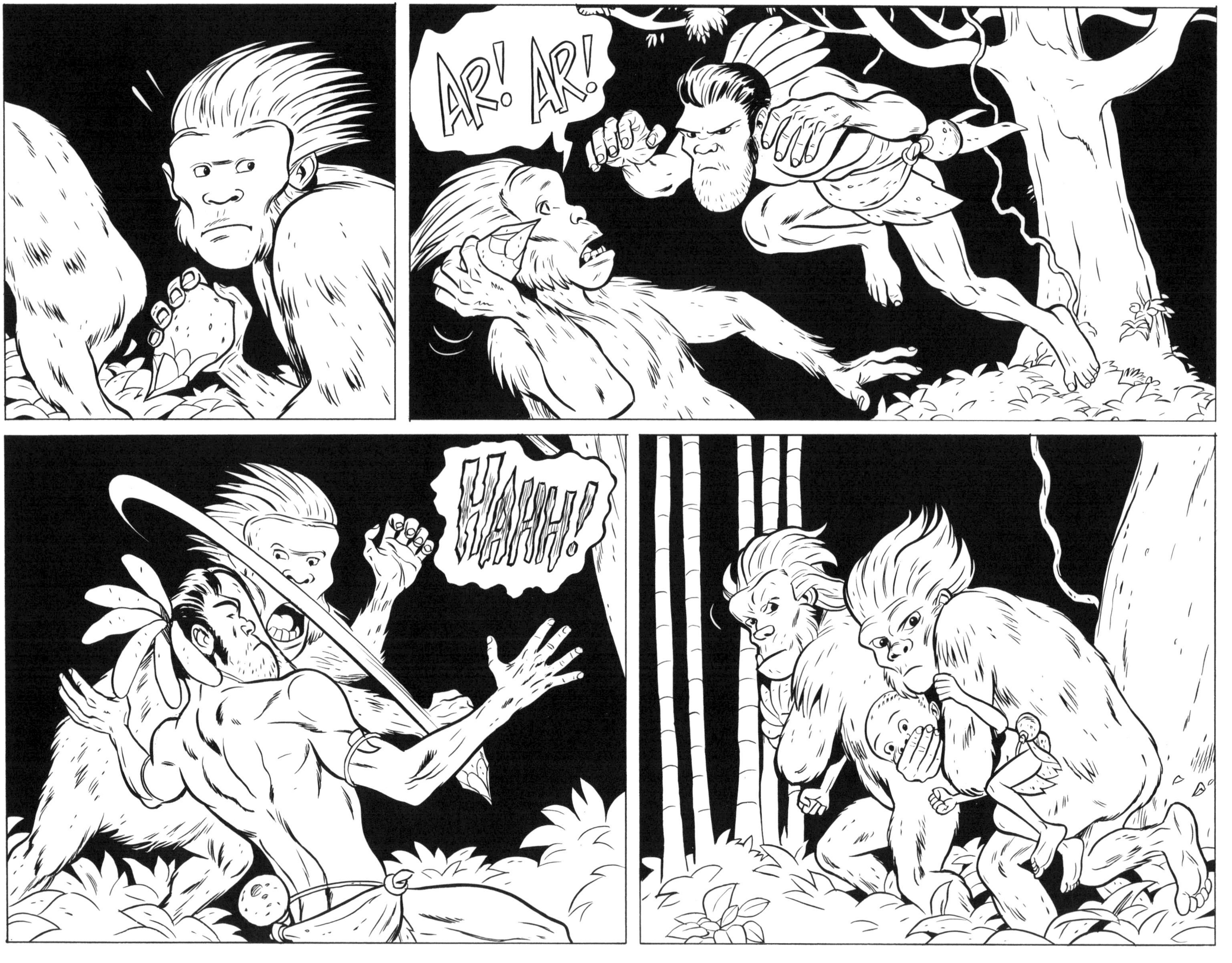
AR! AR!
HAHH!

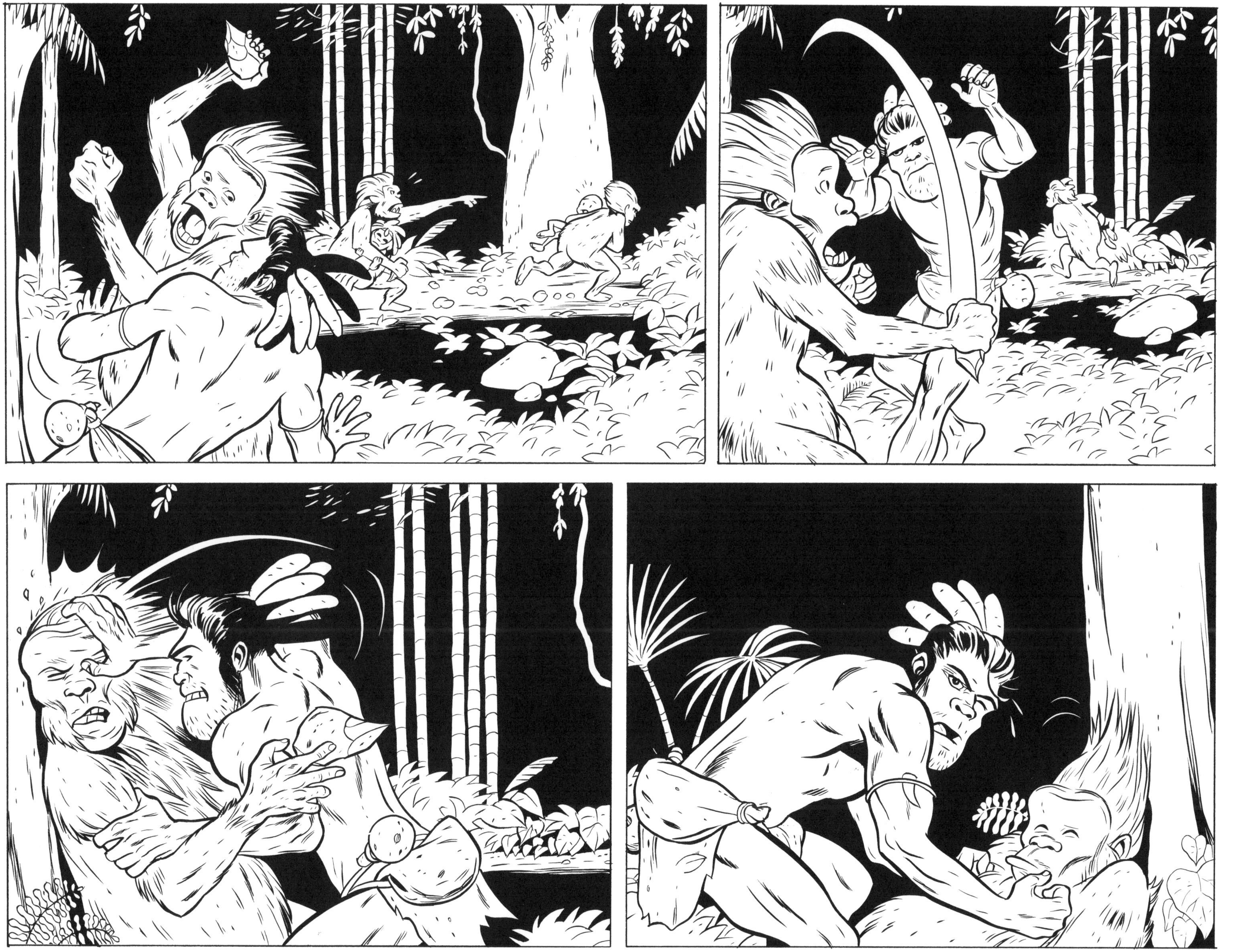

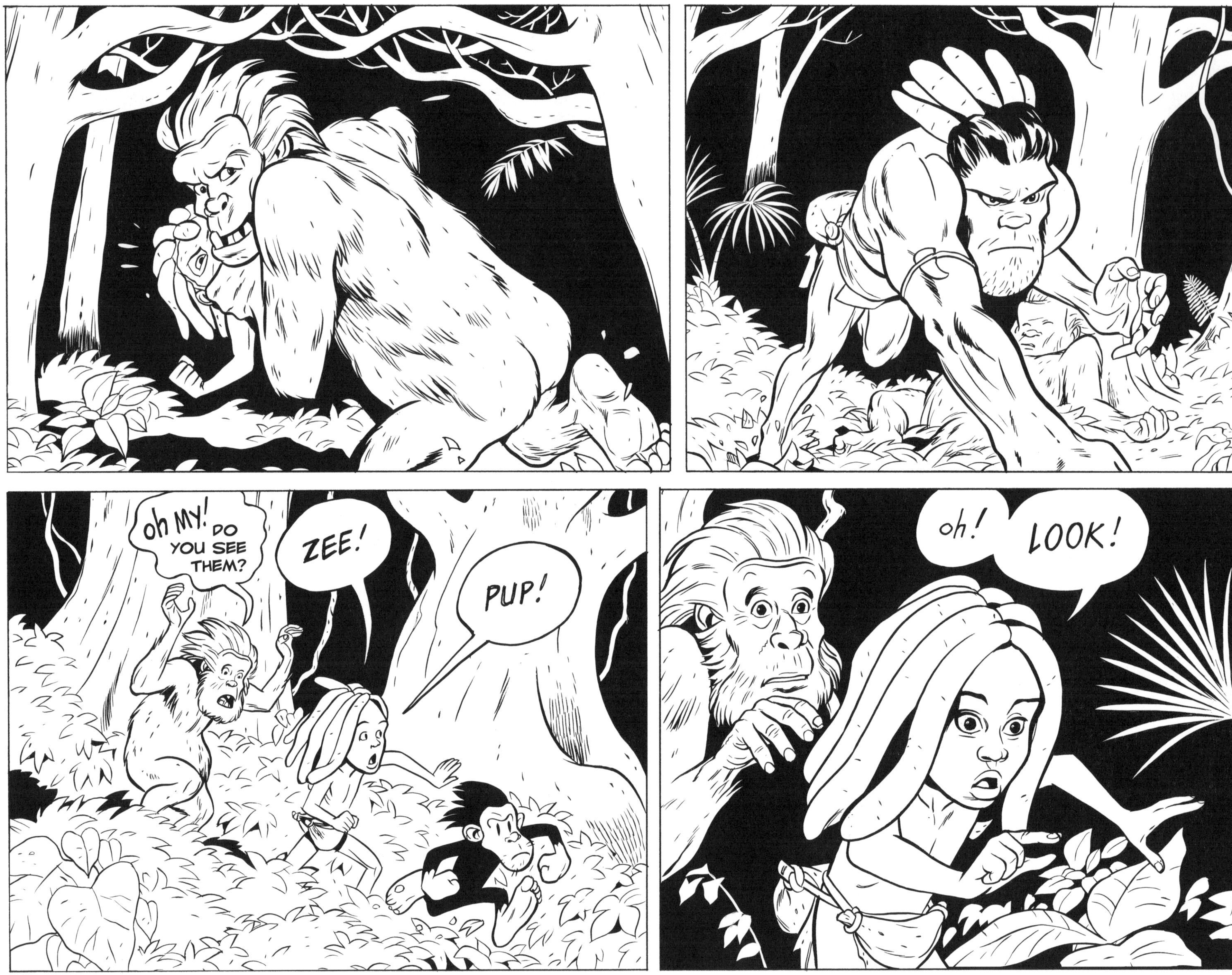
oh MY! DO YOU SEE THEM?
ZEE!
PUP!
oh!
LOOK!

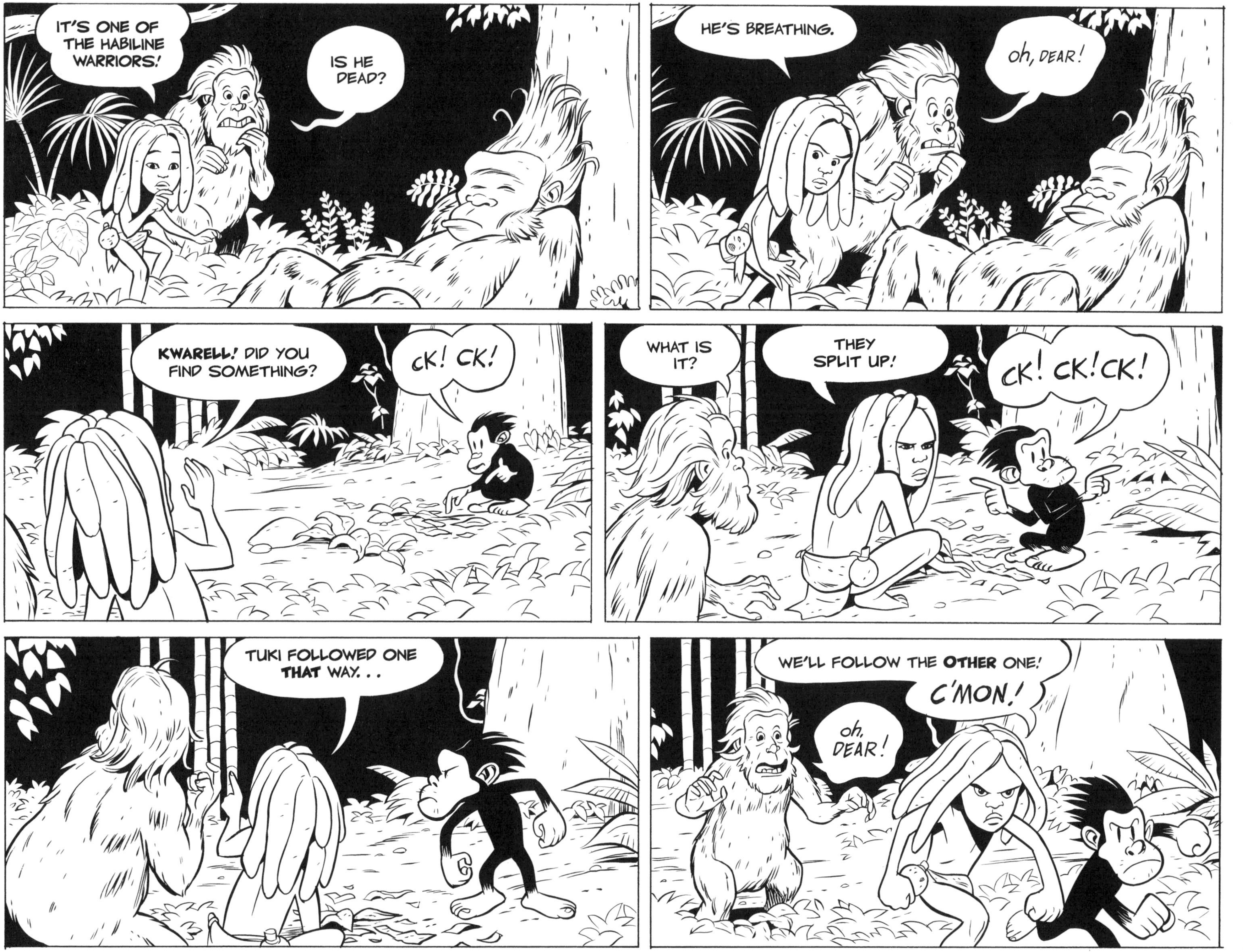
IT'S ONE OF THE HABILINE WARRIORS!
IS HE DEAD?
HE'S BREATHING.
oh, DEAR!
KWARELL! DID YOU FIND SOMETHING?
CK! CK!
WHAT IS IT?
THEY SPLIT UP!
CK! CK! CK!
TUKI FOLLOWED ONE THAT WAY...
WE'LL FOLLOW THE OTHER ONE!
C'MON!
oh, DEAR!

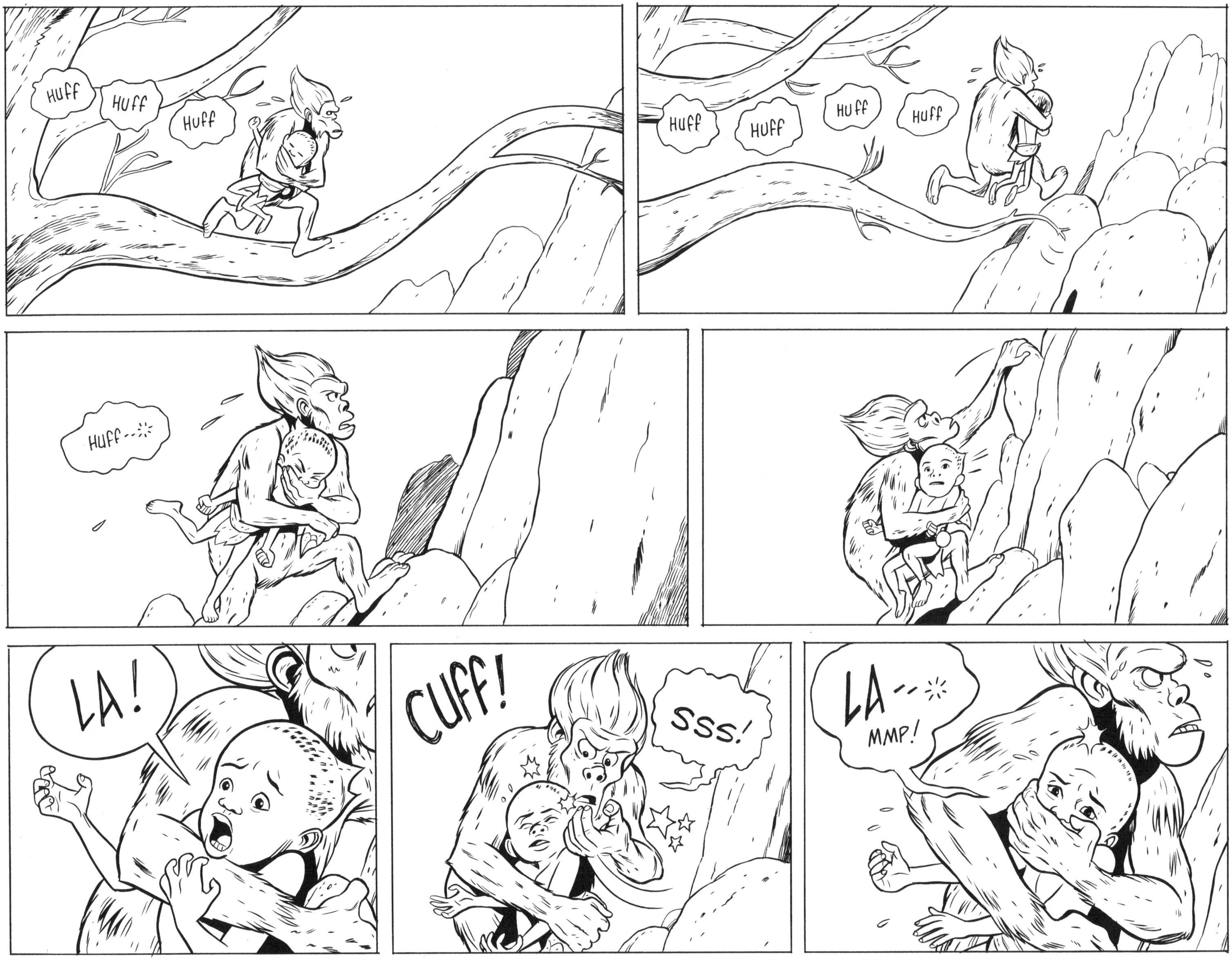

HUFF
HUFF
HUFF
HUFF
HUFF
HUFF
HUFF
HUFF--
LA!
CUFF!
SSS!
LA--
MMP!

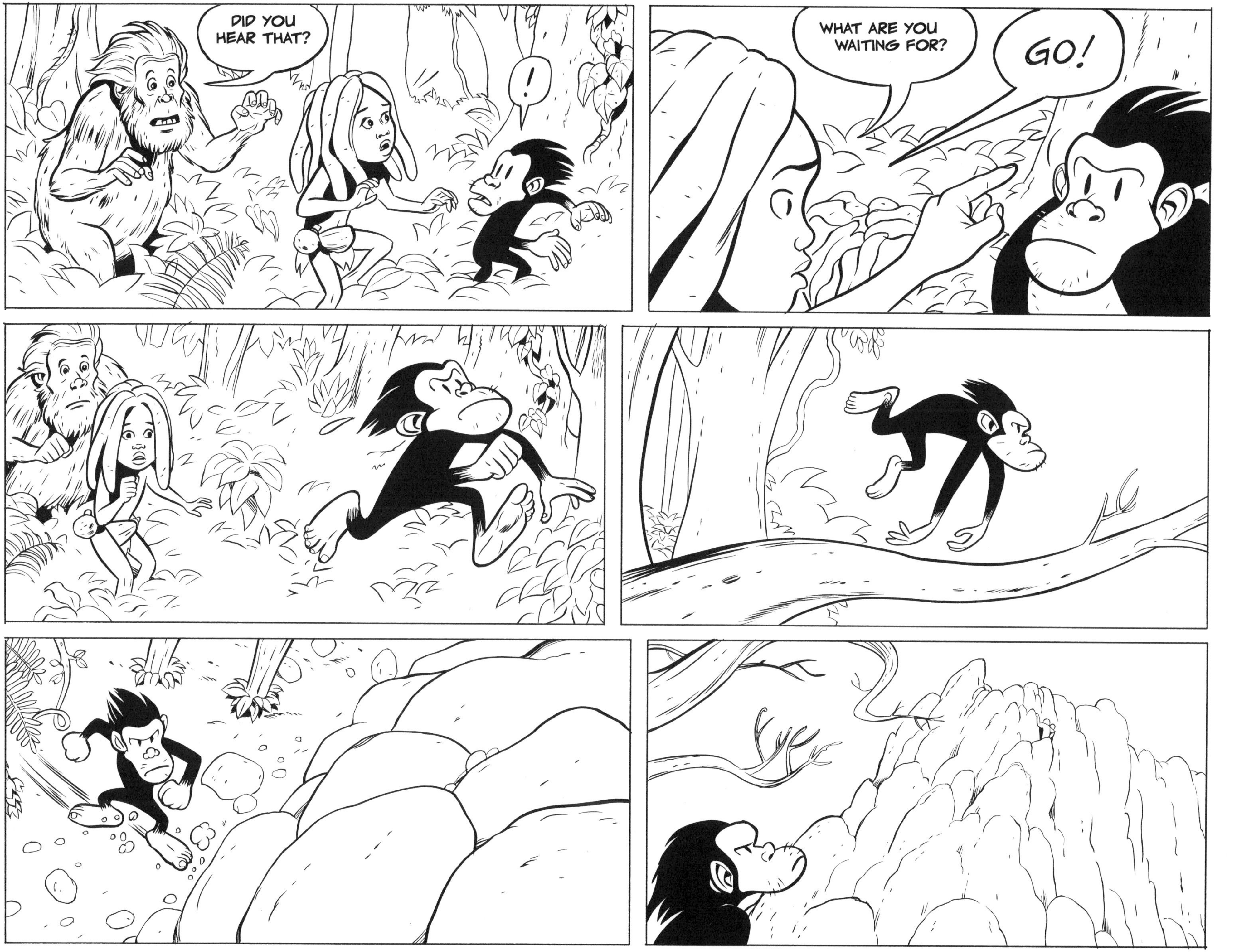
DID YOU HEAR THAT?
!
WHAT ARE YOU WAITING FOR?
GO!

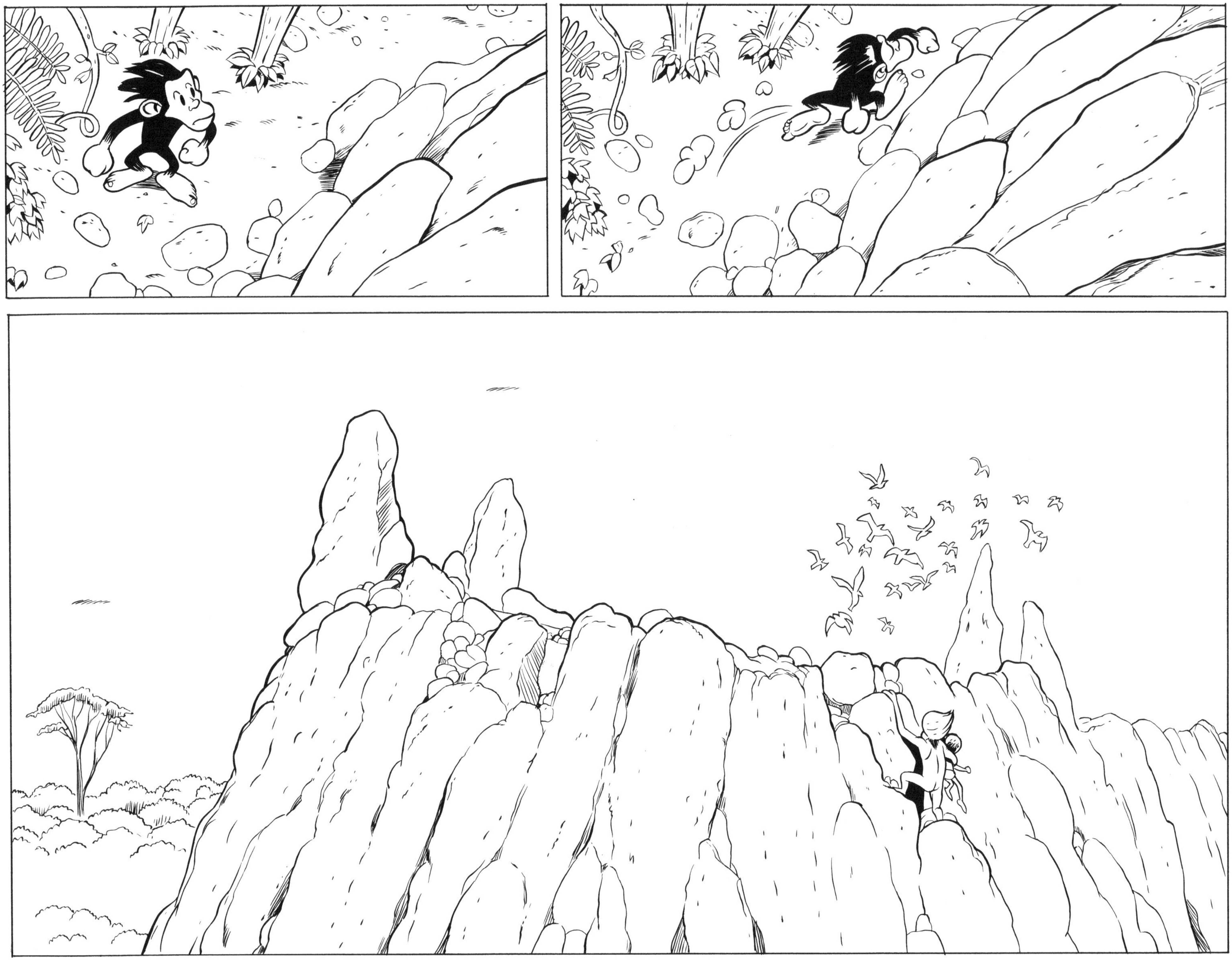

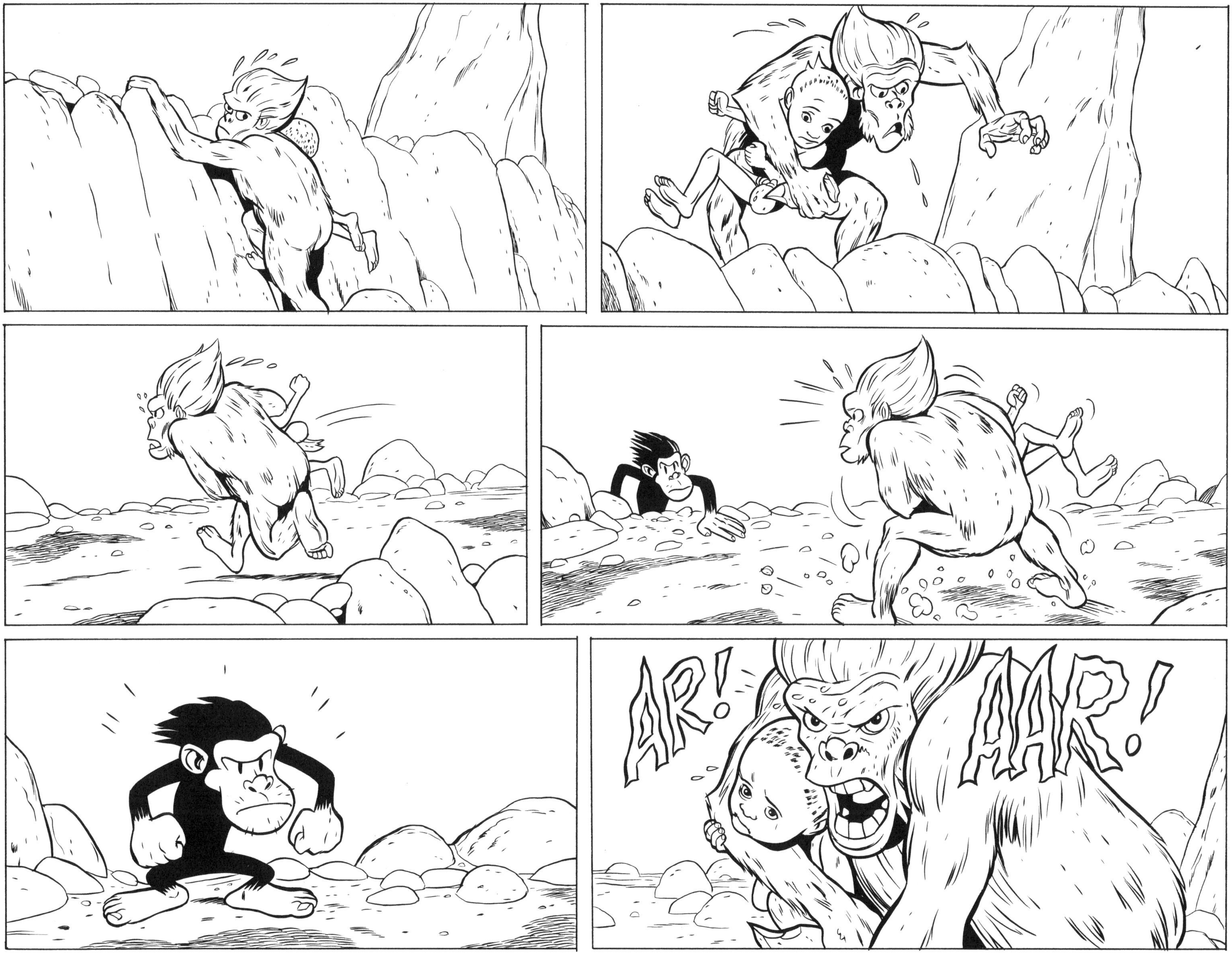
AR!
AAR!

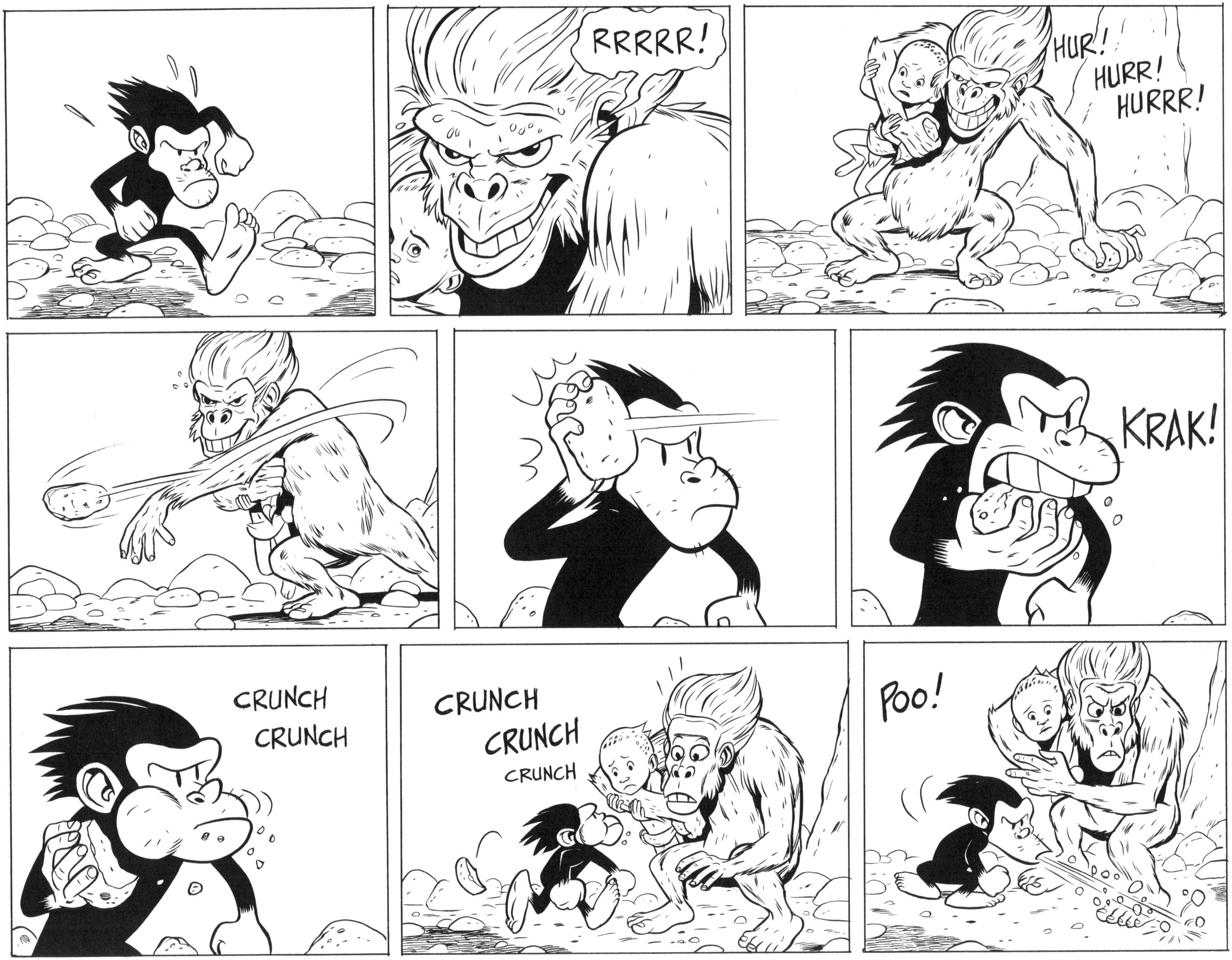
RRRRR!
HUR!
HURR!
HURRR!
KRAK!
CRUNCH
CRUNCH
CRUNCH
CRUNCH
CRUNCH
POO!

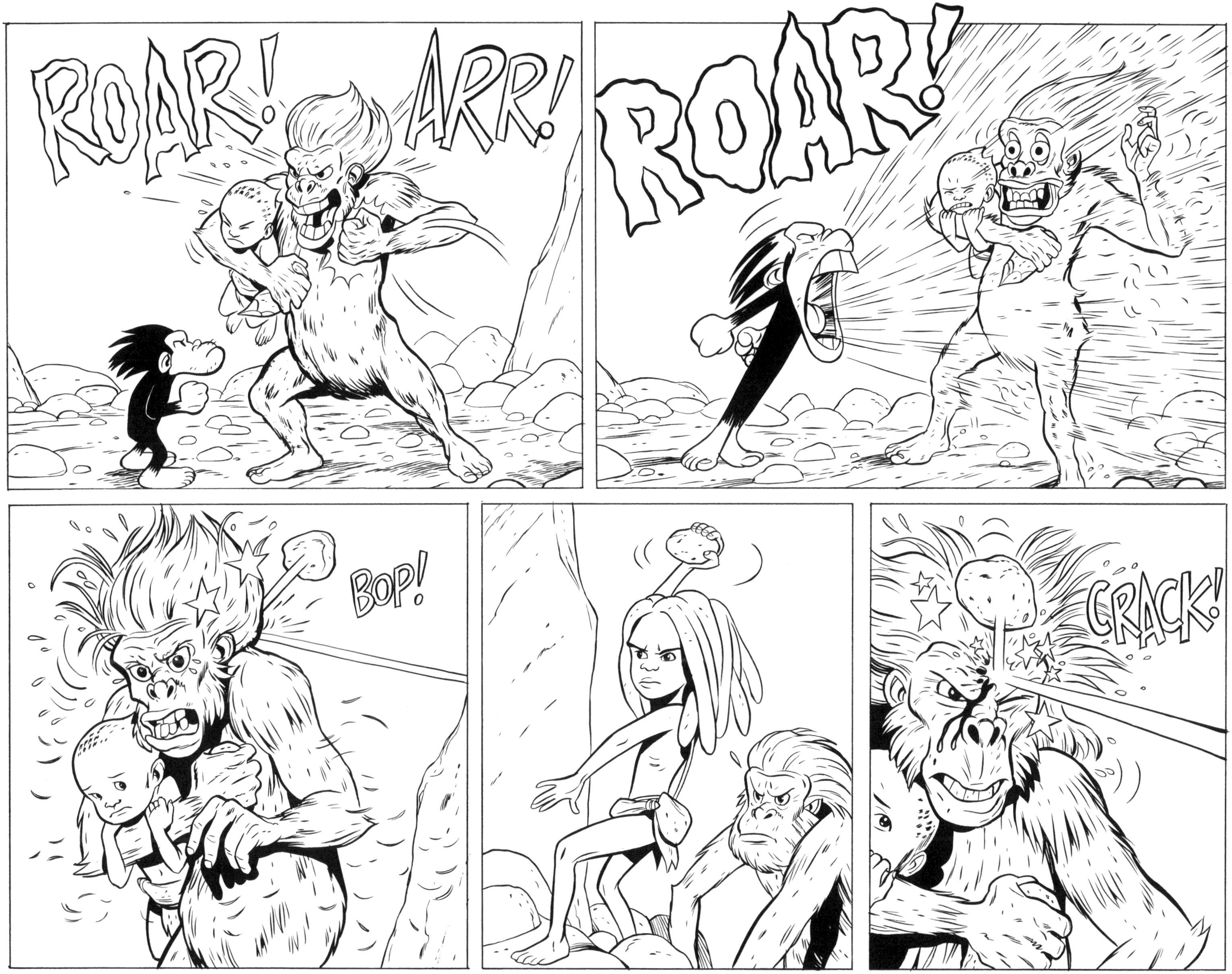
ROAR!
ARR!
ROAR!
BOP!
CRACK!

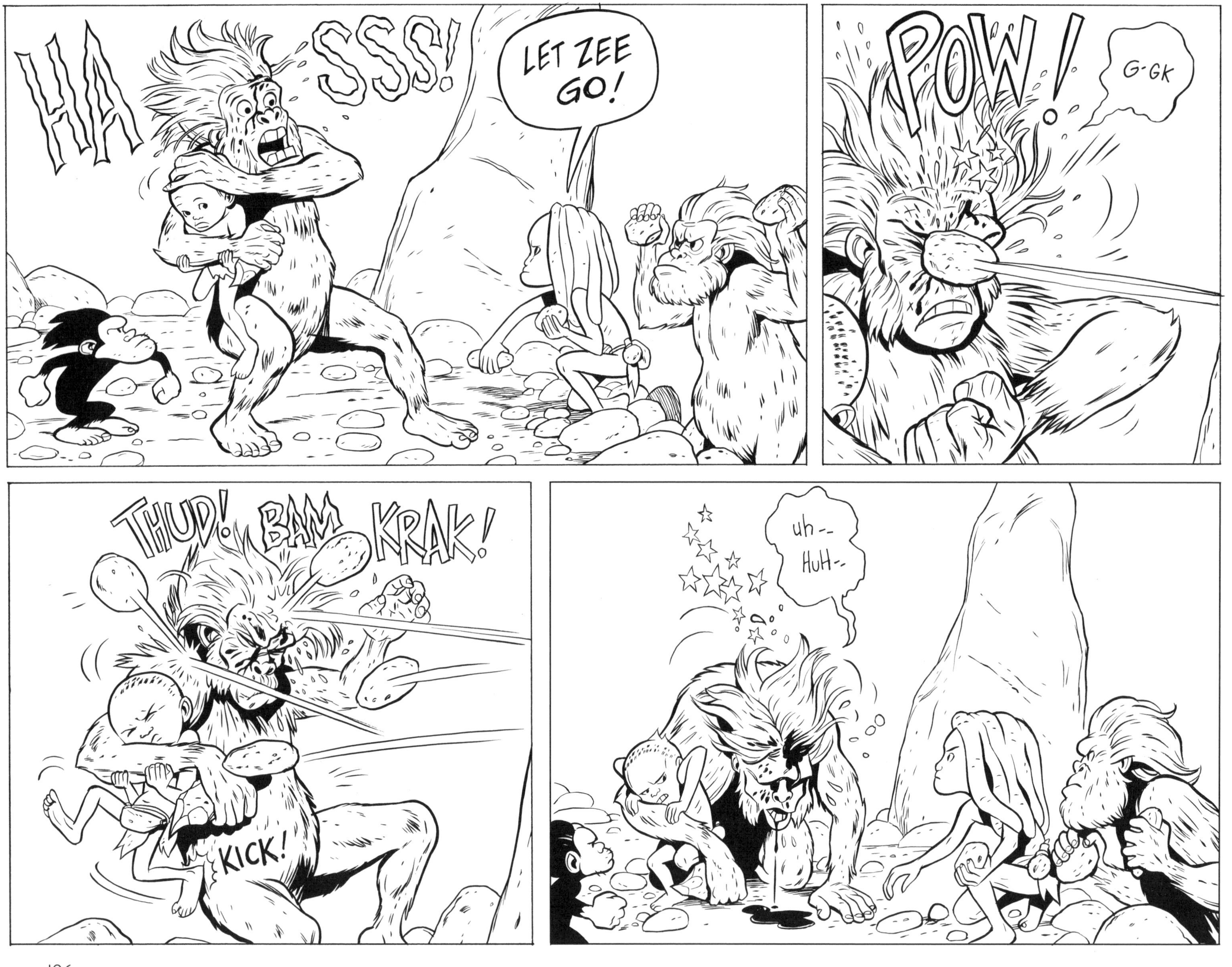
HA
SSSS!
LET ZEE GO!
POW!
G-GK
THUD!
BAM
KRAK!
KICK!
uh--
HuH--

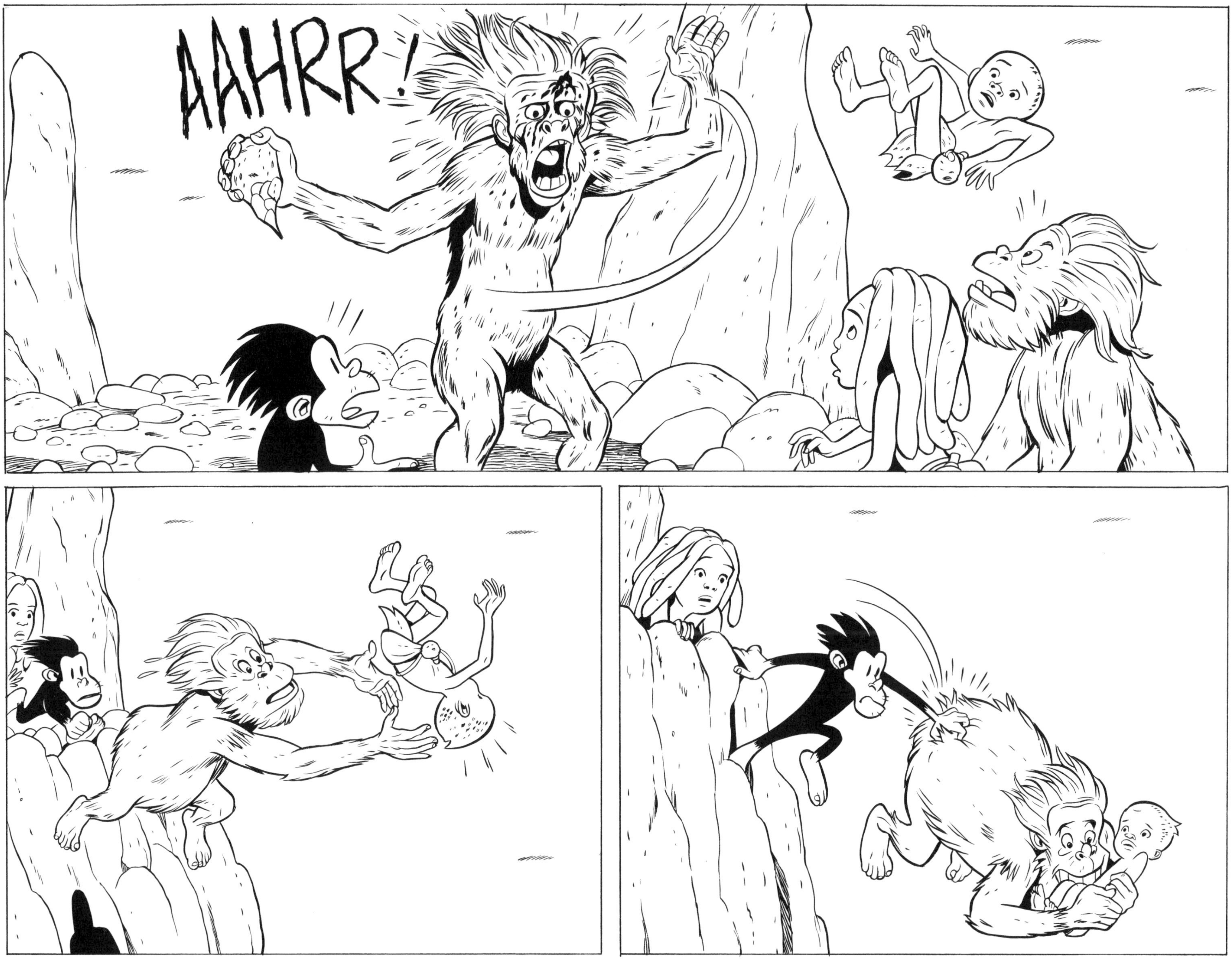
AAHRR!

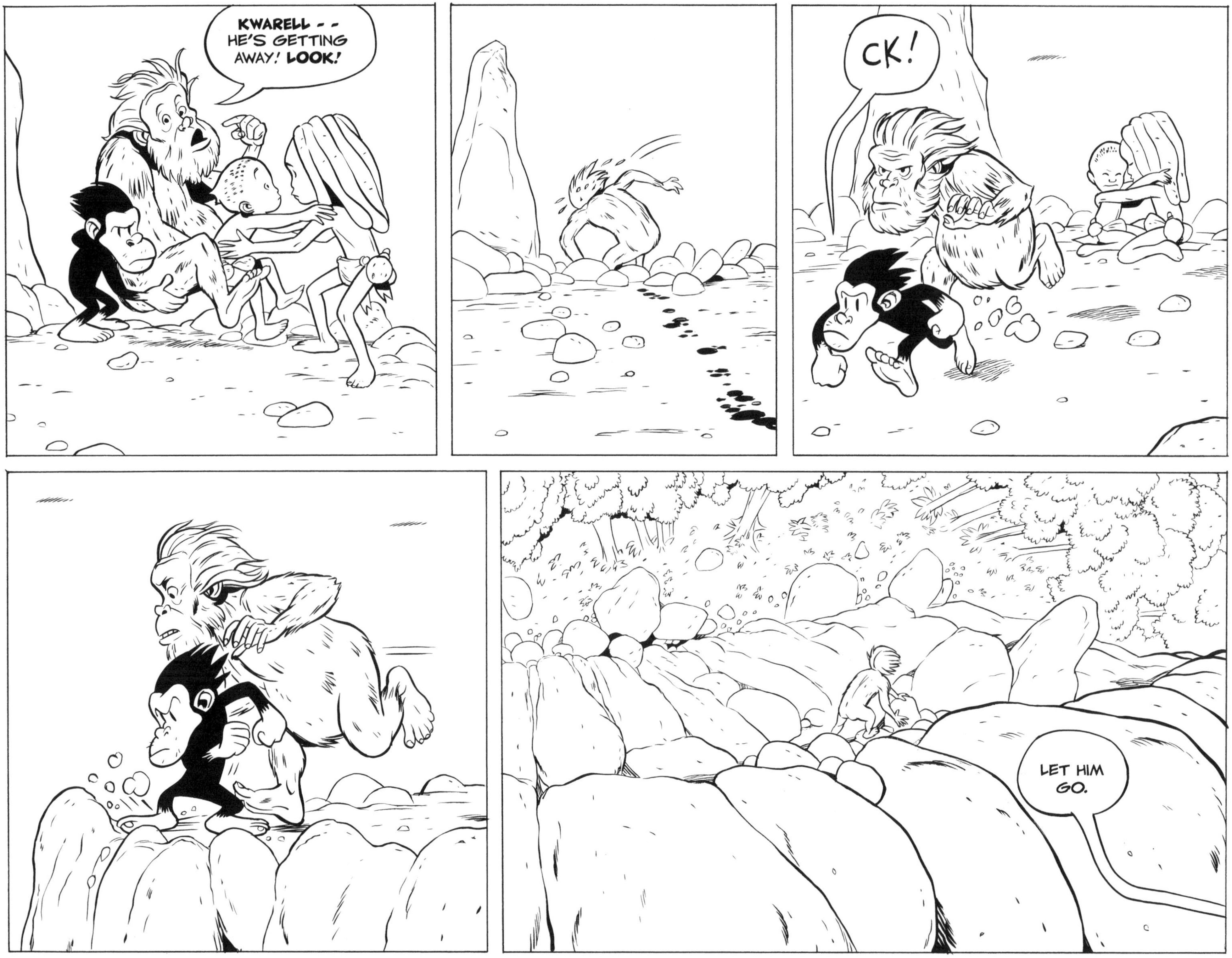
KWARELL - - HE'S GETTING AWAY! LOOK!
CK!
LET HIM GO.

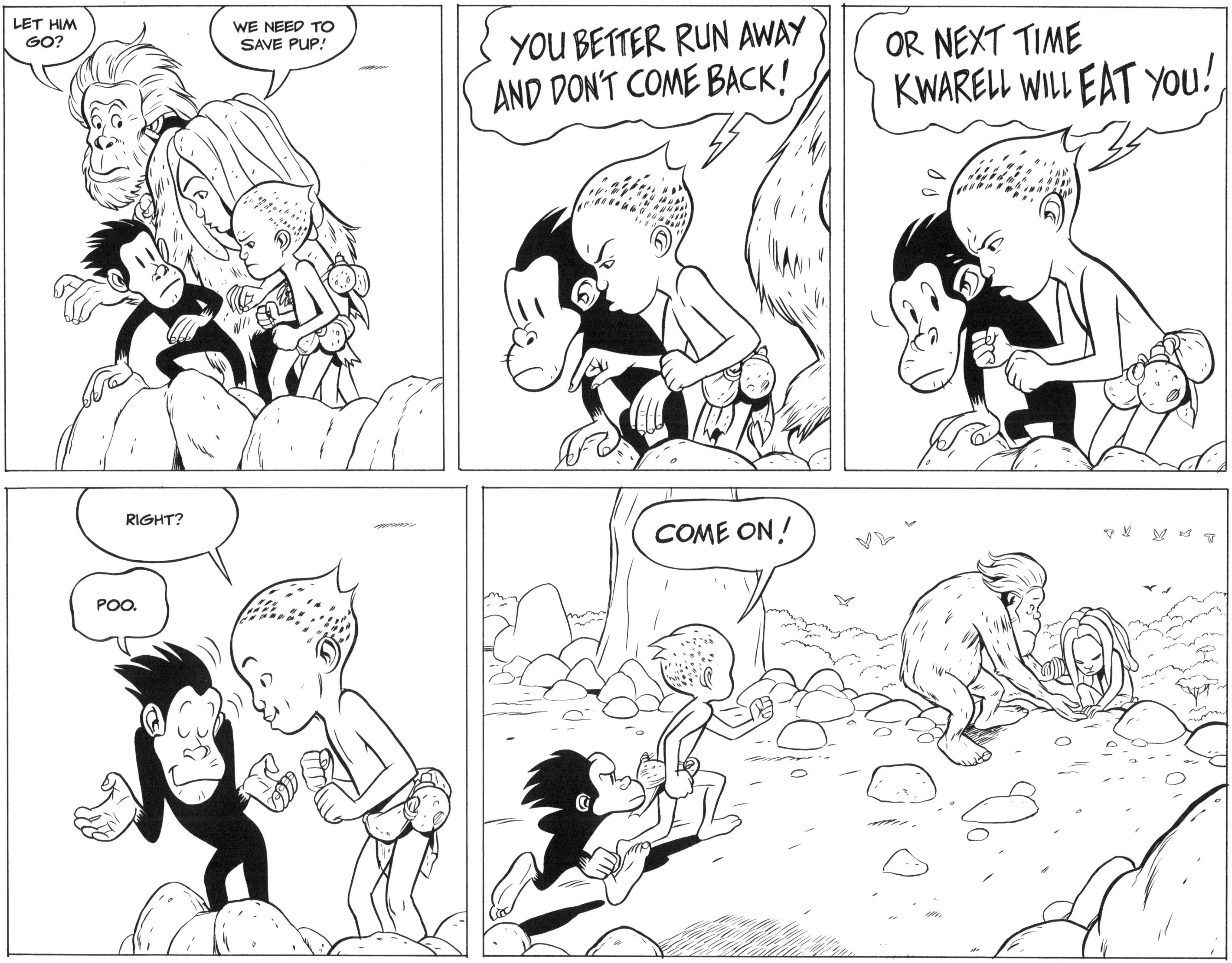
LET HIM GO?
WE NEED TO SAVE PUP!
YOU BETTER RUN AWAY AND DON'T COME BACK!
OR NEXT TIME KWARELL WILL EAT YOU!
RIGHT?
POO.
COME ON!

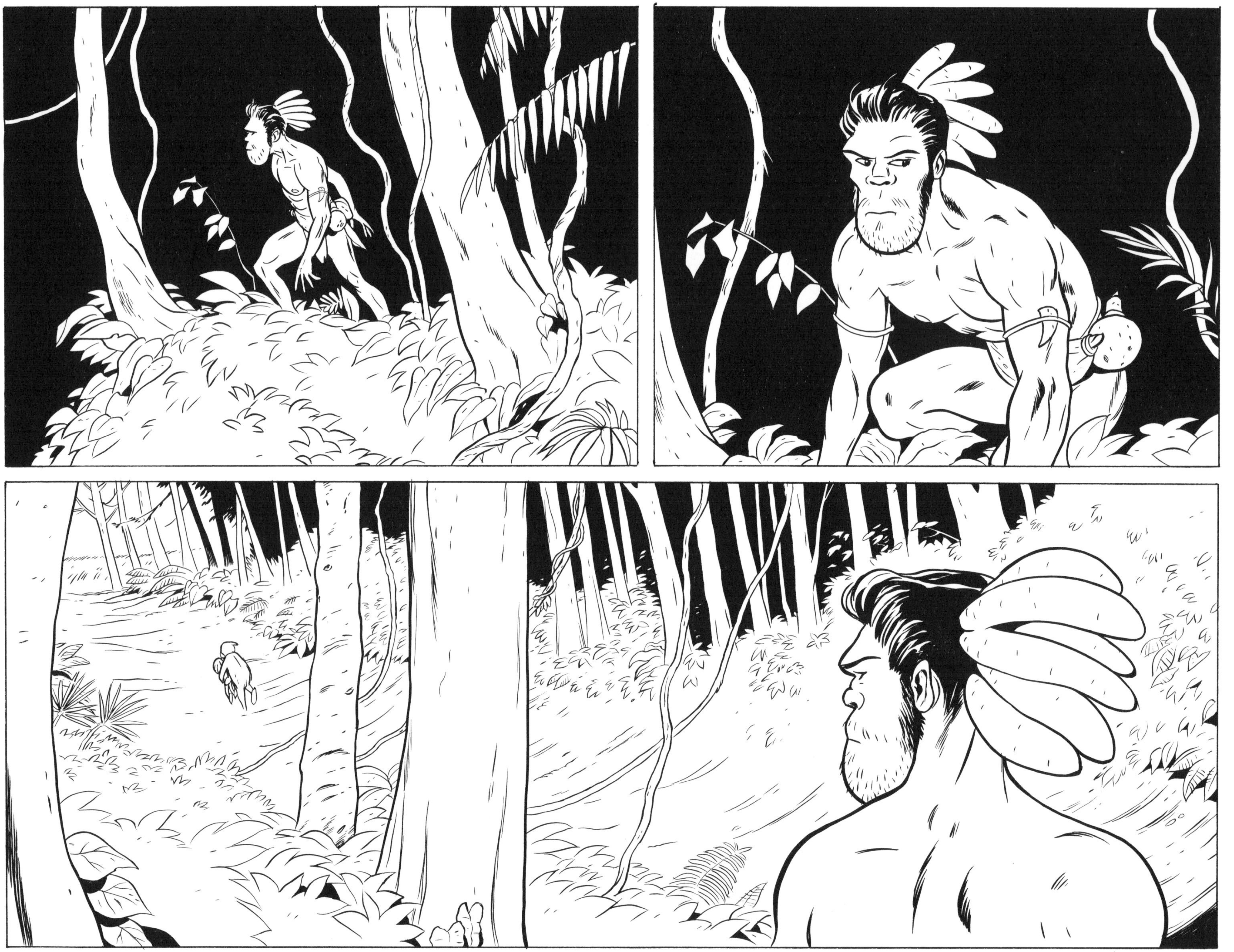

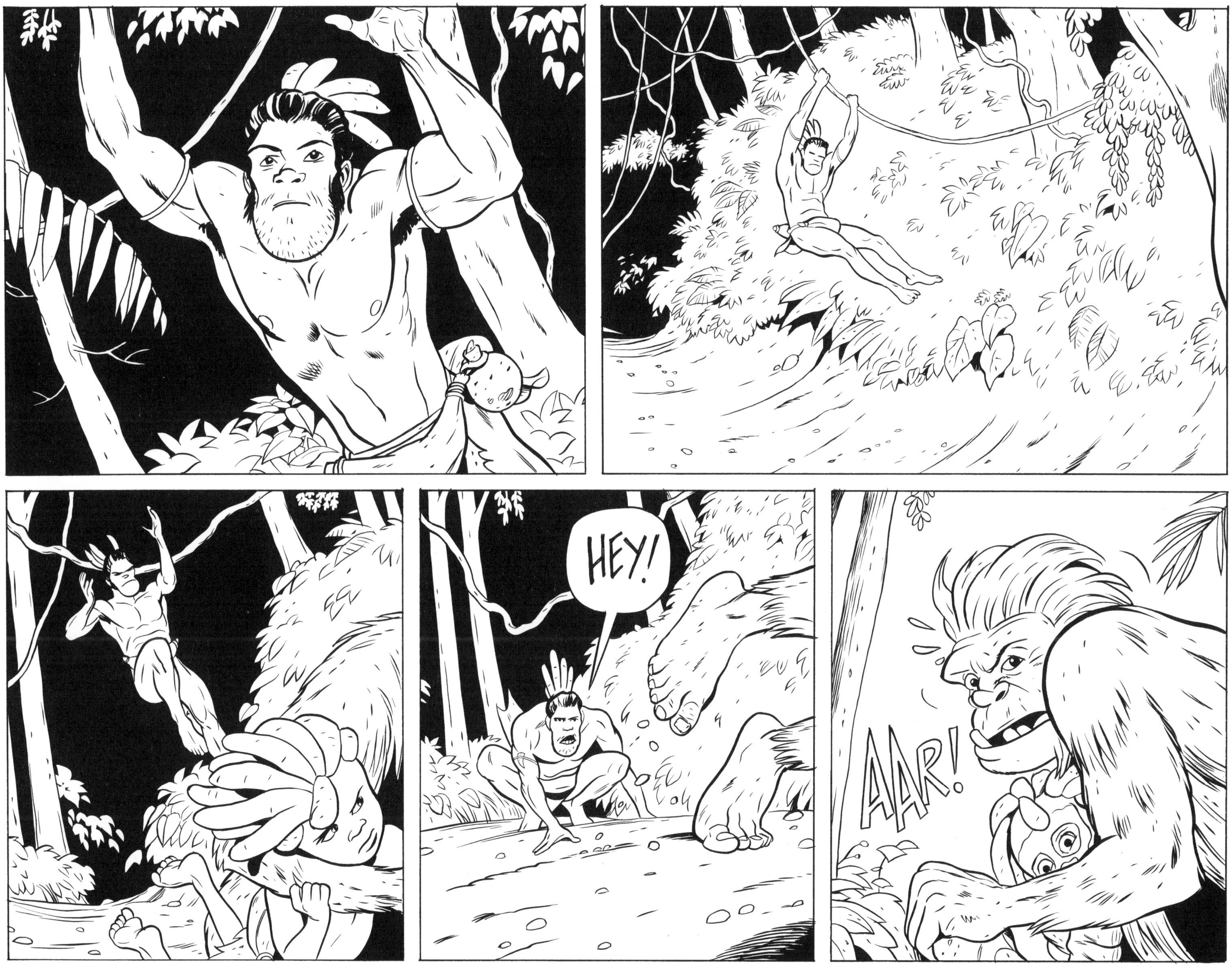
HEY!
AAR!

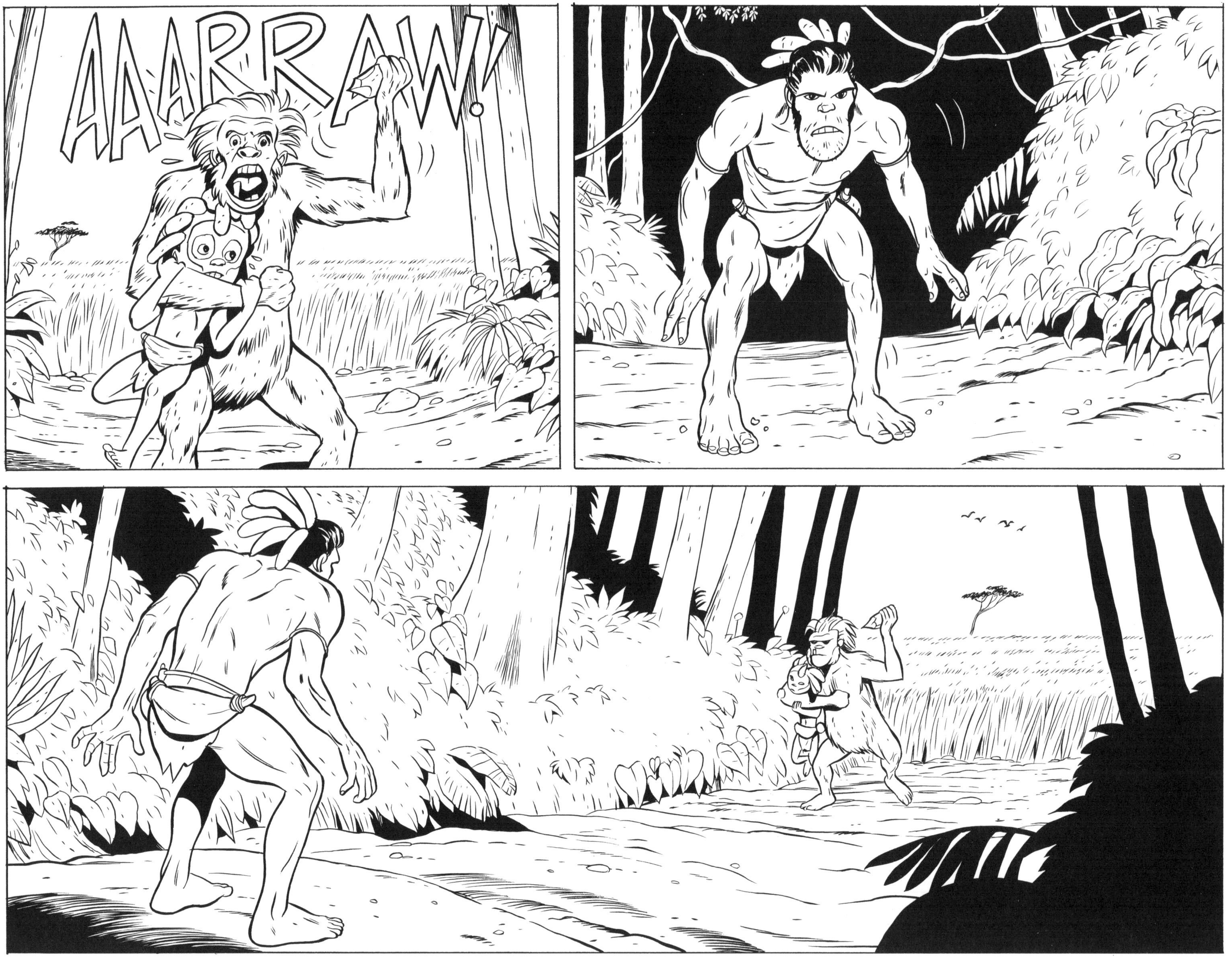
AAARRAW!

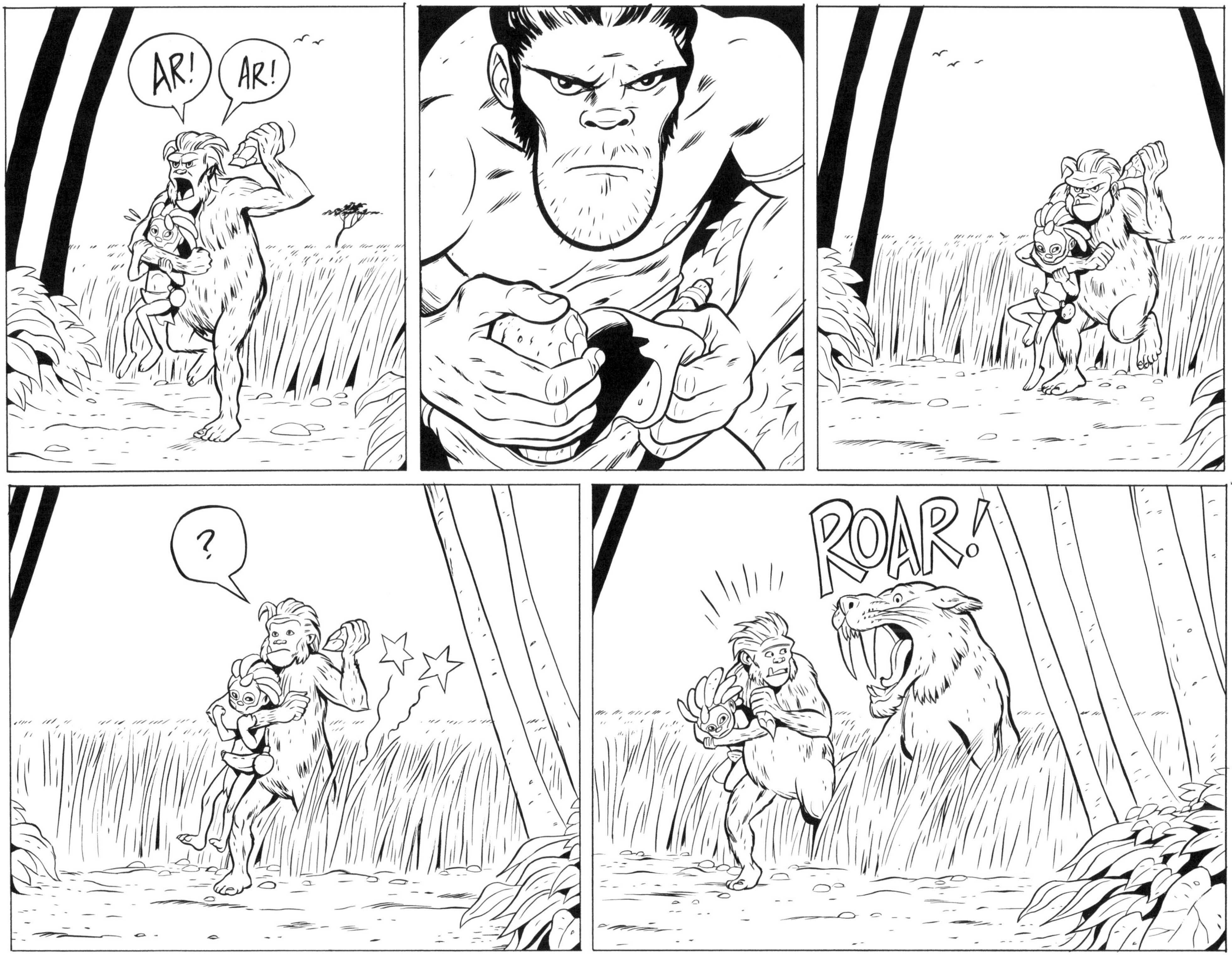

AR!
AR!
?
ROAR!

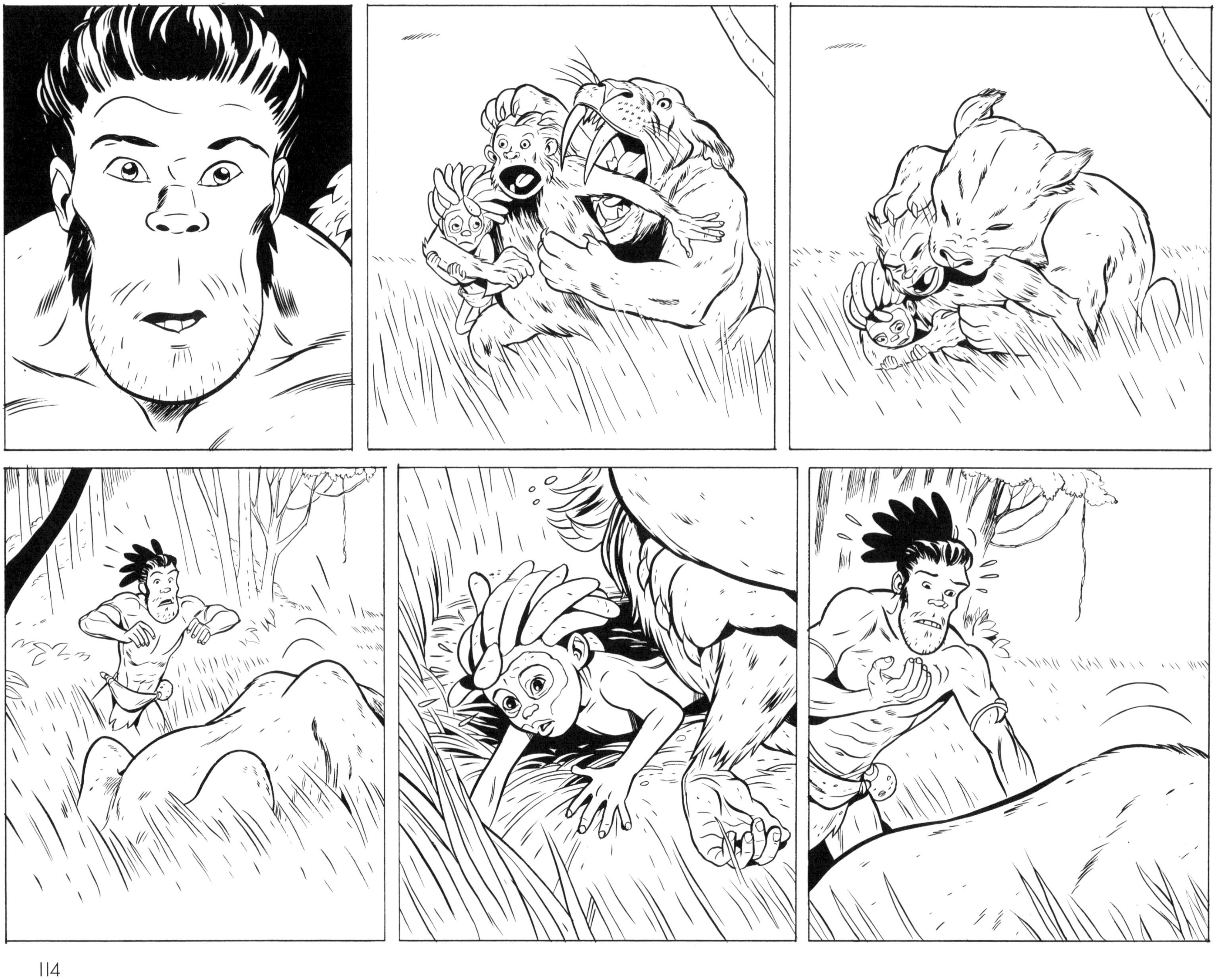

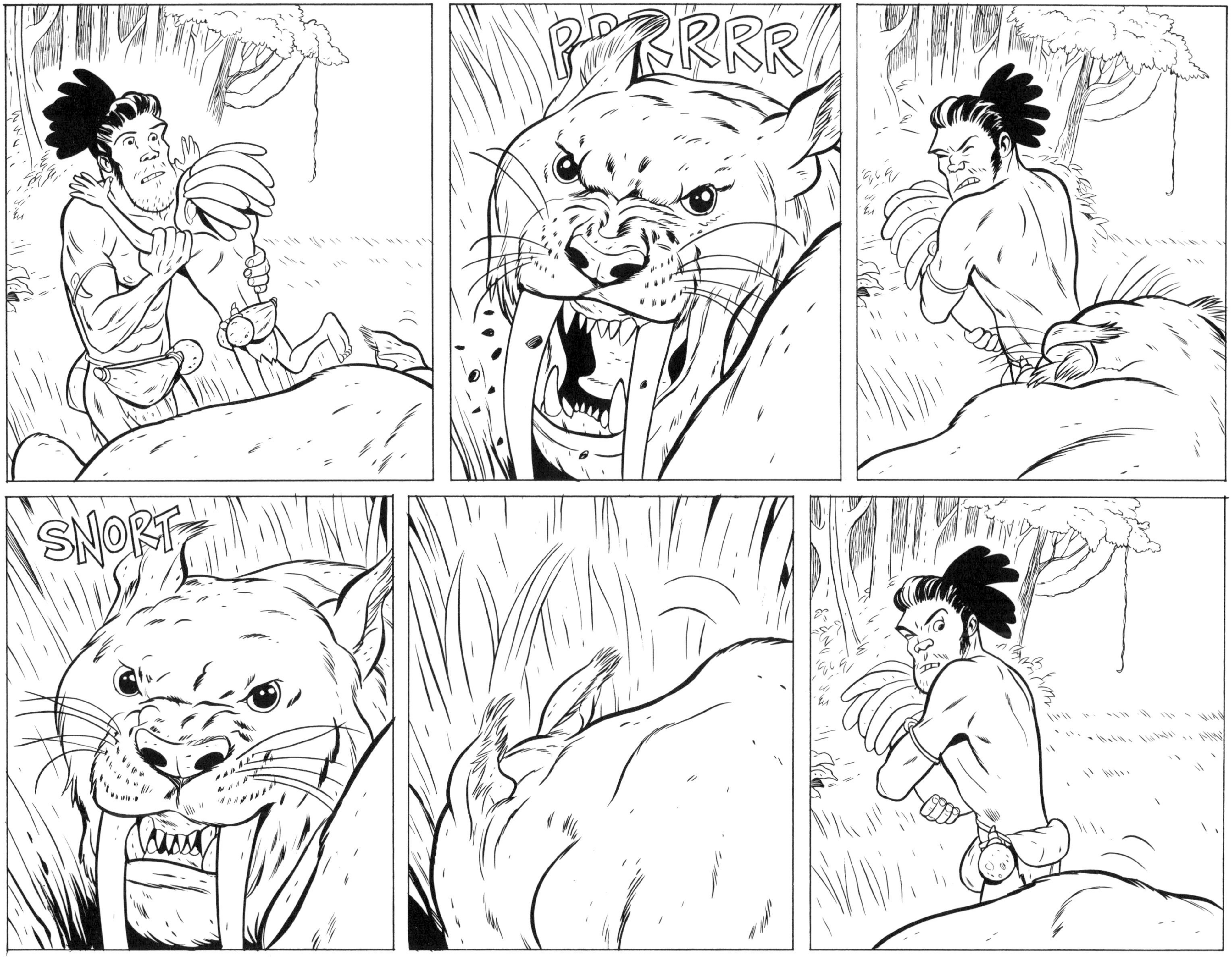
PRRRRRR
SNORT

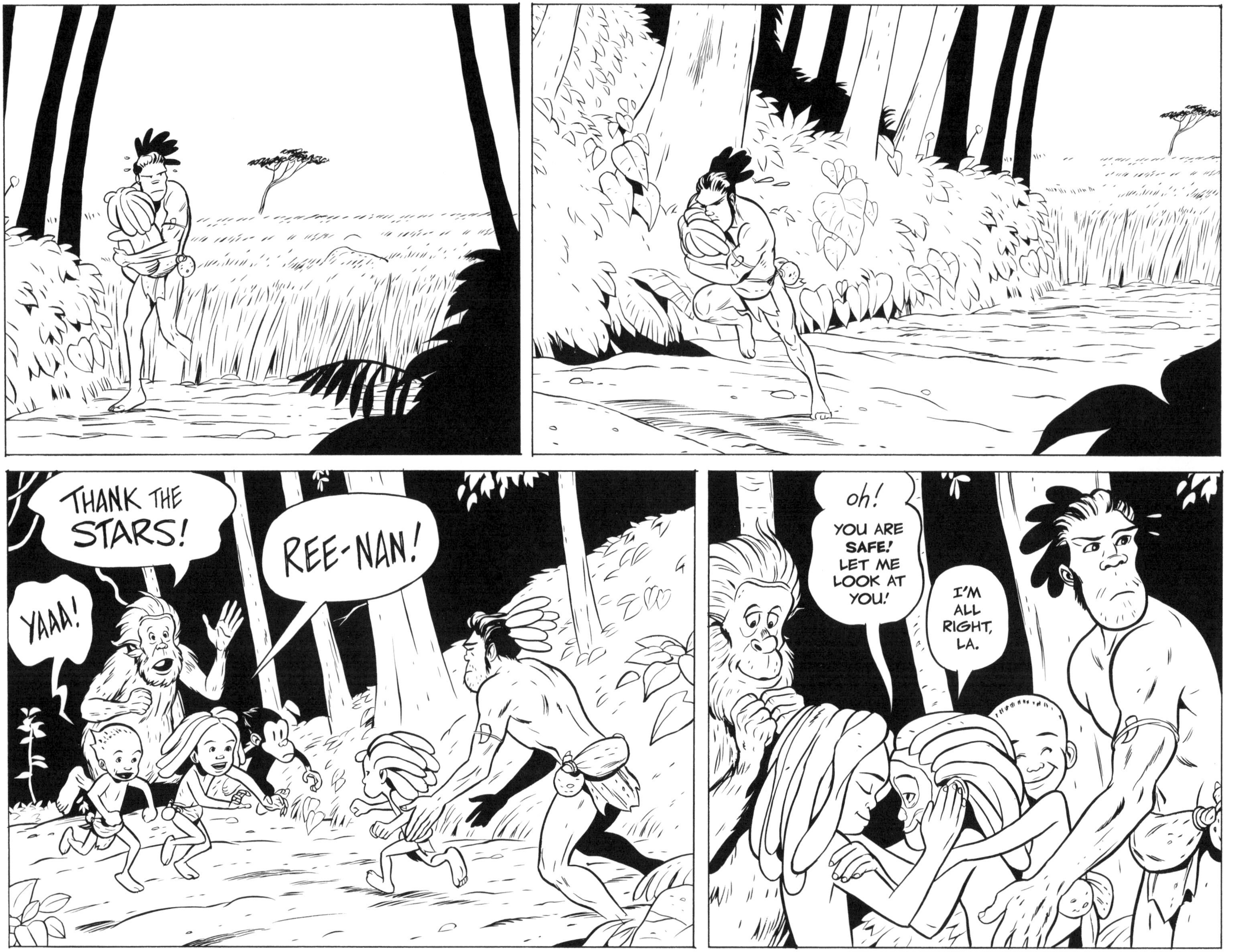
THANK THE STARS!
YAAA!
REE-NAN!
oh!
YOU ARE SAFE! LET ME LOOK AT YOU!
I'M ALL RIGHT, LA.

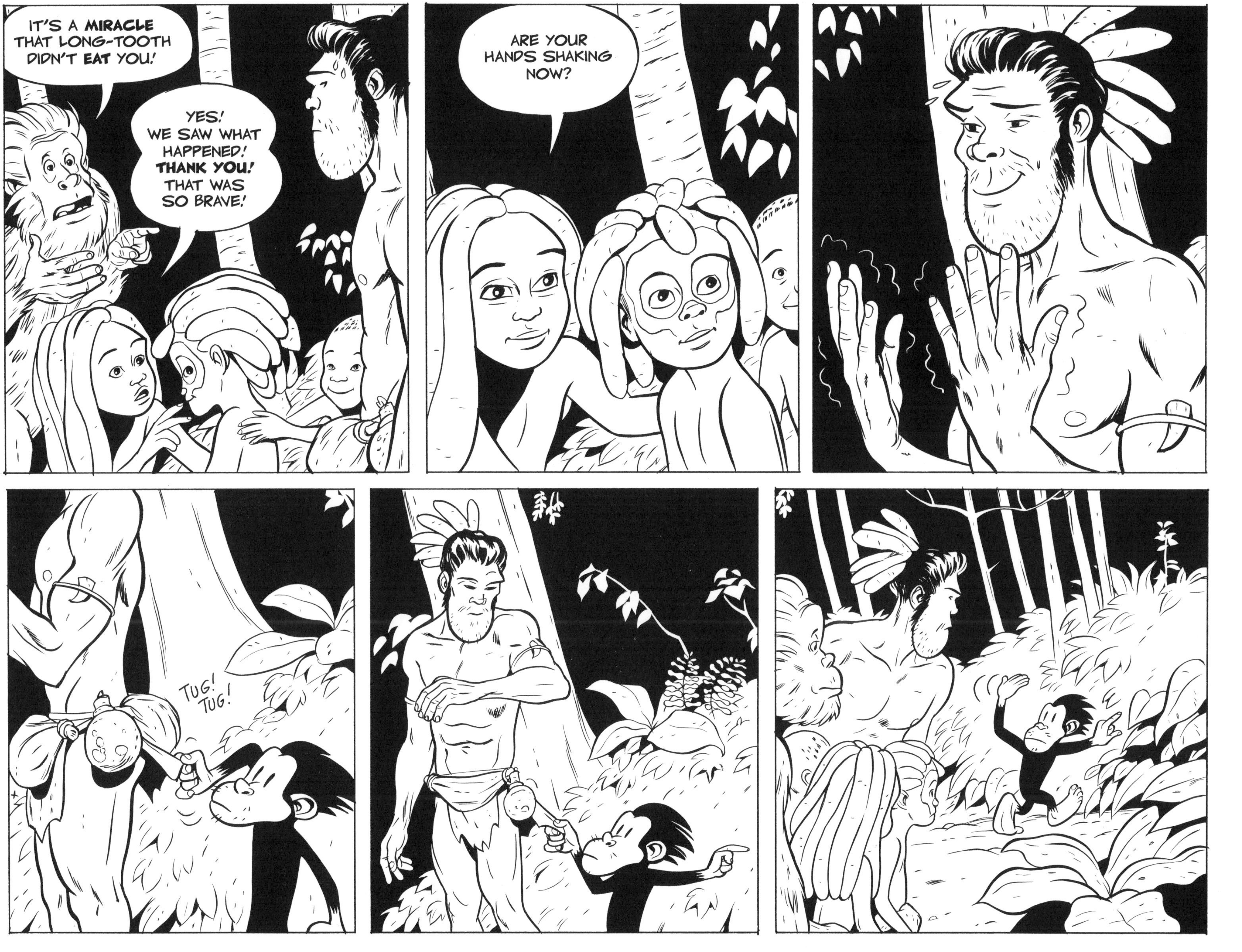
IT'S A MIRACLE THAT LONG-TOOTH DIDN'T EAT YOU!
YES! WE SAW WHAT HAPPENED! THANK YOU! THAT WAS SO BRAVE!
ARE YOUR HANDS SHAKING NOW?
TUG! TUG!

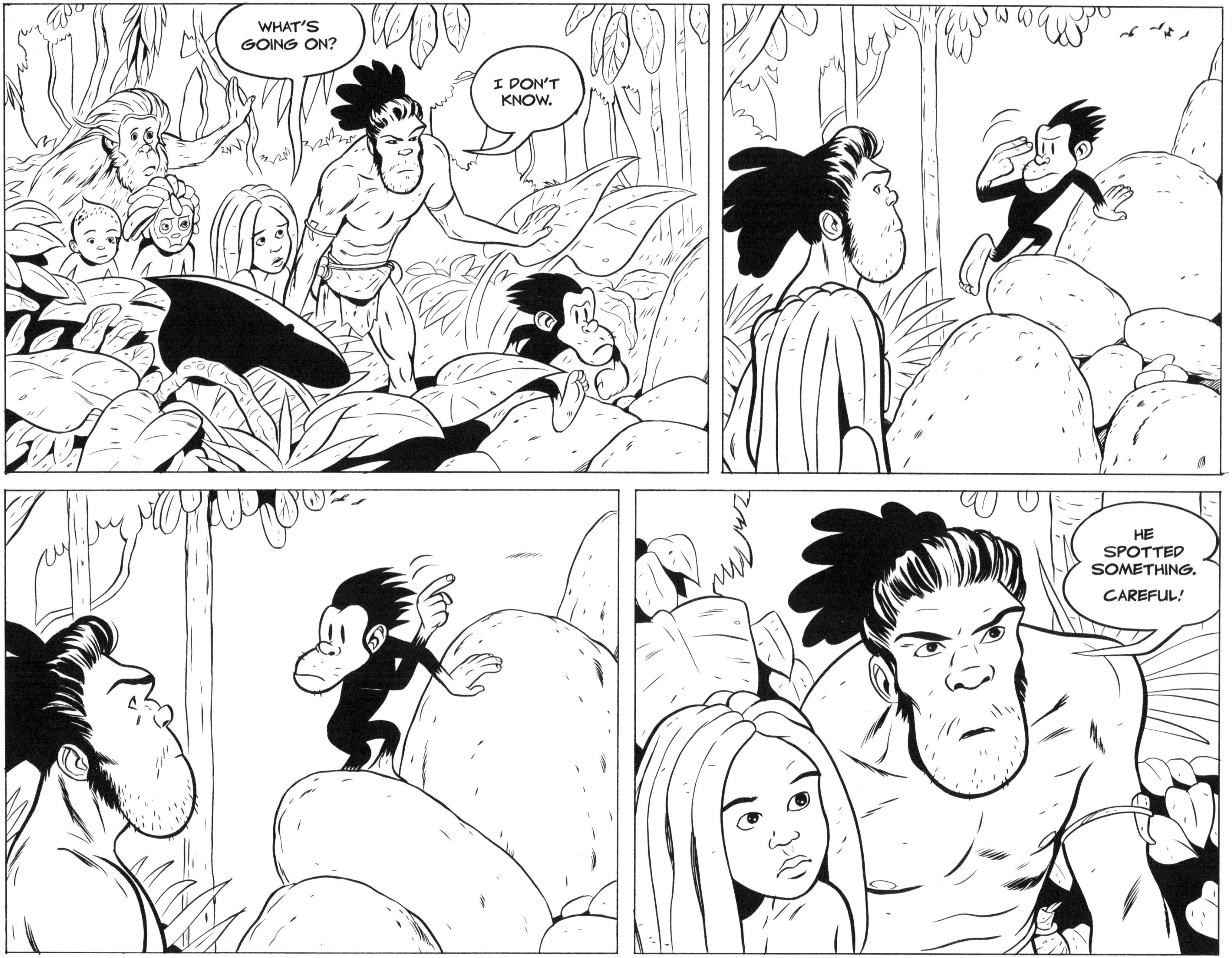
WHAT'S GOING ON?
I DON'T KNOW.
HE SPOTTED SOMETHING.
CAREFUL!

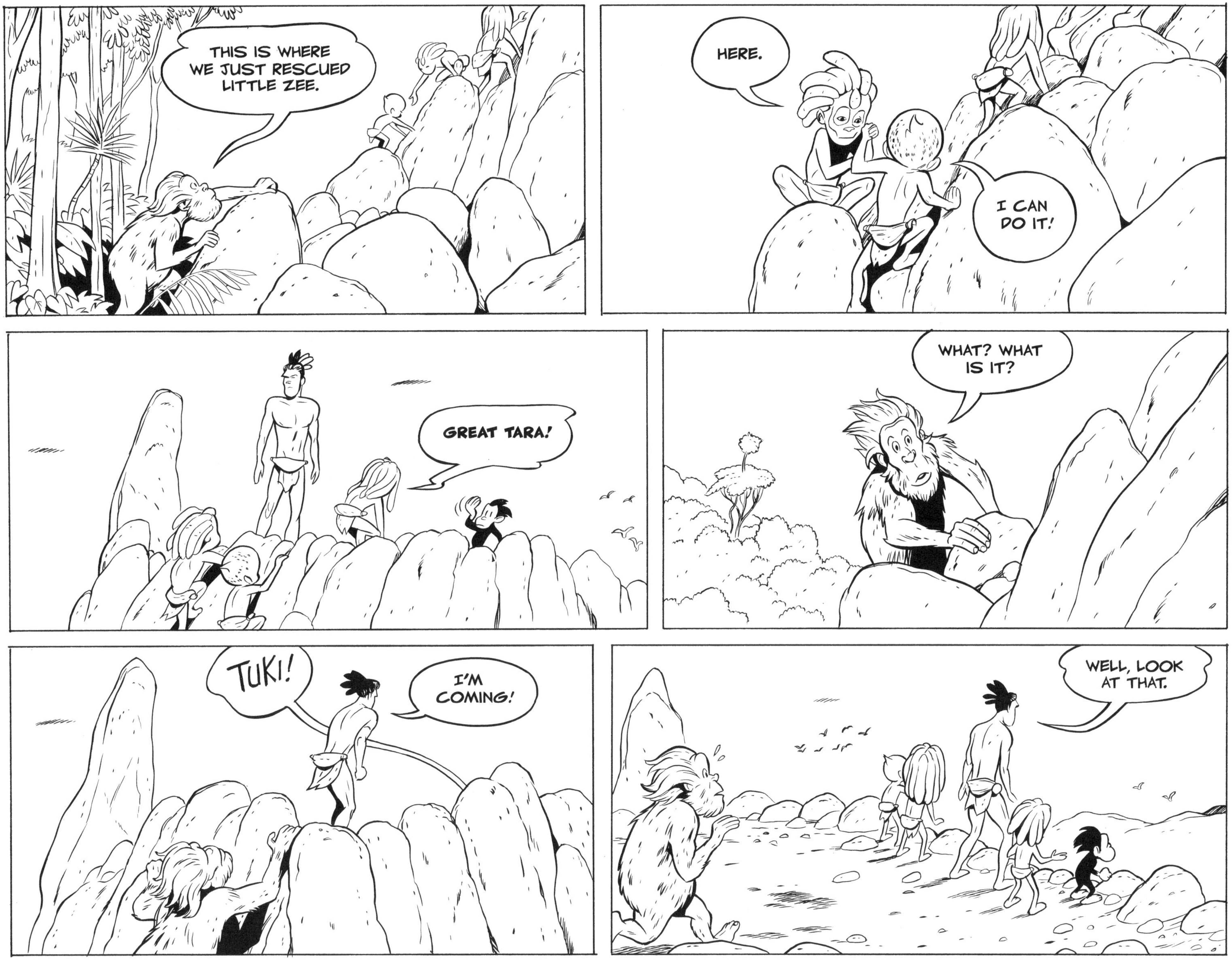
THIS IS WHERE WE JUST RESCUED LITTLE ZEE.
HERE.
I CAN DO IT!
GREAT TARA!
WHAT? WHAT IS IT?
TUKI!
I'M COMING!
WELL, LOOK AT THAT.

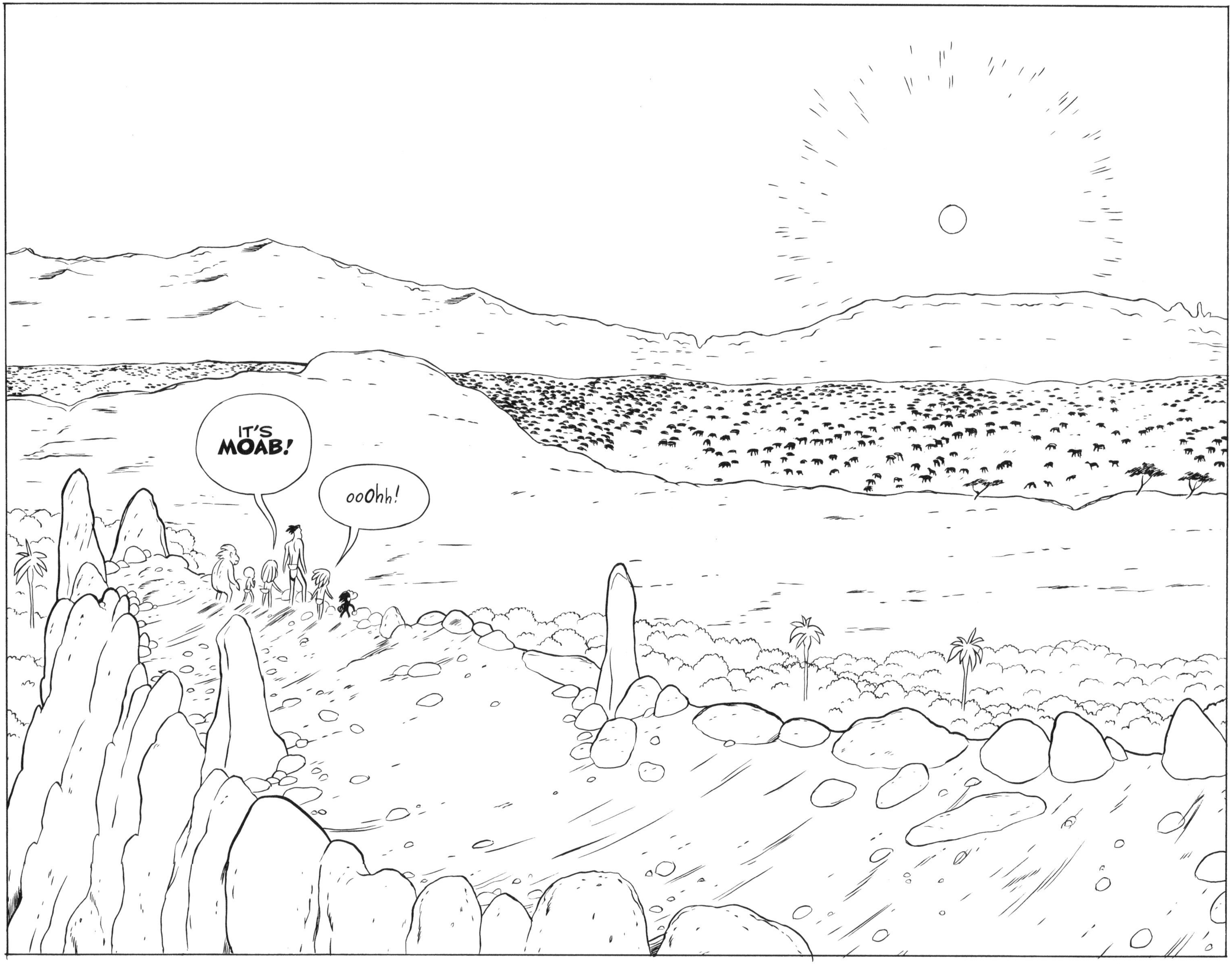
IT'S MOAB!
oooHh!

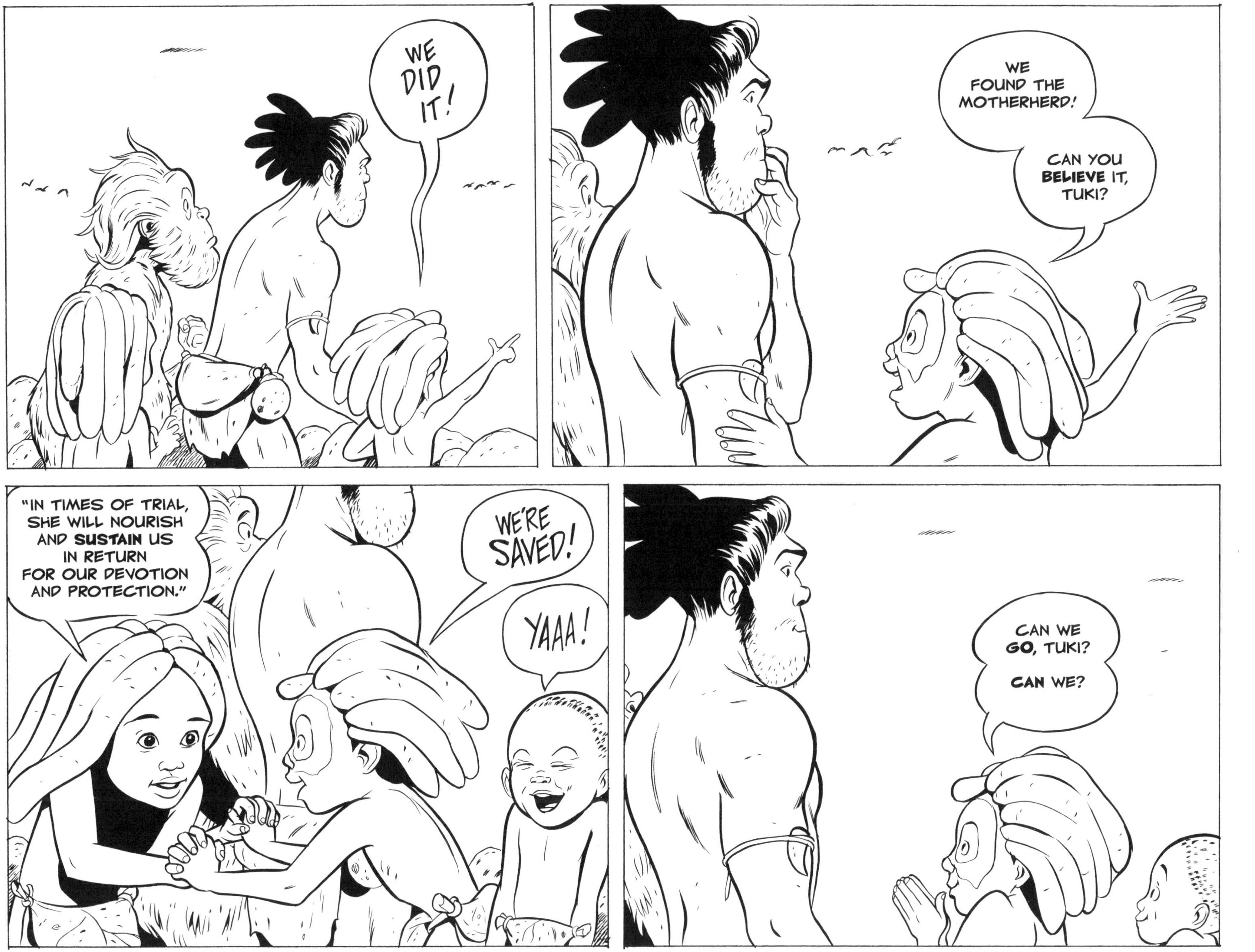
WE DID IT!
WE FOUND THE MOTHERHERD!
CAN YOU **BELIEVE** IT, TUKI?
"IN TIMES OF TRIAL, SHE WILL NOURISH AND **SUSTAIN** US IN RETURN FOR OUR DEVOTION AND PROTECTION."
WE'RE SAVED!
YAAA!
CAN WE **GO**, TUKI?
CAN WE?

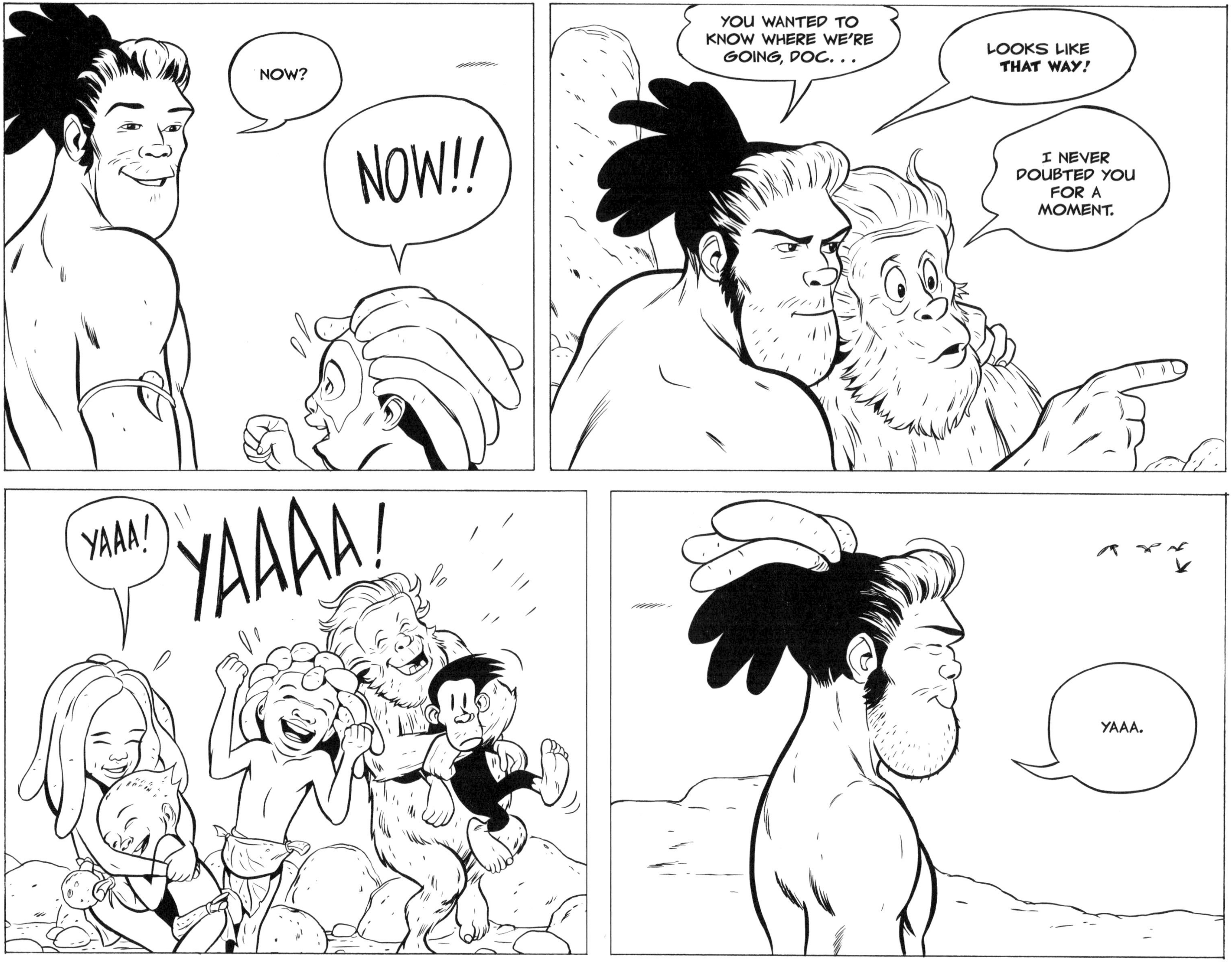
NOW?
NOW!!
YOU WANTED TO KNOW WHERE WE'RE GOING, DOC. . .
LOOKS LIKE THAT WAY!
I NEVER DOUBTED YOU FOR A MOMENT.
YAAA!
YAAAA!
YAAA.

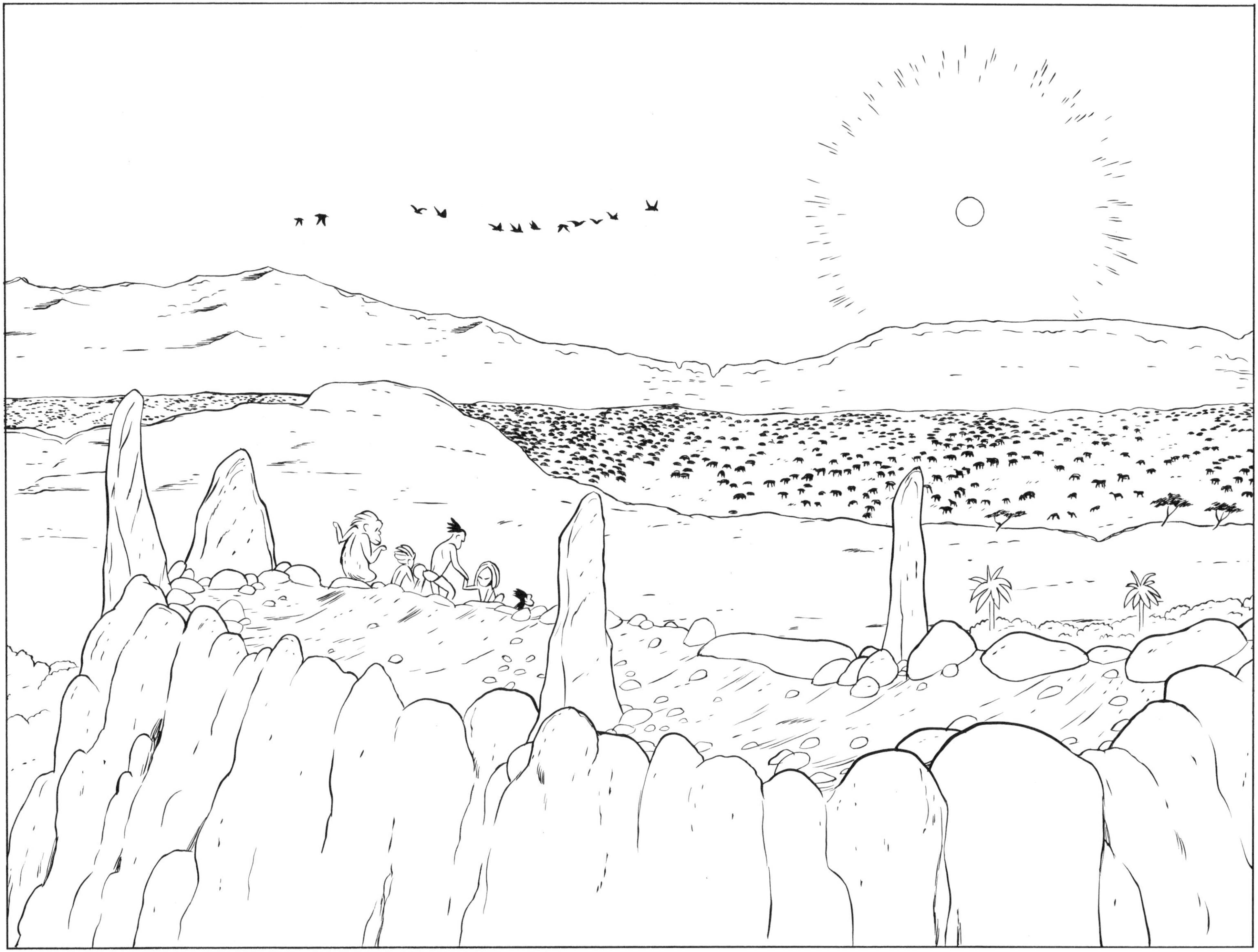

JEFF SMITH

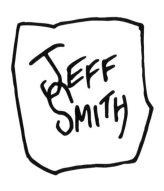

Cartoon Books is

Jeff Smith   Writer and Artist

Vijaya Iyer   Publisher

Kathleen Glosan   Production Manager

Tom Gaadt   Colorist / Pre Press / Design

A Note from the Author

In the first book, TUKI: Fight for Fire, I wrote about my fascination with this particular moment in Earth's history, a fulcrum point where not only was human evolution at a crossroads with multiple human and pre-human species stretched over the African savannas, it was also witness to the discovery of Fire. A momentous shift in technology and power in the world.

And, being how I am, this fascination was quickly blended into a pulp fiction mix of my favorite kinds of stories: wandering heroes, monsters, mystical lost lands and adventure.

I was always interested in evolution and human origins, even from a young age. It is the ultimate question: who are we and where did we come from? In 1974, when I was 14, the famous Lucy was discovered in Ethiopia. A partially complete fossil skeleton of a small female that lived more than 3 million years ago who shared features with both apes and humans. Tons of news coverage in magazines and documentaries followed, and I was hooked.

The idea for TUKI didn't come until much later. The triggering event was a 1995 trip to Africa that Vijaya and I took with Larry and Cory Marder. Larry is the brilliant cartoonist of Beanworld, and was referred to in my circle of friends - folks like Scott McCloud and Dave Sim - as the Nexus of All Comic Book Realities. Larry knew everybody in comics and knew where the bodies were buried. Cory worked with the travel company Abercrombie & Kent and loved Africa. The wildlife, especially elephants, were the joy of her life.

In October of 1995, we set off for Kenya and Tanzania to visit national parks and see the animals. One stop along the way, between Serengeti and Tarangire was Olduvai Gorge. This is the archeological site where Louis and Mary Leakey unearthed evidence of multiple hominid species going back millions of years. Multiple species, representing all of human evolution over time - all lived, loved and survived right there where I was standing! I have talked before about having a vision that day. I looked up at the ridge above, where trees could be seen swaying gently, and saw many different types of early humans walking around, interacting with each other, almost like at a market. I was moved by the experience.

The thought of making a comic about early humans still didn't cross my mind until the early 2010s when reading books about evolution caused me to focus on the year 2 million BCE. There have been overlaps with other humans throughout our past, most recently with Neanderthals in Europe, but 2 million years ago, the overlap matched my vision. Australopithecines and Paranthropus, ancient members of our species, were still around, as well as Homo habilis the tool maker and Homo erectus the fire starter. This is the A-Team! This is where we come from.

I hope you are enjoying the story so far. TUKI: Fight for Fire and TUKI: Fight for Family complete Act One of what I hope will be a six-book saga.

Special thanks to our wonderful and patient Kickstarter supporters for the appendices that continue here in Book 2, where we share how these pages were conceived and built.

See you next time!

Jeff Smith
Key West, March 2022

Opposite:
Olduvai Gorge in Tanzania.

Above: A plaque marks the spot where Mary Leakey discovered the fossilized skull of Paranthropus boisei.

Jeff Smith

TUKI

Fight for Fire

Book One
TUKI Fight for Fire
is available from fine book sellers
and comic shops everywhere.

For more information
visit boneville.com

A Brief Bibliography

Born in Africa: The Quest for the Origins of Human Life by Martin Meredith • Catching Fire: How Cooking Made Us Human by Richard Wrangham
Lone Survivors: How We Came To Be The Only Humans On Earth by Chris Stringer
Prehistoric Life Murals by William Stout • Evolution: The Human Story by Dr. Alice Roberts

Films

NOVA: Becoming Human • National Geographic: The Human Family Tree
Quest for Fire Directed by Jean-Jacques Annaud 1981

SPECIAL THANKS

You know who your friends are when you're in a tough spot and they actually show up. Thank you and a shout out to:

Dave Filipi for being an early reader.

Gib Bickel and the Laughing Ogre Comics Bookstore staff for being our local pickup location for the Kickstarter campaign.

Rich Wagner for hosting the Comic-Con@Home signing events.

Jared Petersen for his expertise in putting together the videos.

Laura Mason and Bruce Peck for their proofing abilities.

Timmy Destefano and Keith Peppers for helping fulfill all the orders.

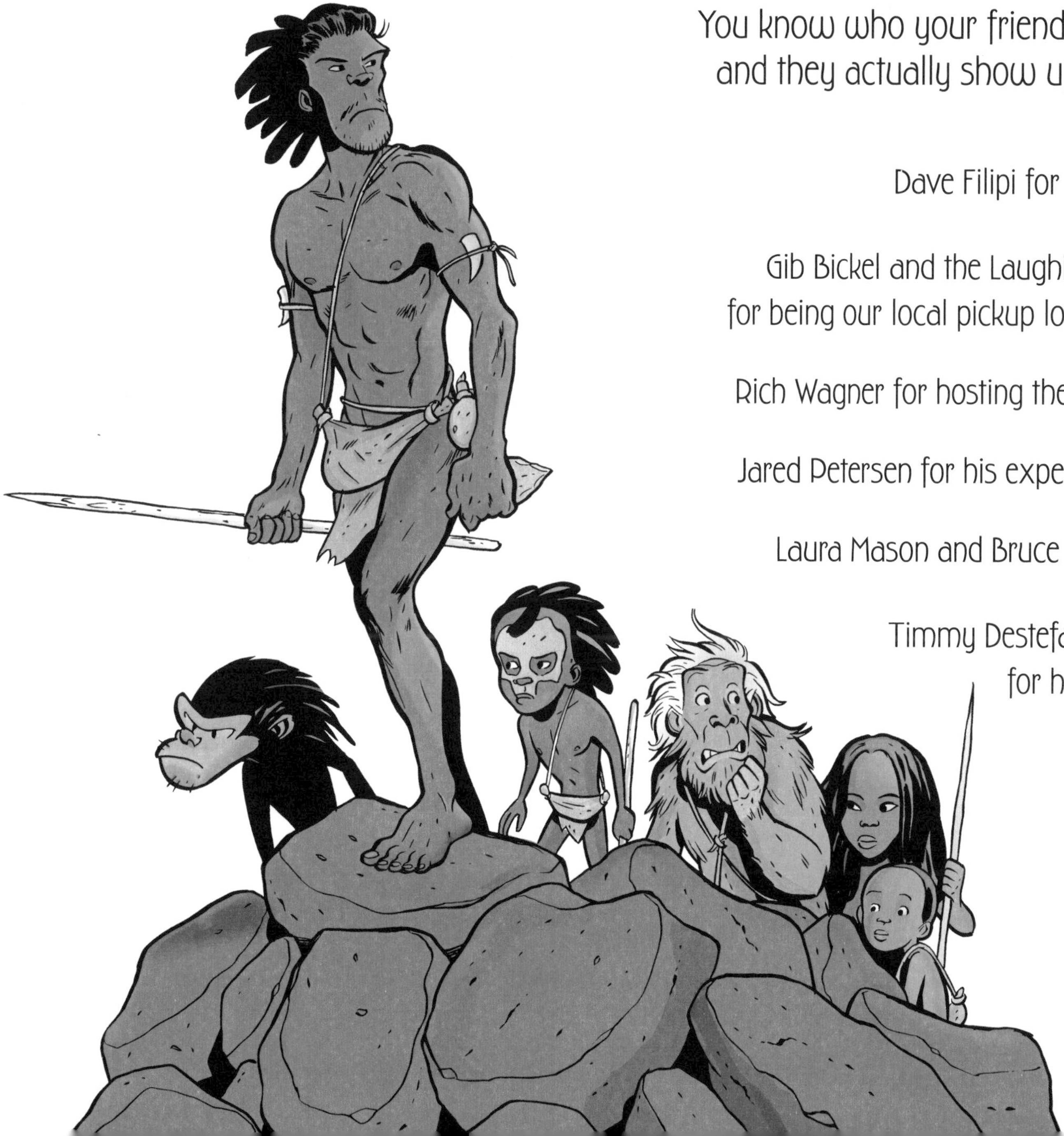

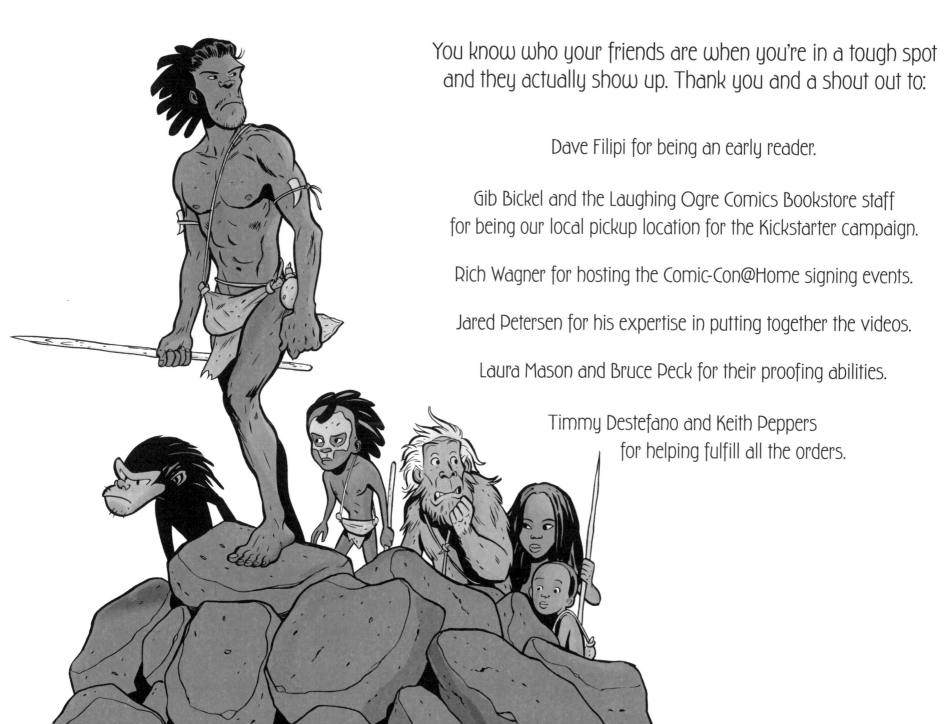

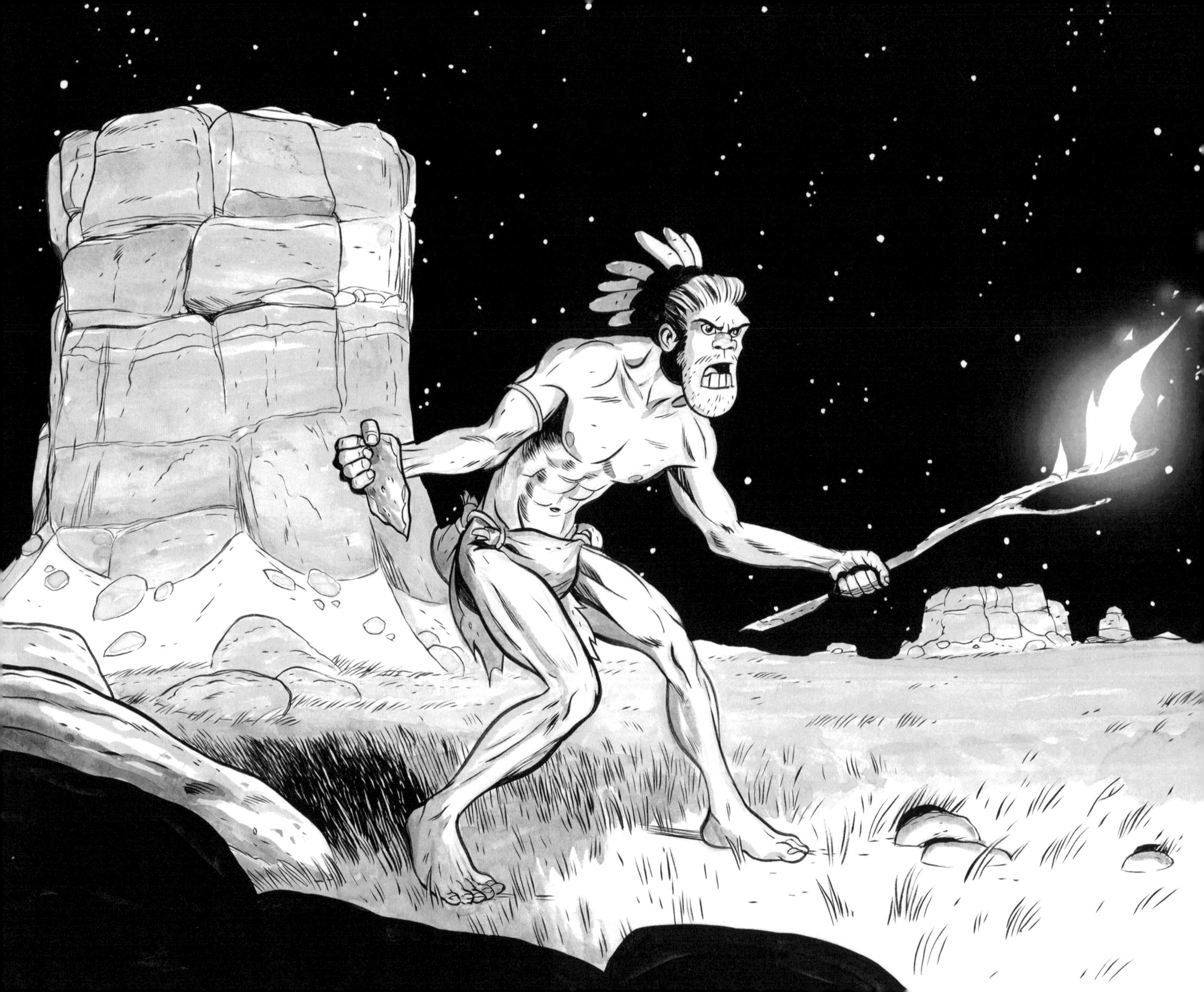

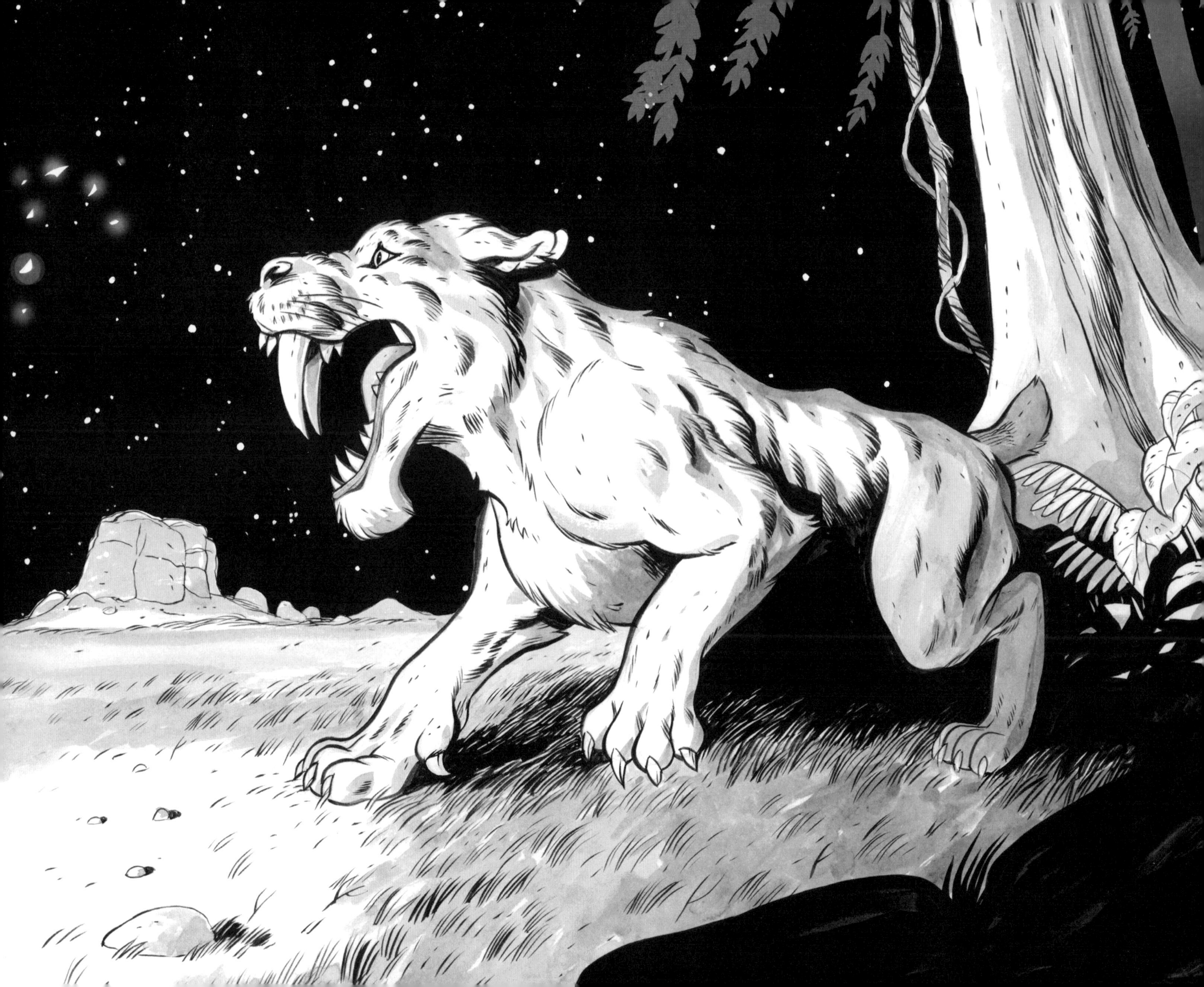

APPENDIX C
The Making of TUKI: Fight for Family

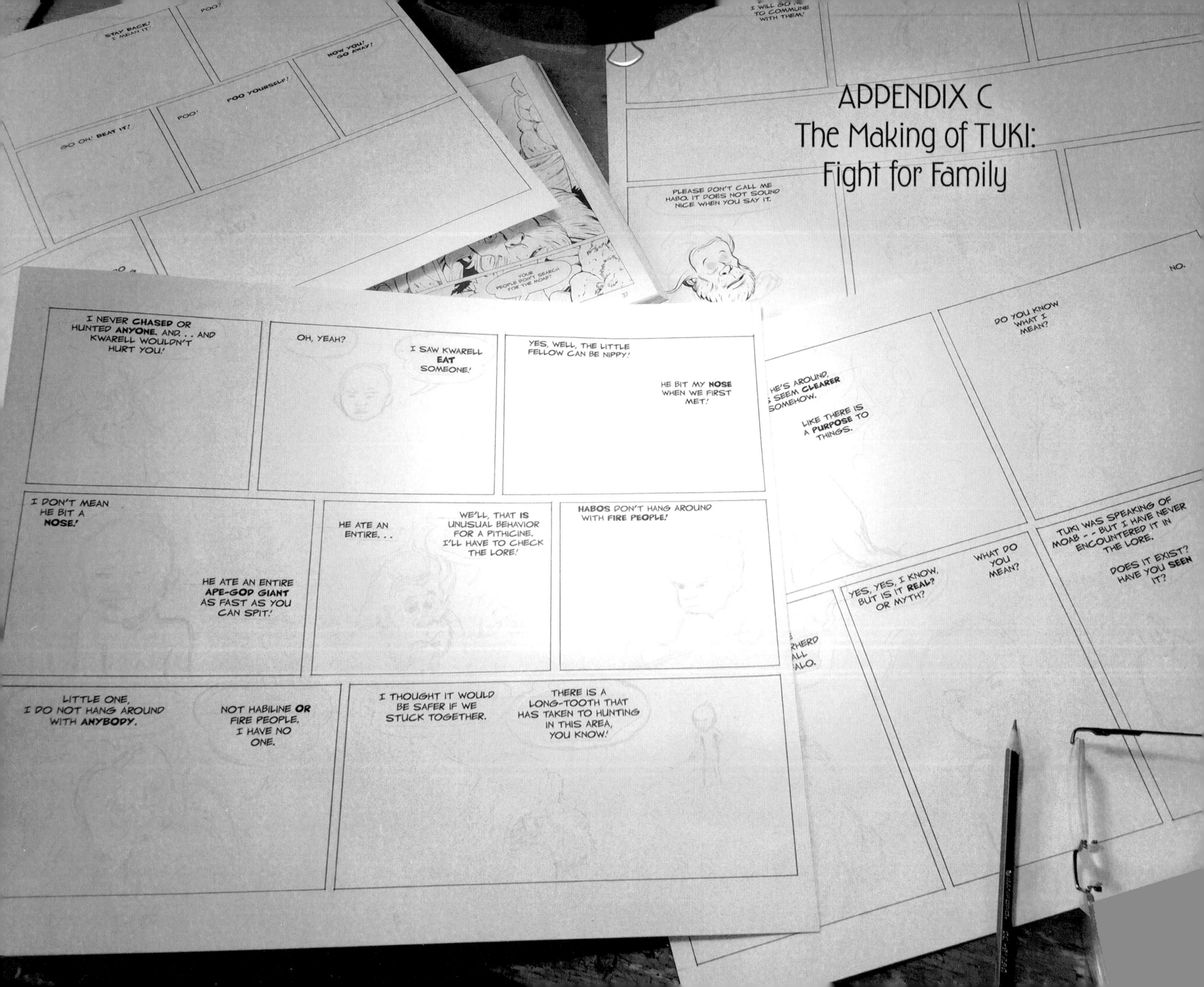
STAY BACK! I MEAN IT!
POO?
HOW YOU! GO AWAY!
POO!
POO YOURSELF!
GO ON! BEAT IT!
I WILL GO TO COMMUNE WITH THEM!
PLEASE DON'T CALL ME HABO. IT DOES NOT SOUND NICE WHEN YOU SAY IT.
YOUR PEOPLE DON'T SEARCH FOR THE MOAB?
NO.
I NEVER CHASED OR HUNTED ANYONE. AND. . . AND KWARELL WOULDN'T HURT YOU!
OH, YEAH?
I SAW KWARELL EAT SOMEONE!
YES, WELL, THE LITTLE FELLOW CAN BE NIPPY!
HE BIT MY NOSE WHEN WE FIRST MET!
DO YOU KNOW WHAT I MEAN?
HE'S AROUND, SEEM CLEARER SOMEHOW.
LIKE THERE IS A PURPOSE TO THINGS.
I DON'T MEAN HE BIT A NOSE!
HE ATE AN ENTIRE APE-GOD GIANT AS FAST AS YOU CAN SPIT!
HE ATE AN ENTIRE. . .
WE'LL, THAT IS UNUSUAL BEHAVIOR FOR A PITHICINE. I'LL HAVE TO CHECK THE LORE!
HABOS DON'T HANG AROUND WITH FIRE PEOPLE!
TUKI WAS SPEAKING OF MOAB - - BUT I HAVE NEVER ENCOUNTERED IT IN THE LORE.
DOES IT EXIST? HAVE YOU SEEN IT?
WHAT DO YOU MEAN?
YES, YES, I KNOW, BUT IS IT REAL? OR MYTH?
LITTLE ONE, I DO NOT HANG AROUND WITH ANYBODY.
NOT HABILINE OR FIRE PEOPLE. I HAVE NO ONE.
I THOUGHT IT WOULD BE SAFER IF WE STUCK TOGETHER.
THERE IS A LONG-TOOTH THAT HAS TAKEN TO HUNTING IN THIS AREA, YOU KNOW!

Out of Her Comfort Zone:
Building Chapter 2

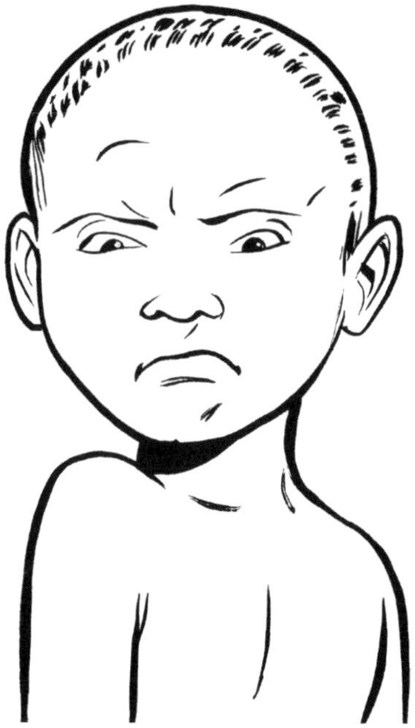

Let's get in the weeds!

Zee is suddenly alone with Doc, a Habiline, and she is not having it.

I know how I want it to end, but the first attempt to feel out how a scene like this would go is a quick off-the-cuff paragraph. Next an equally quick run at it with drawings; this usually sparks enough energy to see the way forward and start a more complete pass of the whole scene.

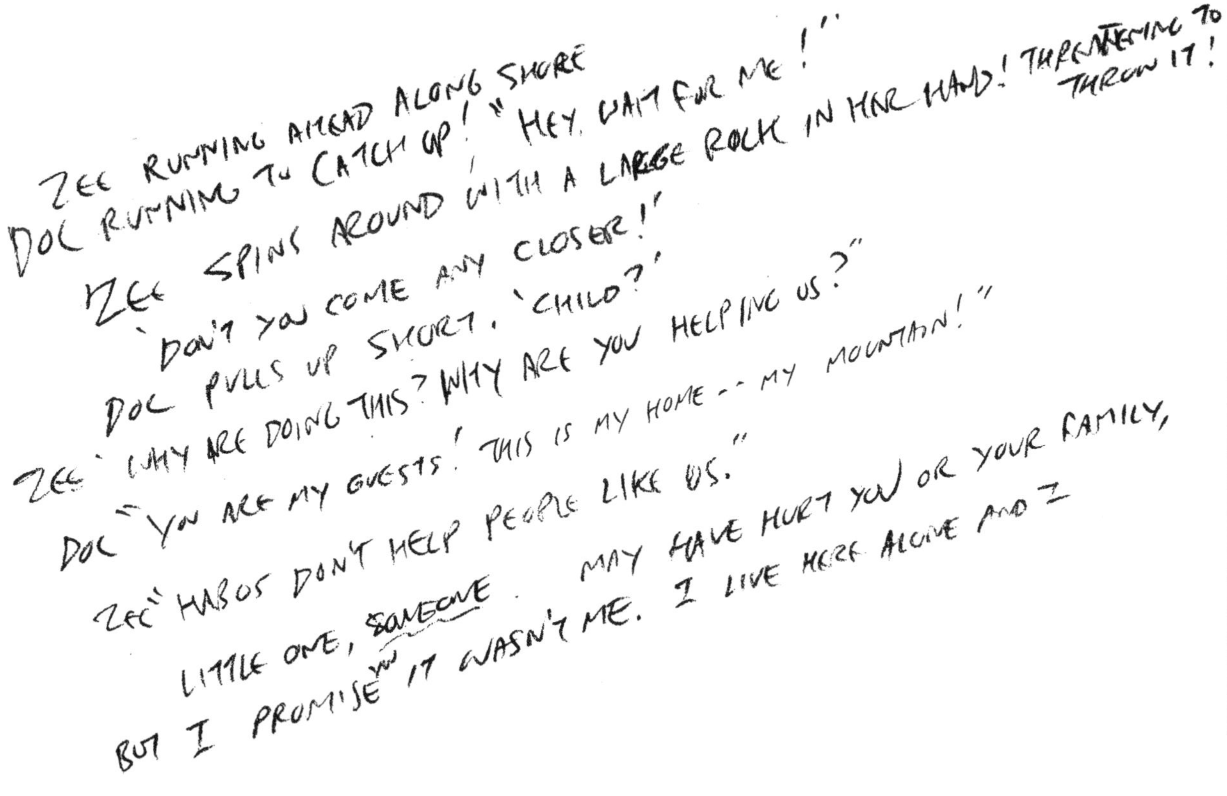

ZEE RUNNING AHEAD ALONG SHORE
DOC RUNNING TO CATCH UP! "HEY, WAIT FOR ME!"
ZEE SPINS AROUND WITH A LARGE ROCK IN HER HAND! THREATENING TO THROW IT!
"DON'T YOU COME ANY CLOSER!"
DOC PULLS UP SHORT. 'CHILD?'
ZEE 'WHY ARE DOING THIS? WHY ARE YOU HELPING US?"
DOC "YOU ARE MY GUESTS! THIS IS MY HOME -- MY MOUNTAIN!"
ZEE "HABOS DON'T HELP PEOPLE LIKE US."
LITTLE ONE, SOMEONE MAY HAVE HURT YOU OR YOUR FAMILY,
BUT I PROMISE YOU IT WASN'T ME. I LIVE HERE ALONE AND I

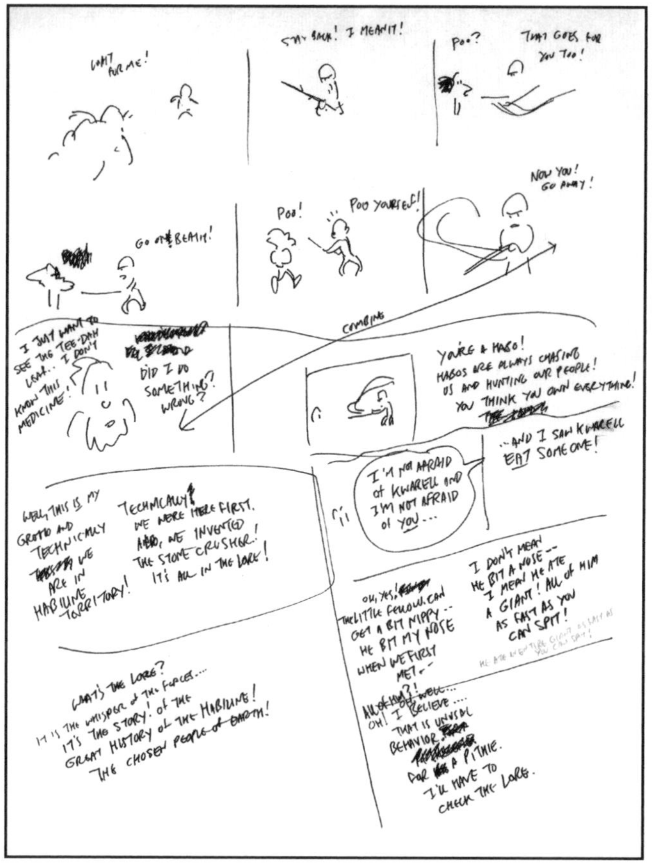

STAY BACK! I MEAN IT!
POO?
THAT GOES FOR YOU TOO!
POO!
POO YOURSELF!
NOW YOU! GO AWAY!
I'M NOT AFRAID OF KWARELL AND I'M NOT AFRAID OF YOU...
...AND I SAW KWARELL EAT SOMEONE!

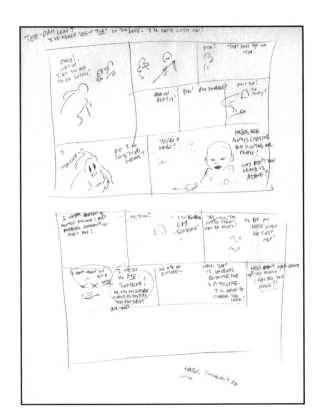

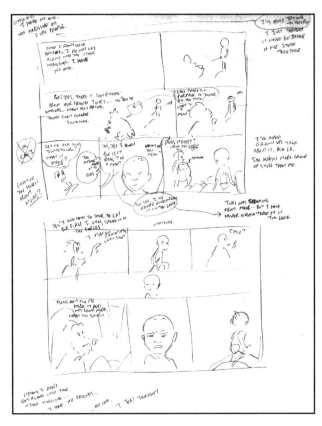

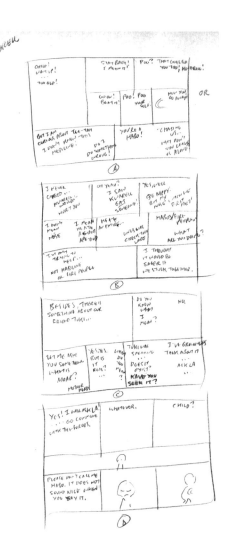

I've got the scene down in four pages. The dialog is still a bit trial by error, with arrows moving things around, but by the end, I know what everybody needs to say. I decided to make a panel map (seen to the right) to decide exactly what is said in what panel.

At this point I'm ready to commit to laying out the full size pages on 14" x 17" 2-ply Bristol board. The live area of a TUKI page is 12" x 16". The lettering (my own bonefont) is printed out and pasted to the board and the characters penciled in.

PANEL MAP FOR "THE DOCTOR, KUNKEL & ZEE"

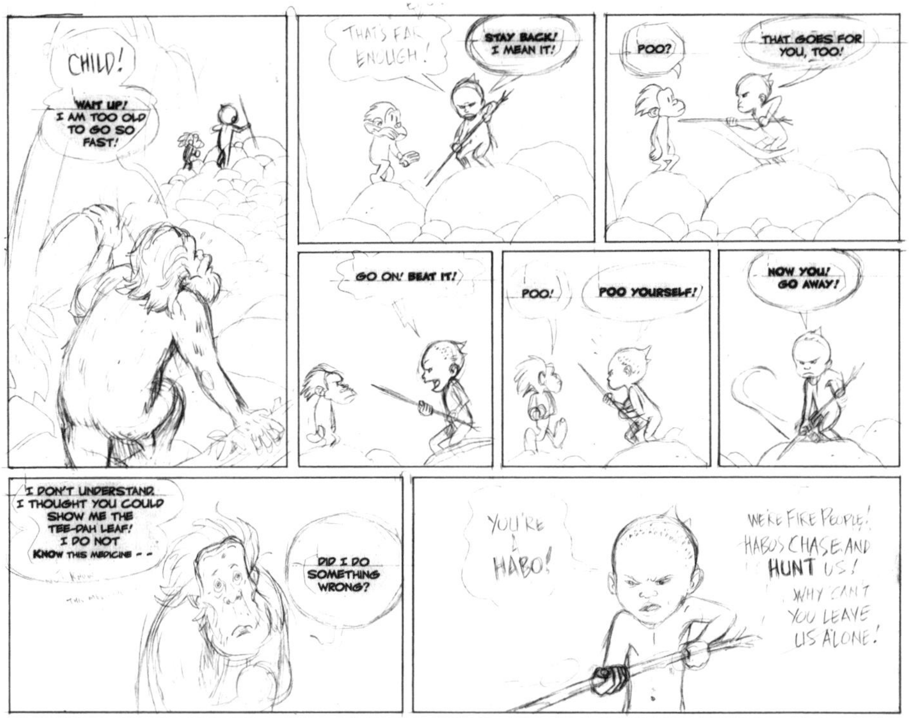
CHILD!
WAIT UP! I AM TOO OLD TO GO SO FAST!
THAT'S FAIR ENOUGH!
STAY BACK! I MEAN IT!
POO?
THAT GOES FOR YOU, TOO!
GO ON! BEAT IT!
POO!
POO YOURSELF!
NOW YOU! GO AWAY!
I DON'T UNDERSTAND. I THOUGHT YOU COULD SHOW ME THE TEE-DAH LEAF! I DO NOT KNOW THIS MEDICINE - -
DID I DO SOMETHING WRONG?
YOU'RE A HABO!
WE'RE FIRE PEOPLE! HABOS CHASE AND HUNT US! WHY CAN'T YOU LEAVE US ALONE!

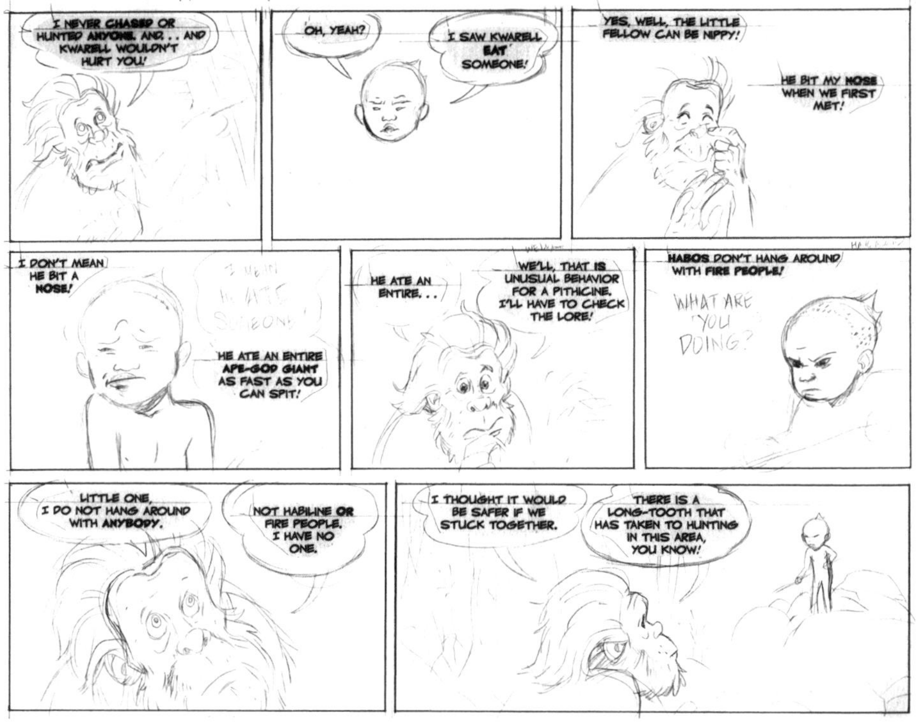
I NEVER CHASED OR HUNTED ANYONE! AND. . . AND KWARELL WOULDN'T HURT YOU!
OH, YEAH?
I SAW KWARELL EAT SOMEONE!
YES, WELL, THE LITTLE FELLOW CAN BE NIPPY!
HE BIT MY NOSE WHEN WE FIRST MET!
I DON'T MEAN HE BIT A NOSE!
HE ATE AN ENTIRE APE-GOD GIANT AS FAST AS YOU CAN SPIT!
HE ATE AN ENTIRE. . .
WE'LL, THAT IS UNUSUAL BEHAVIOR FOR A PITHICINE. I'LL HAVE TO CHECK THE LORE!
HABOS DON'T HANG AROUND WITH FIRE PEOPLE!
WHAT ARE YOU DOING?
LITTLE ONE, I DO NOT HANG AROUND WITH ANYBODY.
NOT HABILINE OR FIRE PEOPLE. I HAVE NO ONE.
I THOUGHT IT WOULD BE SAFER IF WE STUCK TOGETHER.
THERE IS A LONG-TOOTH THAT HAS TAKEN TO HUNTING IN THIS AREA, YOU KNOW!

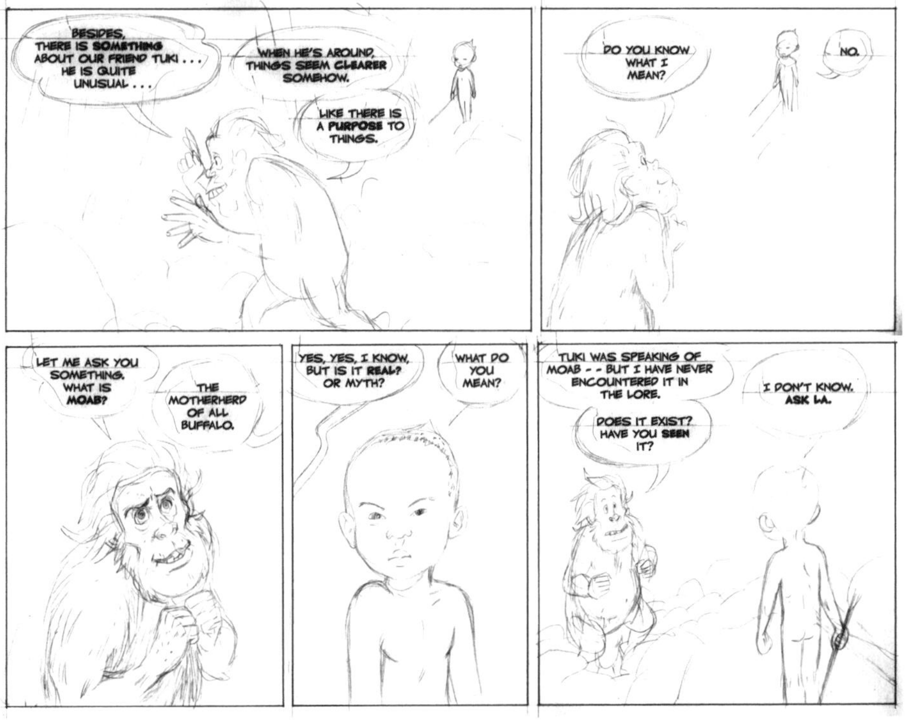
BESIDES, THERE IS SOMETHING ABOUT OUR FRIEND TUKI . . . HE IS QUITE UNUSUAL . . .
WHEN HE'S AROUND, THINGS SEEM CLEARER SOMEHOW.
LIKE THERE IS A PURPOSE TO THINGS.
DO YOU KNOW WHAT I MEAN?
NO.
LET ME ASK YOU SOMETHING. WHAT IS MOAB?
THE MOTHERHERD OF ALL BUFFALO.
YES, YES, I KNOW. BUT IS IT REAL? OR MYTH?
WHAT DO YOU MEAN?
TUKI WAS SPEAKING OF MOAB - - BUT I HAVE NEVER ENCOUNTERED IT IN THE LORE.
DOES IT EXIST? HAVE YOU SEEN IT?
I DON'T KNOW. ASK LA.

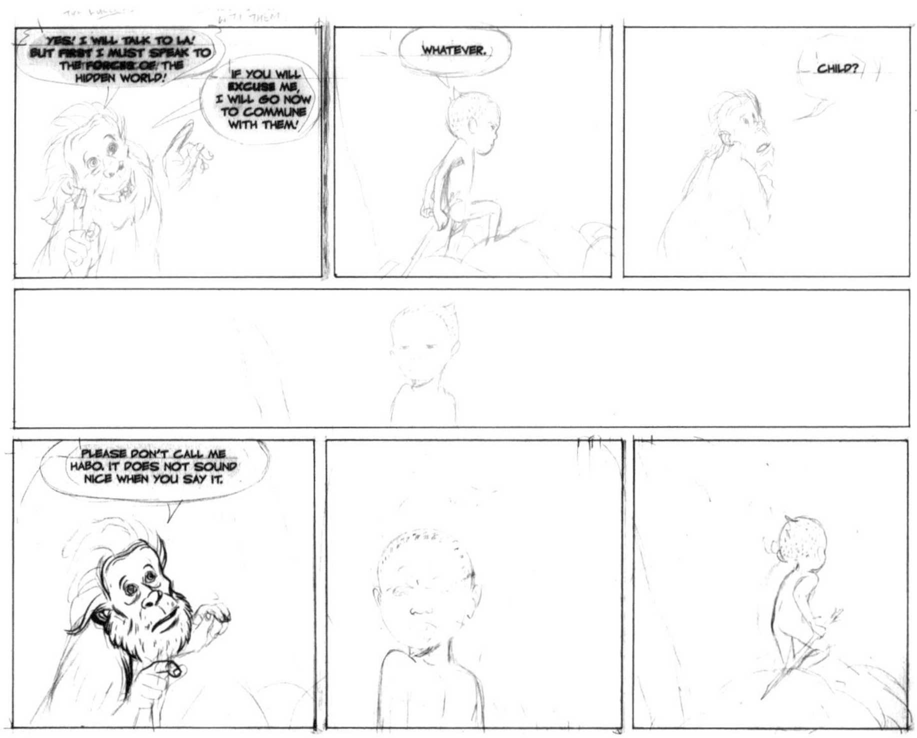
YES! I WILL TALK TO LA! BUT FIRST I MUST SPEAK TO THE FORCES OF THE HIDDEN WORLD!
IF YOU WILL EXCUSE ME, I WILL GO NOW TO COMMUNE WITH THEM!
WHATEVER.
CHILD?
PLEASE DON'T CALL ME HABO. IT DOES NOT SOUND NICE WHEN YOU SAY IT.

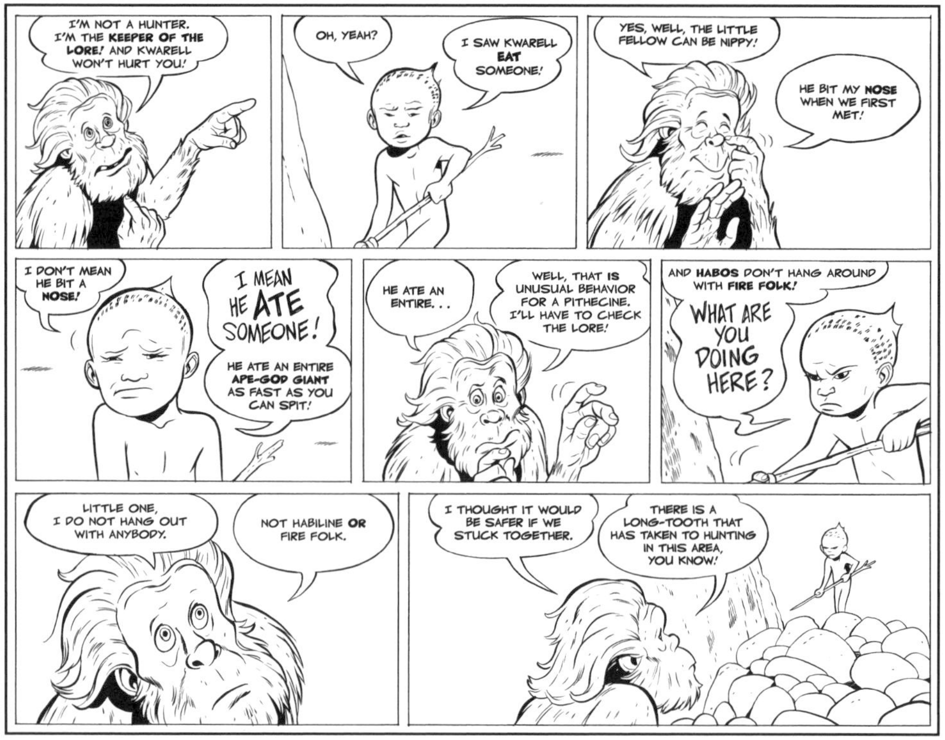
I'M NOT A HUNTER. I'M THE KEEPER OF THE LORE! AND KWARELL WON'T HURT YOU!
OH, YEAH?
I SAW KWARELL EAT SOMEONE!
YES, WELL, THE LITTLE FELLOW CAN BE NIPPY!
HE BIT MY NOSE WHEN WE FIRST MET!
I DON'T MEAN HE BIT A NOSE!
I MEAN HE ATE SOMEONE!
HE ATE AN ENTIRE APE-GOD GIANT AS FAST AS YOU CAN SPIT!
HE ATE AN ENTIRE. . .
WELL, THAT IS UNUSUAL BEHAVIOR FOR A PITHECINE. I'LL HAVE TO CHECK THE LORE!
AND HABOS DON'T HANG AROUND WITH FIRE FOLK!
WHAT ARE YOU DOING HERE?
LITTLE ONE, I DO NOT HANG OUT WITH ANYBODY.
NOT HABILINE OR FIRE FOLK.
I THOUGHT IT WOULD BE SAFER IF WE STUCK TOGETHER.
THERE IS A LONG-TOOTH THAT HAS TAKEN TO HUNTING IN THIS AREA, YOU KNOW!

Here is one of the pages inked. I picked this one to show a little set dressing, which means digitally dropping in some background detail.

Although the framing of each panel is slightly different throughout the page, there are really only two backgrounds - the sky behind Zee, and a rock wall behind Doc. I designed a bit of tropical flora to dress the set behind Doc, sometimes facing right or left depending on our vantage point.

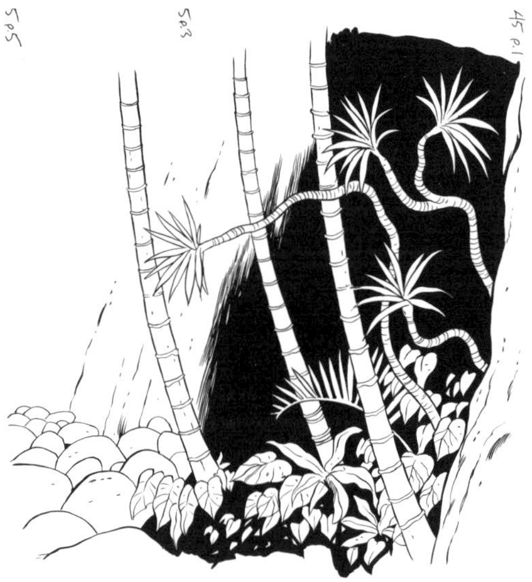

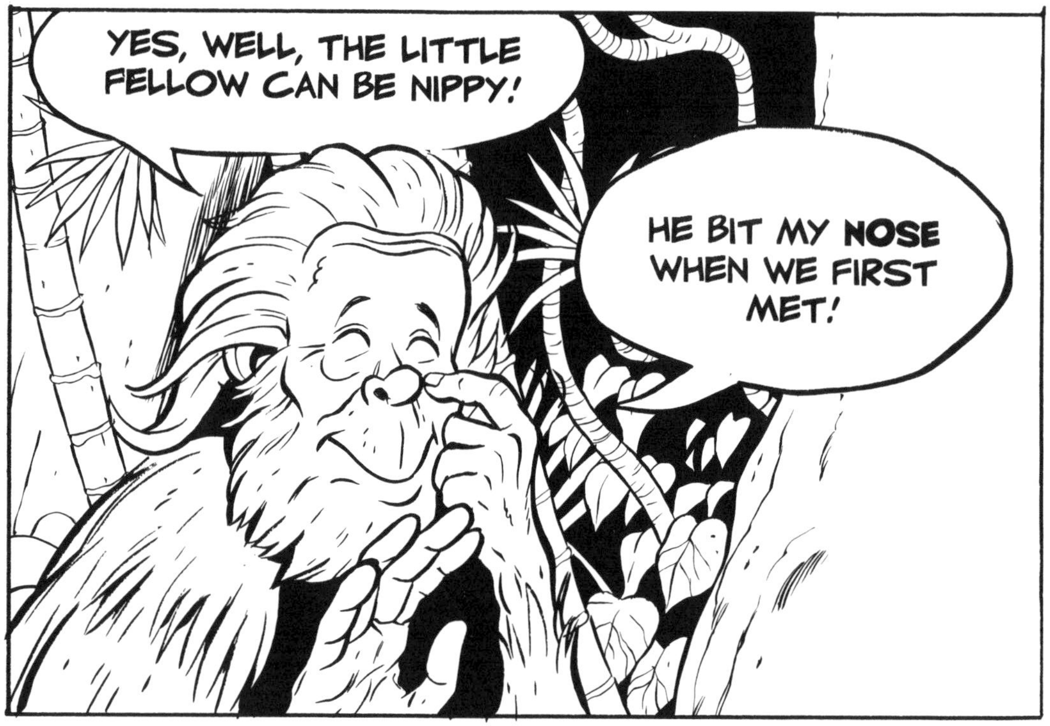
YES, WELL, THE LITTLE FELLOW CAN BE NIPPY!
HE BIT MY NOSE WHEN WE FIRST MET!

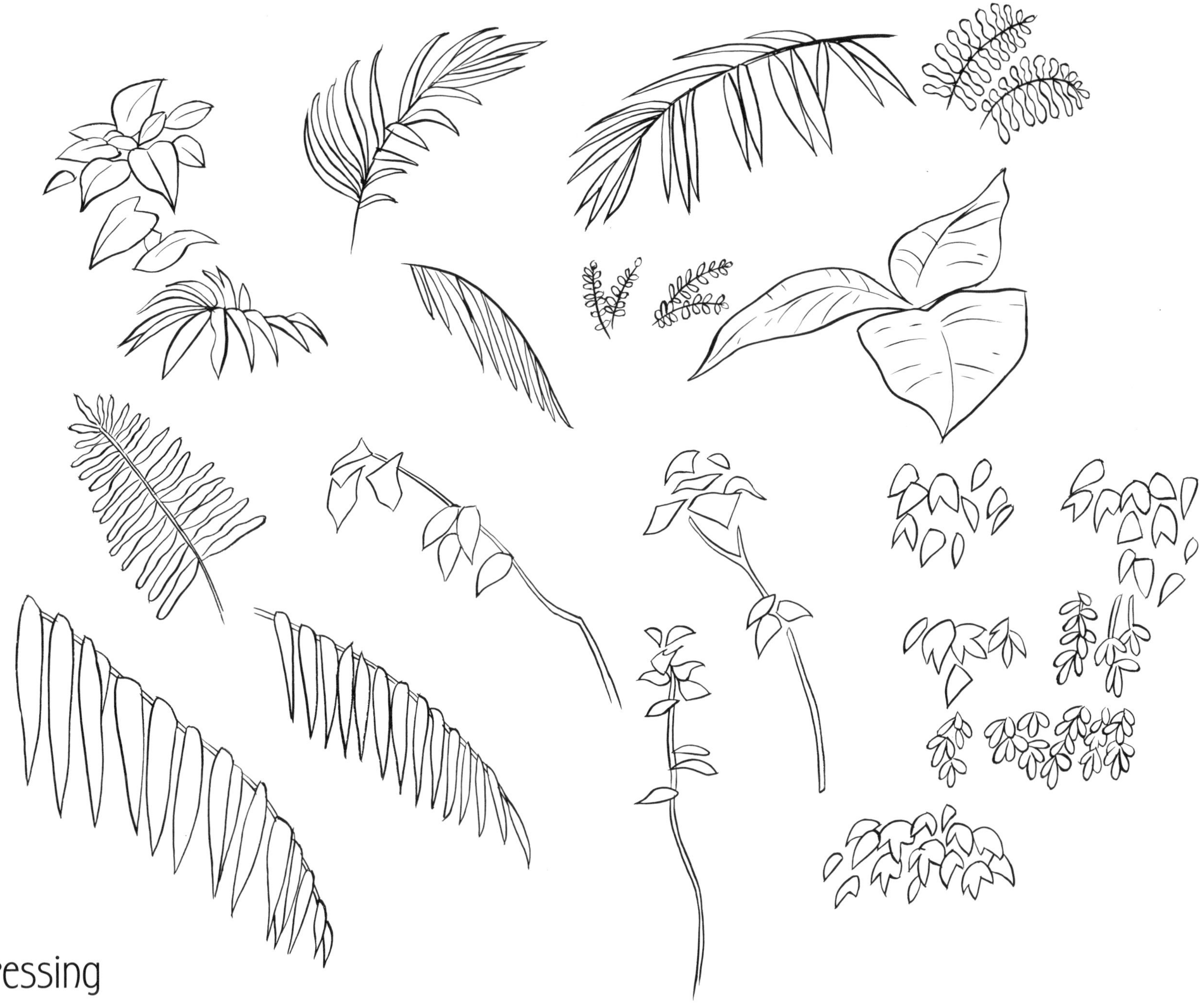

Set Dressing

A lot of this story takes place in a jungle. I came up with a series of little bits we could use in different configurations.

Like the tropical plants I made for Doc, these were designed not to attract too much attention, but give the world a bit of life and keep the story going.

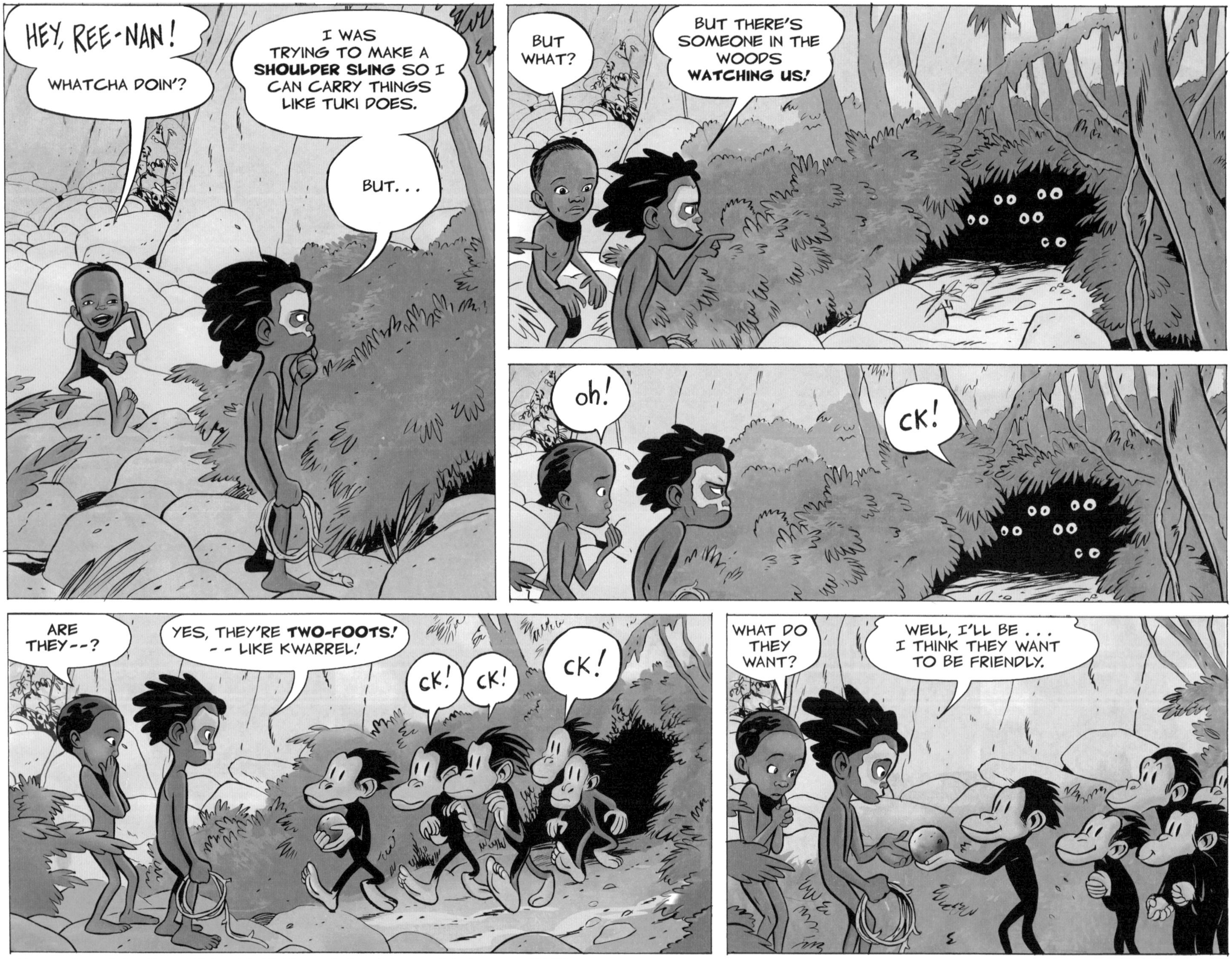
HEY, REE-NAN!
WHATCHA DOIN'?
I WAS TRYING TO MAKE A SHOULDER SLING SO I CAN CARRY THINGS LIKE TUKI DOES.
BUT. . .
BUT WHAT?
BUT THERE'S SOMEONE IN THE WOODS WATCHING US!
oh!
CK!
ARE THEY--?
YES, THEY'RE TWO-FOOTS! --LIKE KWARREL!
CK!
CK!
CK!
WHAT DO THEY WANT?
WELL, I'LL BE . . . I THINK THEY WANT TO BE FRIENDLY.

Above: As originally published in Tuki comic book issue #4, January 2016

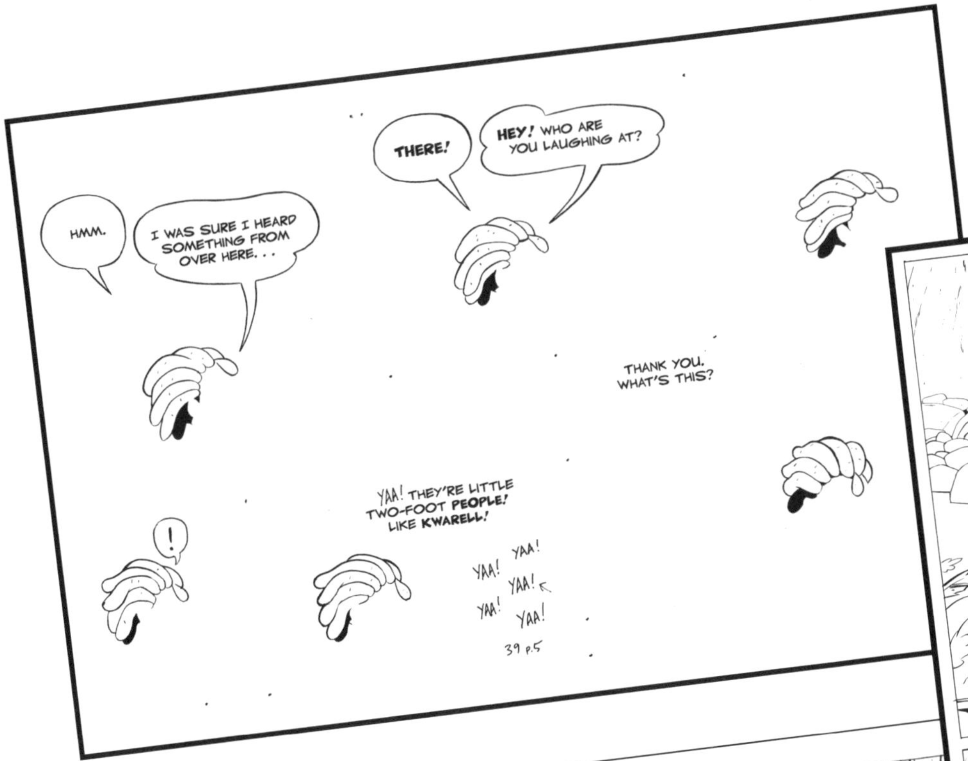
HMM.
I WAS SURE I HEARD SOMETHING FROM OVER HERE. . .
THERE!
HEY! WHO ARE YOU LAUGHING AT?
THANK YOU. WHAT'S THIS?
YAA! THEY'RE LITTLE TWO-FOOT PEOPLE! LIKE KWARELL!
!
YAA! YAA!
YAA! YAA!
YAA! YAA!
39 p.5

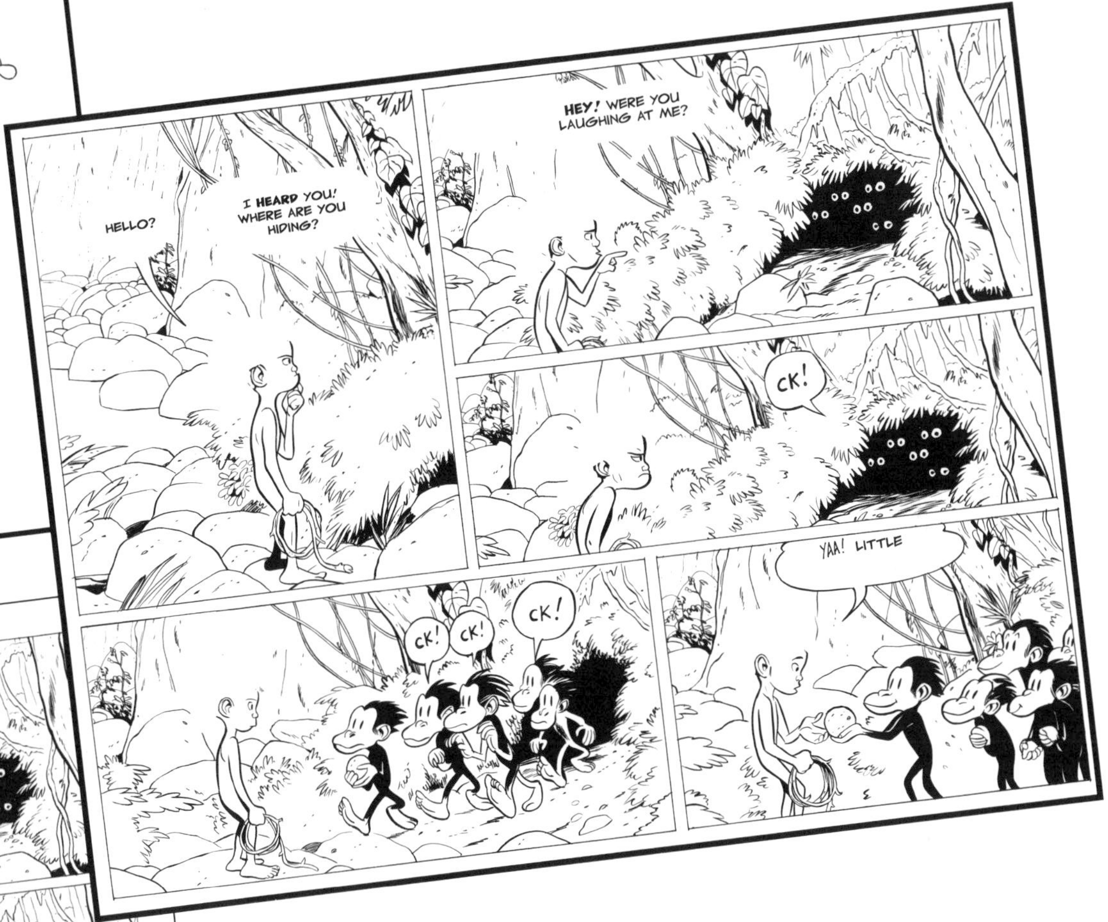
HELLO?
I HEARD YOU! WHERE ARE YOU HIDING?
HEY! WERE YOU LAUGHING AT ME?
CK!
CK!
CK!
CK!
YAA! LITTLE

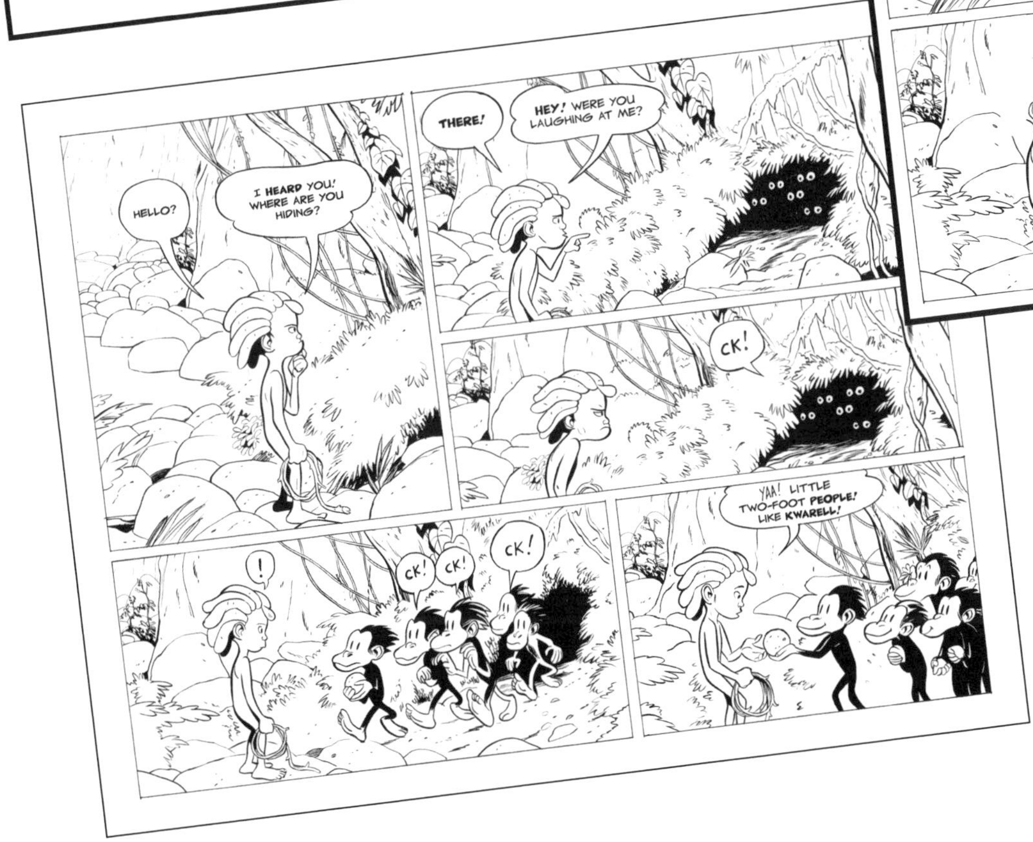
HELLO?
I HEARD YOU! WHERE ARE YOU HIDING?
THERE!
HEY! WERE YOU LAUGHING AT ME?
CK!
!
CK!
CK!
CK!
YAA! LITTLE TWO-FOOT PEOPLE! LIKE KWARELL!

The second half of chapter 2 involves the character Pup. This scene was from the earlier version of TUKI: Save the Humans, and a few things needed to be changed. First, this is now a solo moment for Pup, so Zee would have to be taken out of every panel. Also, Pup's hair is off model from the newer stuff. Tom Gaadt, who does the coloring and photoshop here at Cartoon Books, removed Zee and erased Pup's hair. Meanwhile, I drew new dreds and a tree with vines for Pup to make his coil of rope.

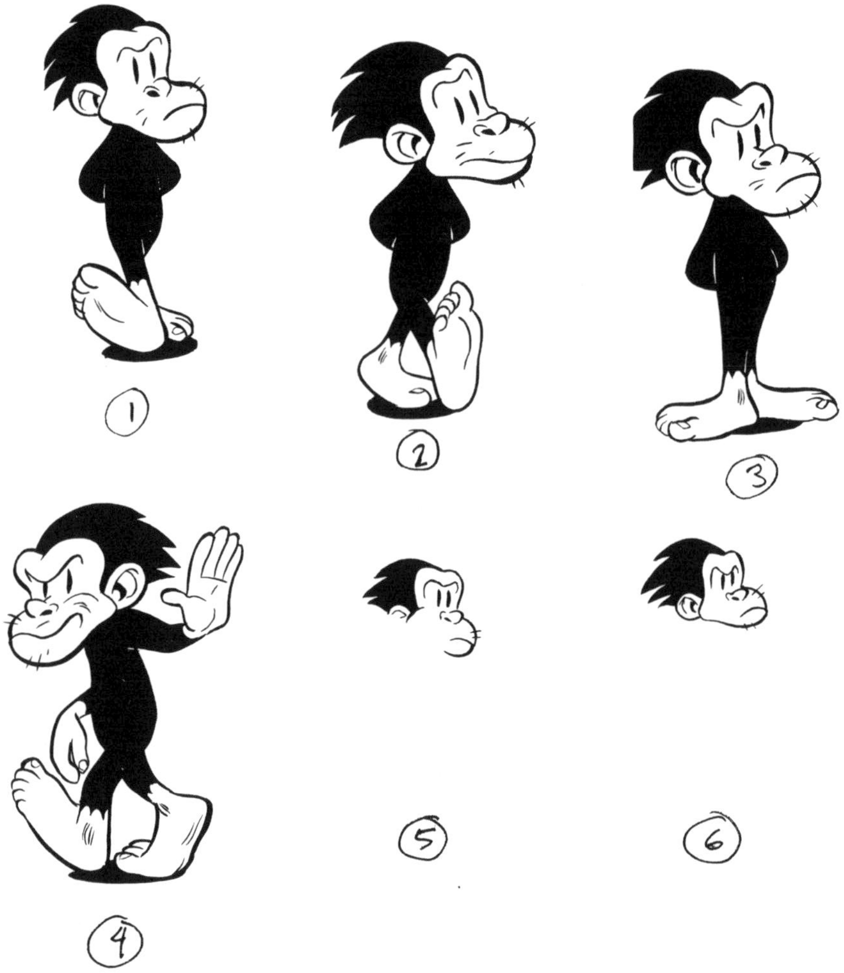

1
2
3
4
5
6

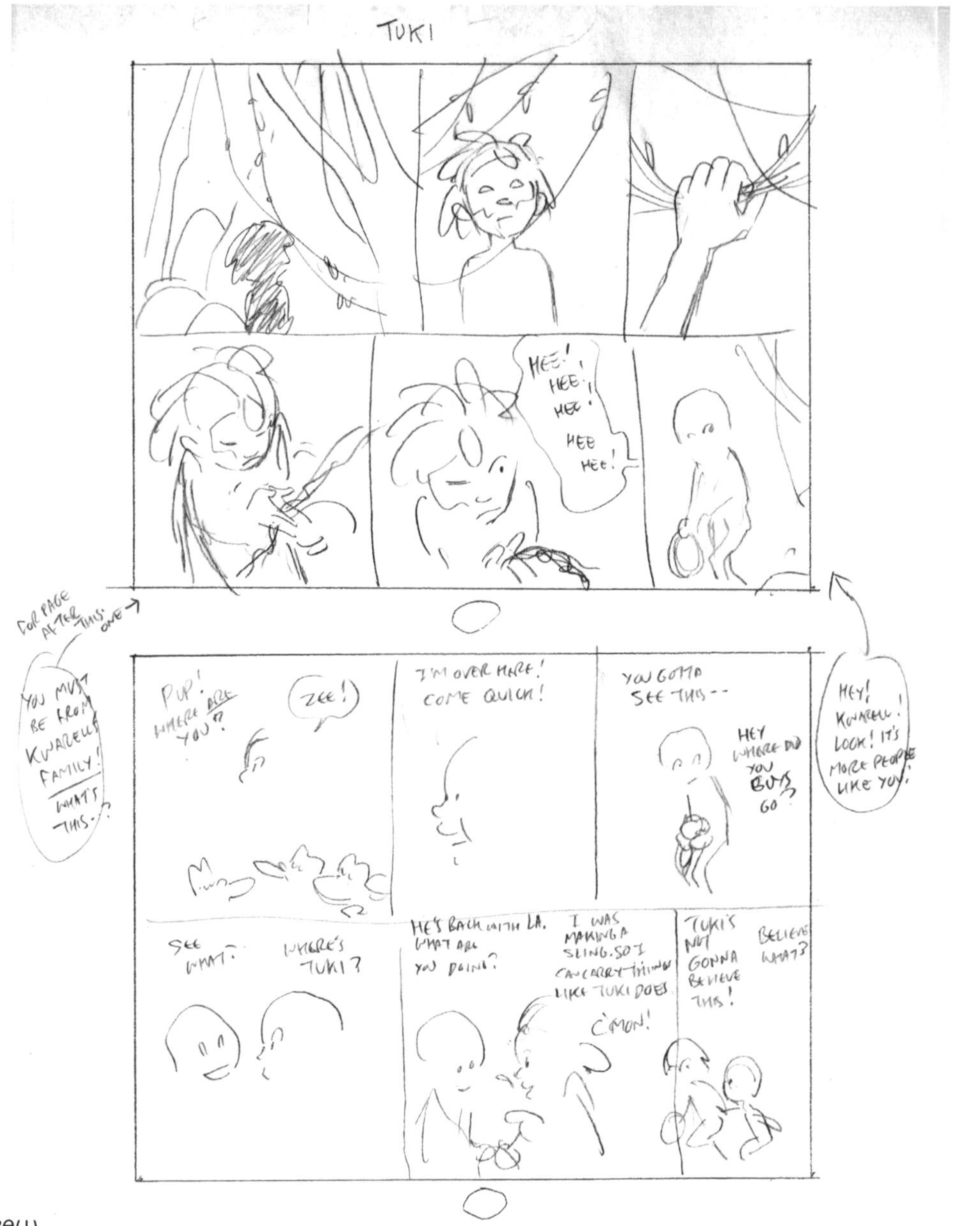

TUKI
HEE! HEE! HEE! HEE! HEE!
FOR PAGE AFTER THIS ONE
YOU MUST BE FROM KWARELL'S FAMILY! WHAT'S THIS..?
PUP! WHERE ARE YOU?!
ZEE!
I'M OVER HERE! COME QUICK!
YOU GOTTA SEE THIS --
HEY WHERE DID YOU GUYS GO?
HEY! KWARELL! LOOK! IT'S MORE PEOPLE LIKE YOU!
SEE WHAT?
WHERE'S TUKI?
HE'S BACK WITH LA. WHAT ARE YOU DOING?
I WAS MAKING A SLING SO I CAN CARRY THINGS LIKE TUKI DOES
C'MON!
TUKI'S NOT GONNA BELIEVE THIS!
BELIEVE WHAT?

But wait! There's more!

Kwarell was a little off model in this scene as well, so I redrew him with better construction in a similar style to what I used on the Bone cousins. All that's left is to whip up some new opening and closing pages and we're through!

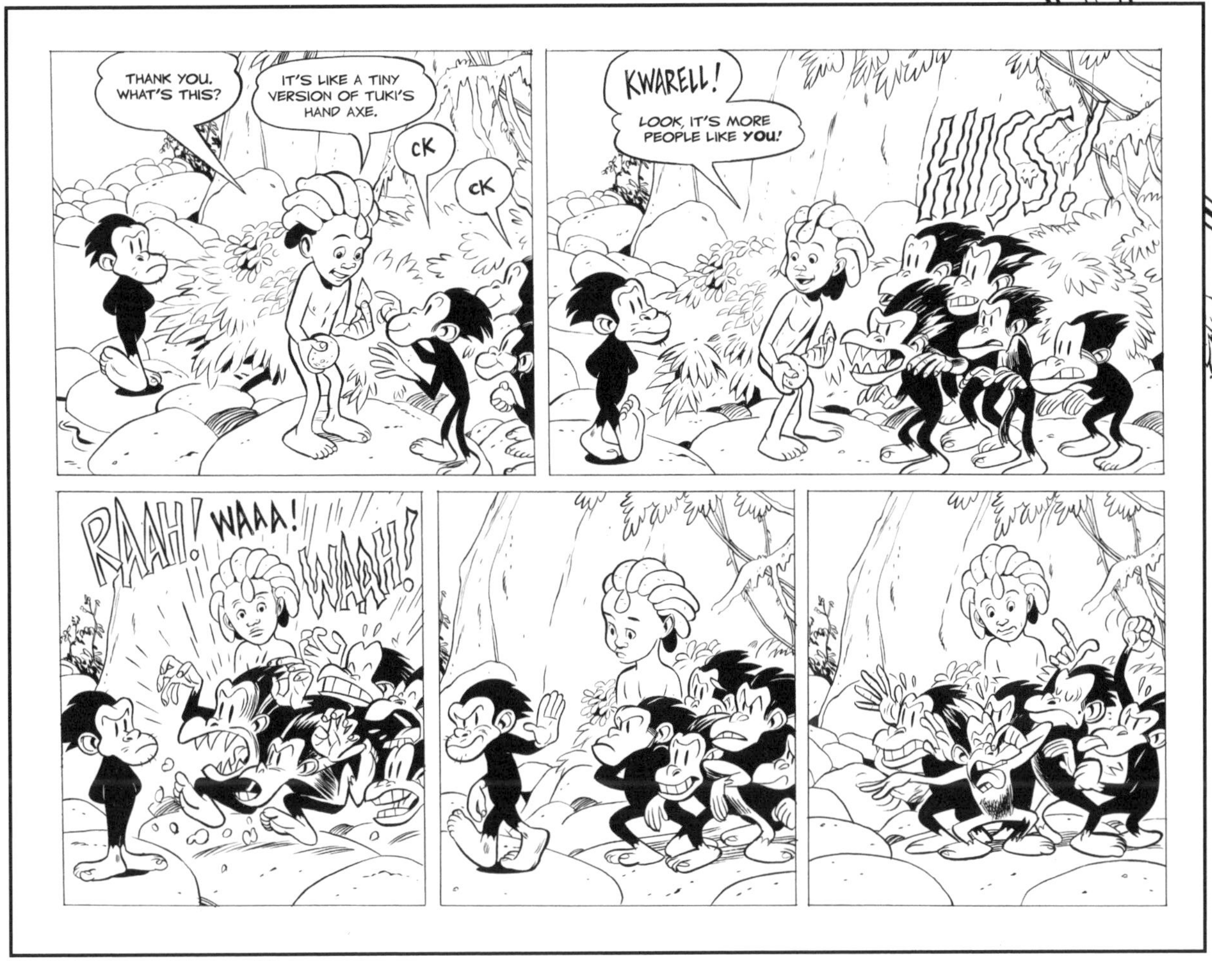
THANK YOU. WHAT'S THIS?
IT'S LIKE A TINY VERSION OF TUKI'S HAND AXE.
CK
CK
KWARELL!
LOOK, IT'S MORE PEOPLE LIKE **YOU!**
HISS!
RAAH!
WAAA!
WAAH!

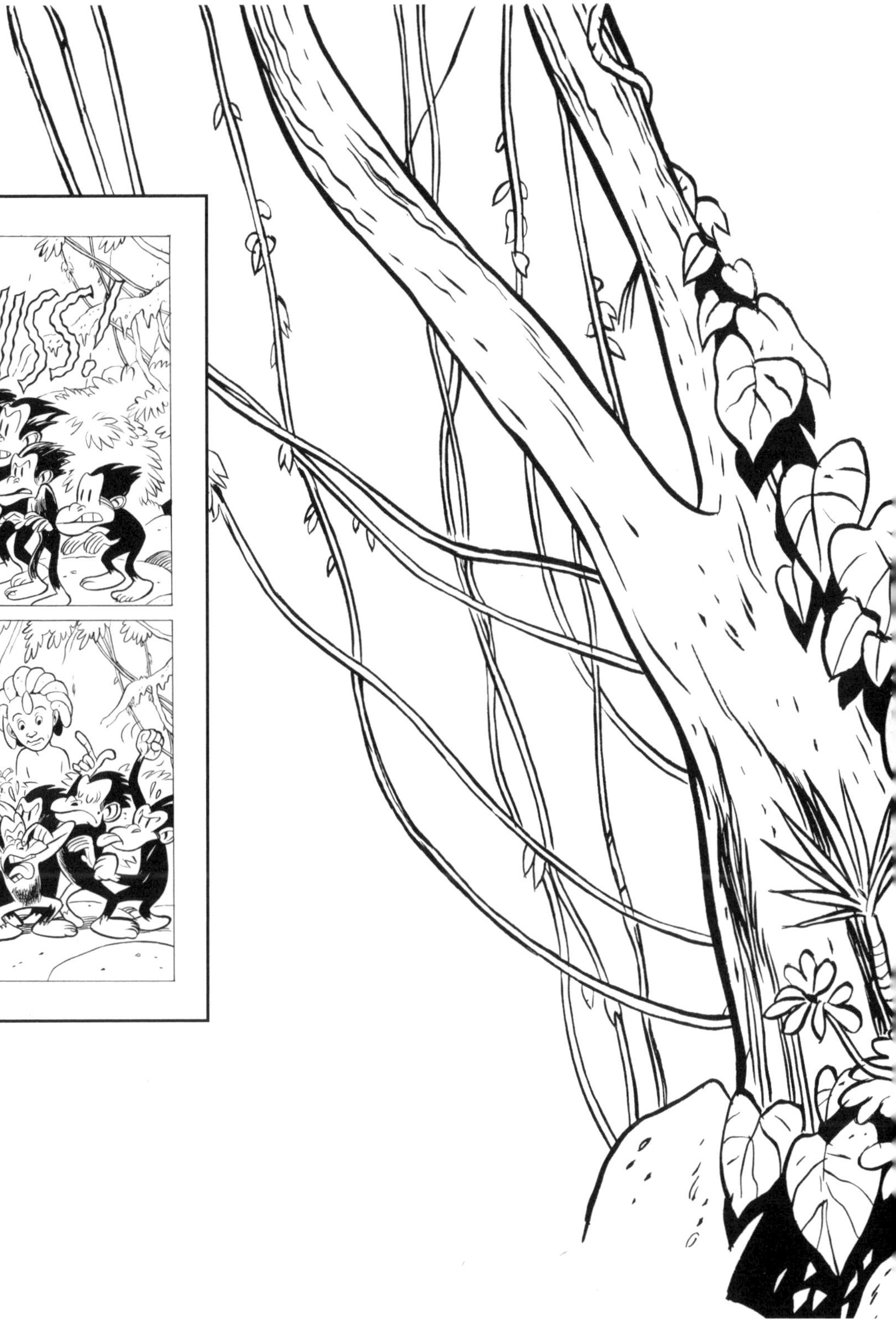

Chapter 2 is complete!

Piece of cake!

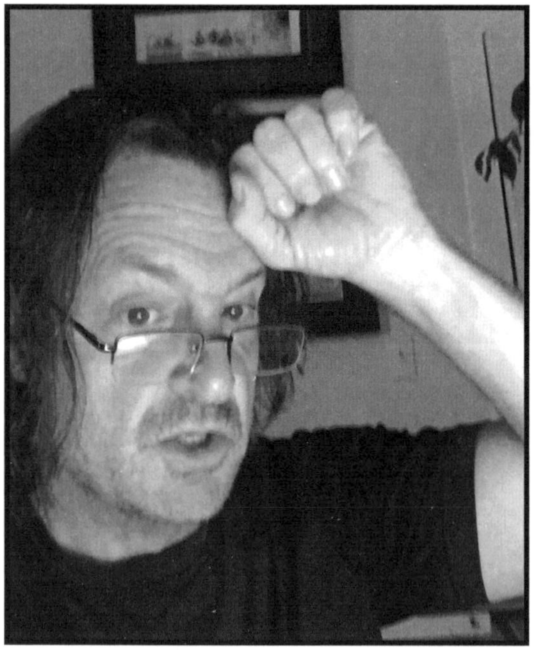

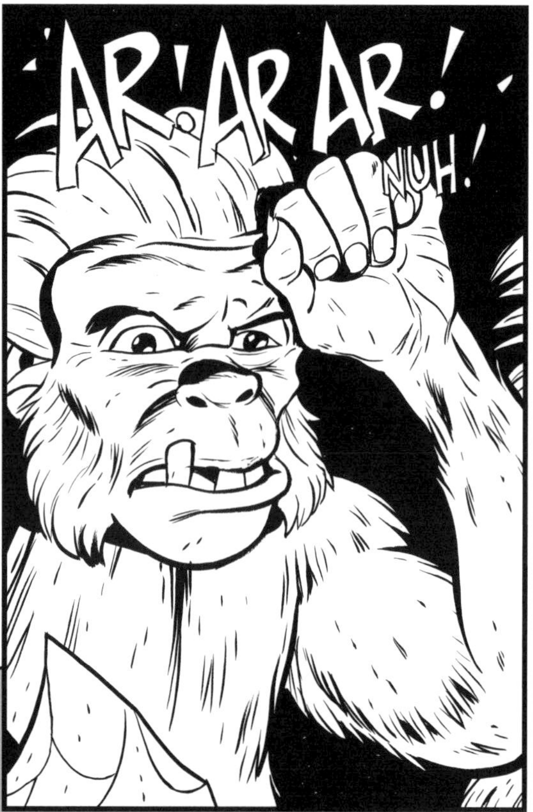
AR! AR AR!
NUH!

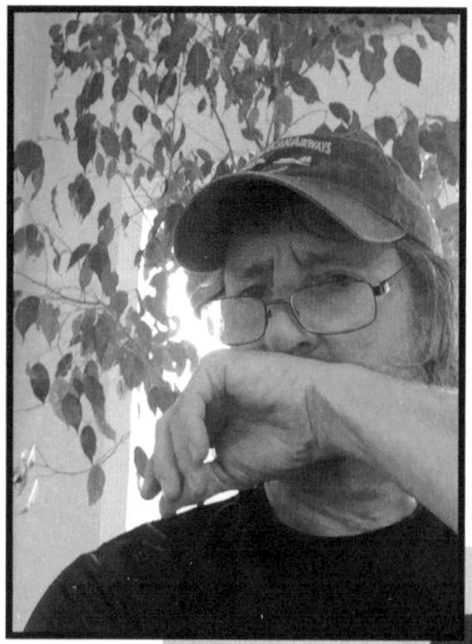

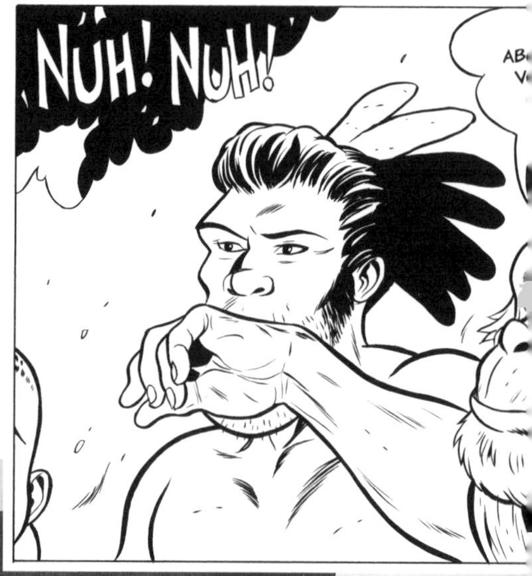
NUH! NUH!

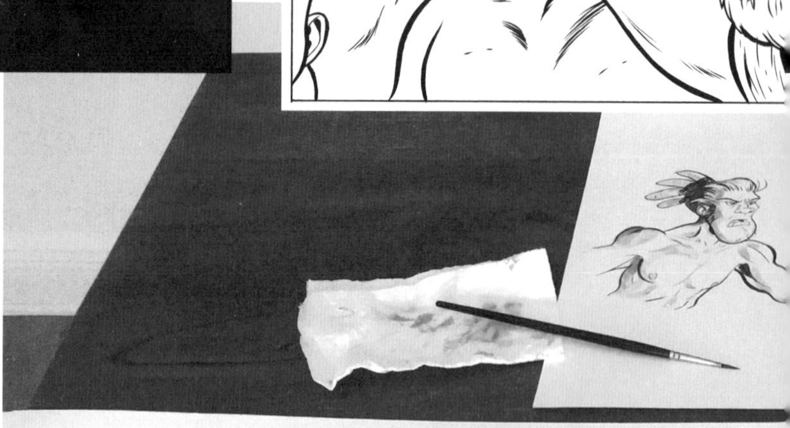

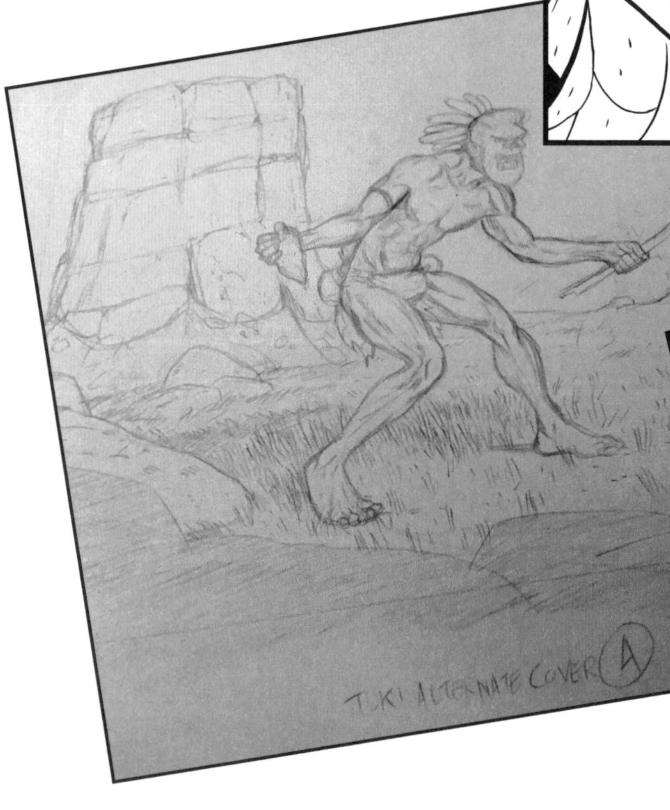
TUKI ALTERNATE COVER (A)

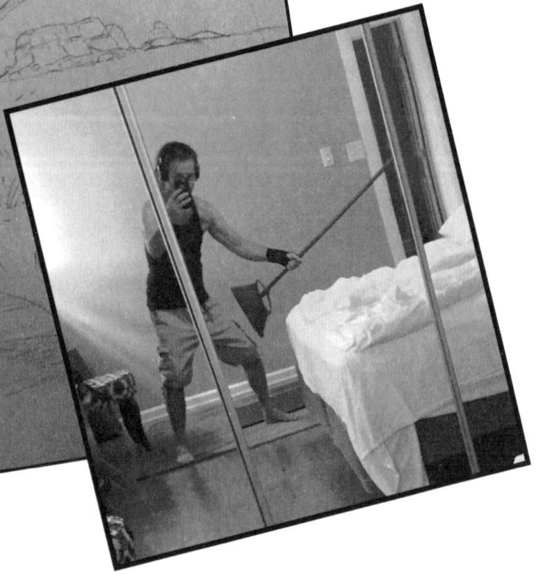

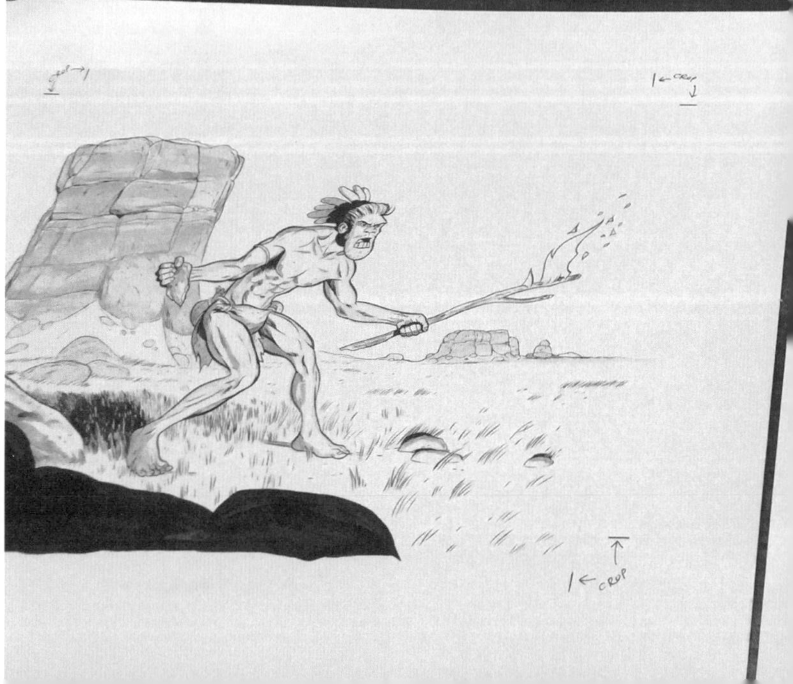

Photo Reference

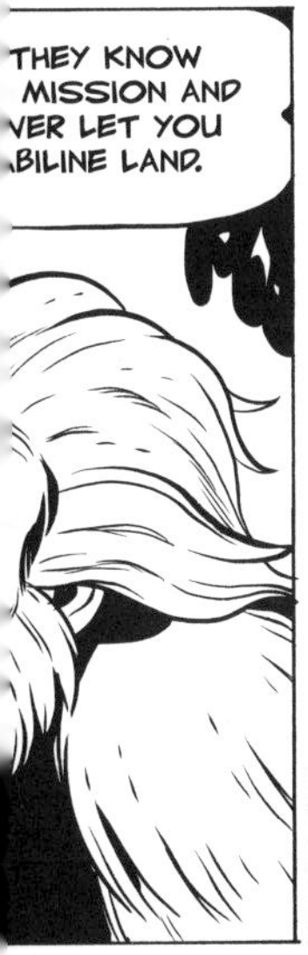
THEY KNOW
MISSION AND
VER LET YOU
BILINE LAND.

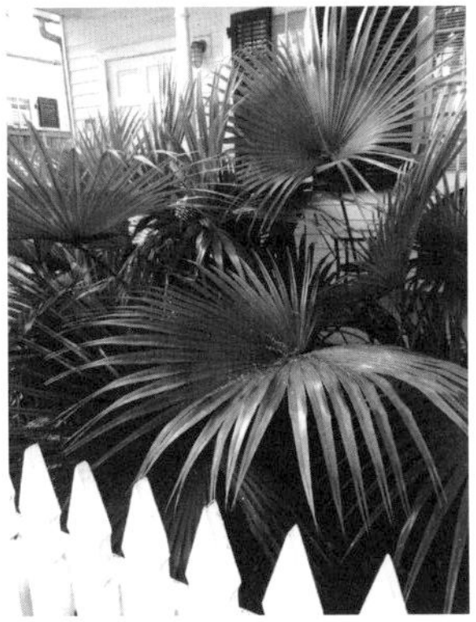

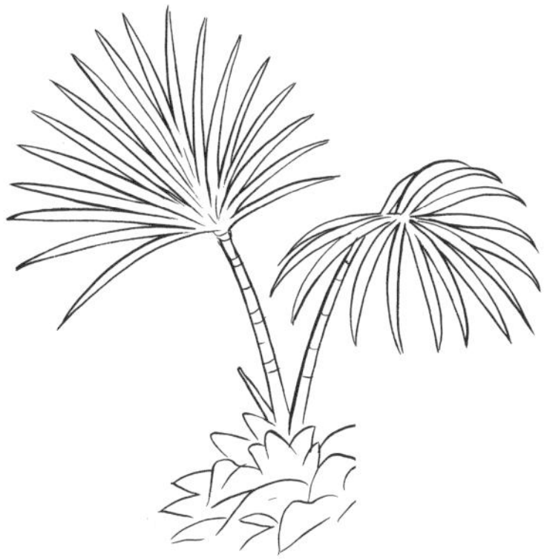

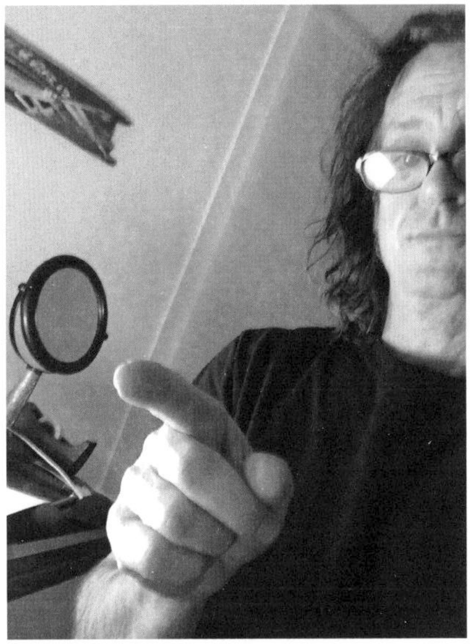

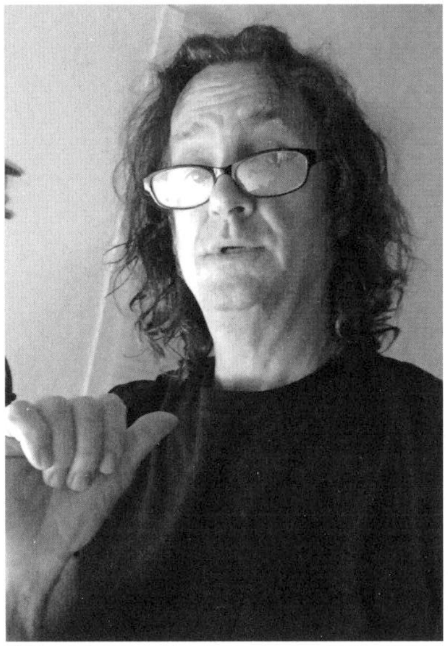

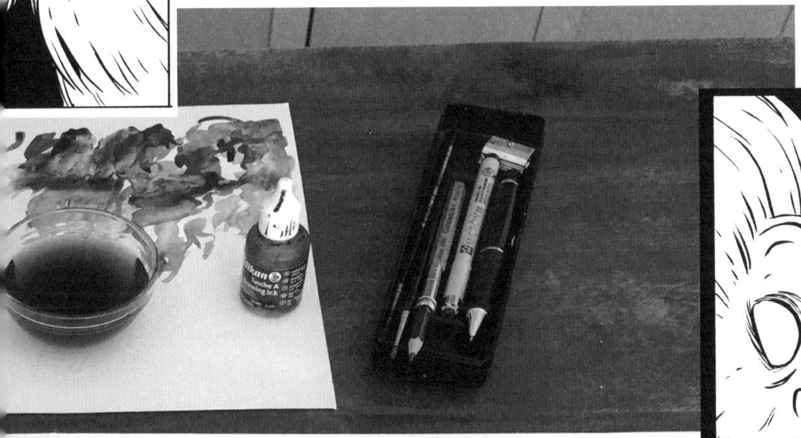

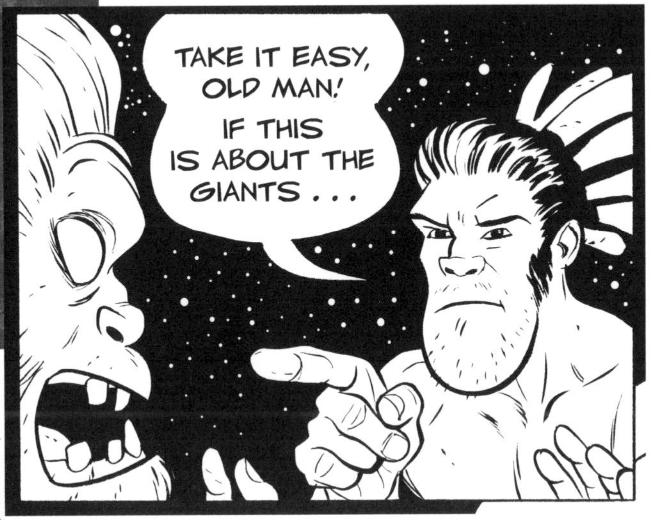
TAKE IT EASY, OLD MAN!
IF THIS IS ABOUT THE GIANTS . . .

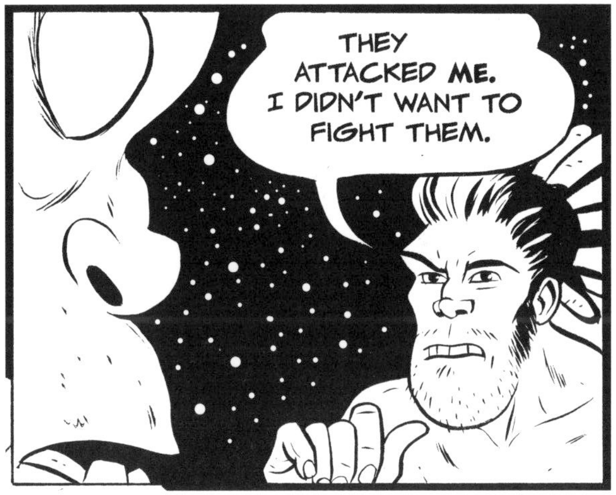
THEY ATTACKED ME. I DIDN'T WANT TO FIGHT THEM.

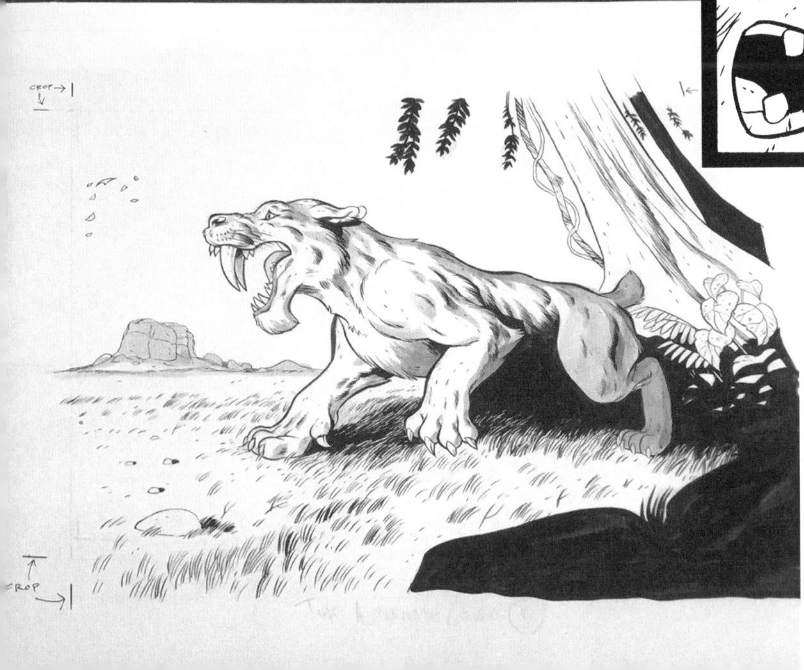

How Do You Hold a Torch?

When I need a little help posing a character, a selfie is just the thing! Whether it's for hands, poses or even palms and landscapes, photo reference is a must!

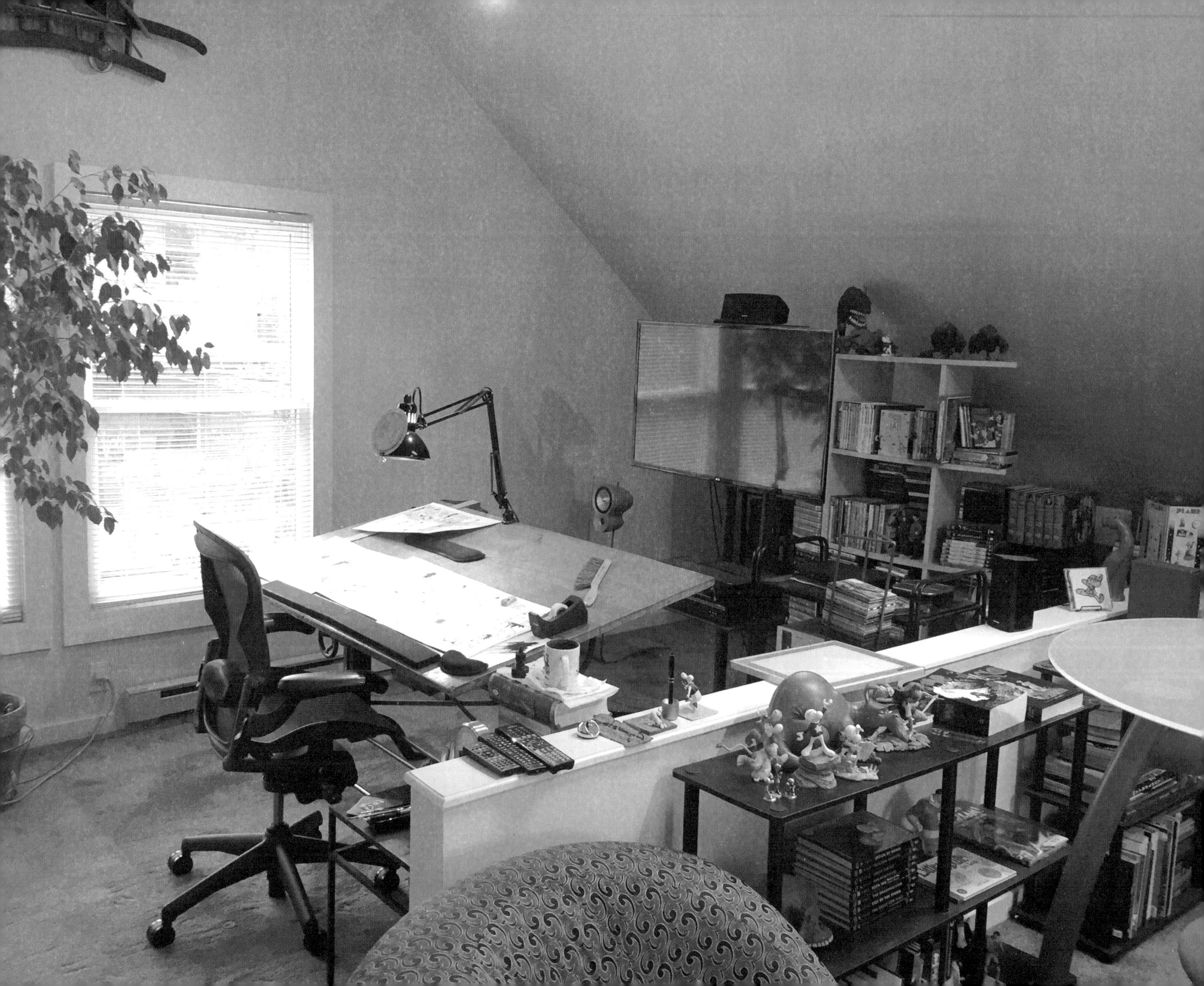

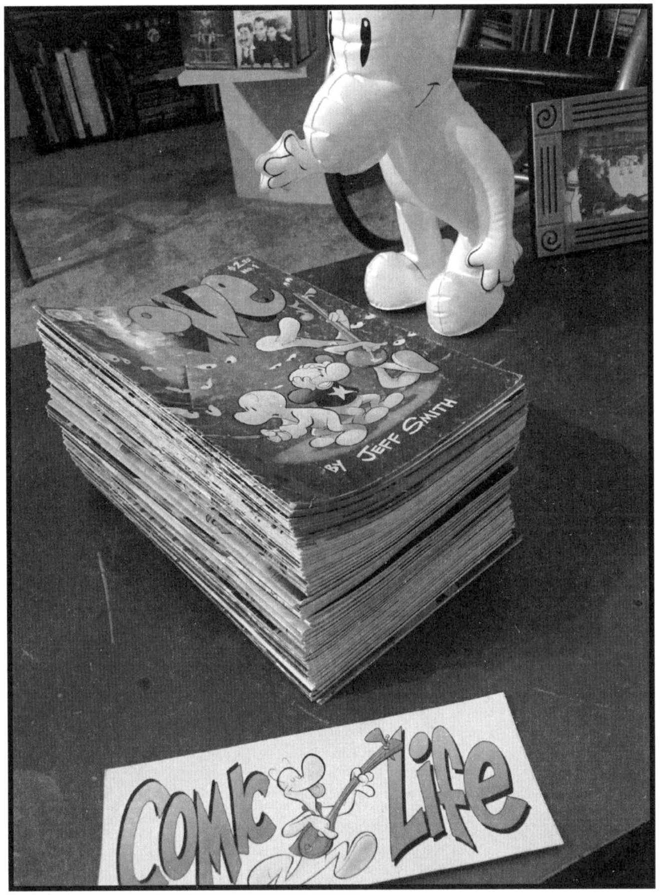
BY JEFF SMITH
Life

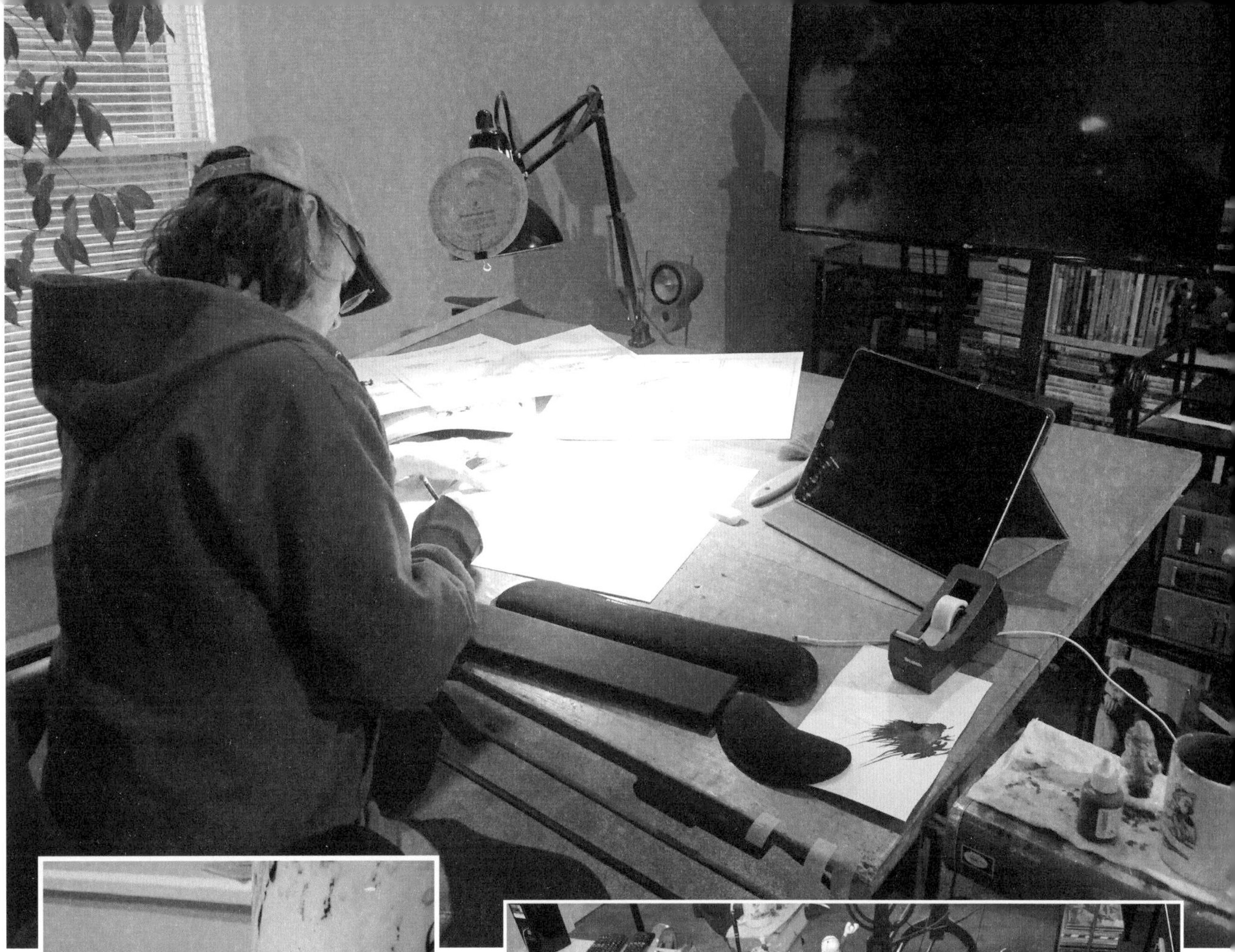

Workspaces

My German Village studio near downtown Columbus.

This page clockwise from the top:
My original reading copies of all 55 issues of Bone;
Me at the drawing board; some of my projects from the past 30 years; a Christmas decoration that sits next to my bottle of ink. It was a hand painted gift from my mother not long after Vijaya and I started dating.

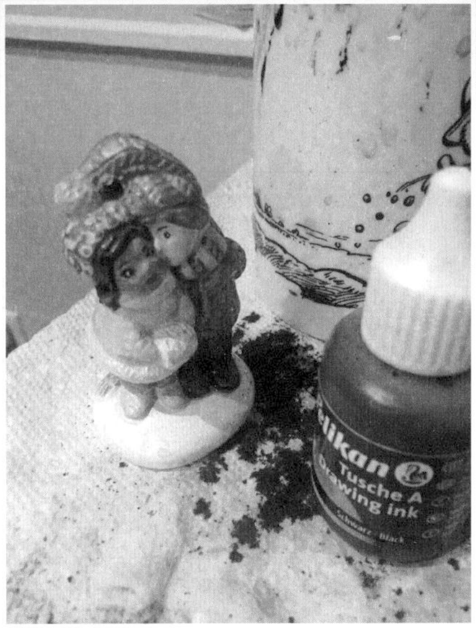
Tusche A
drawing ink

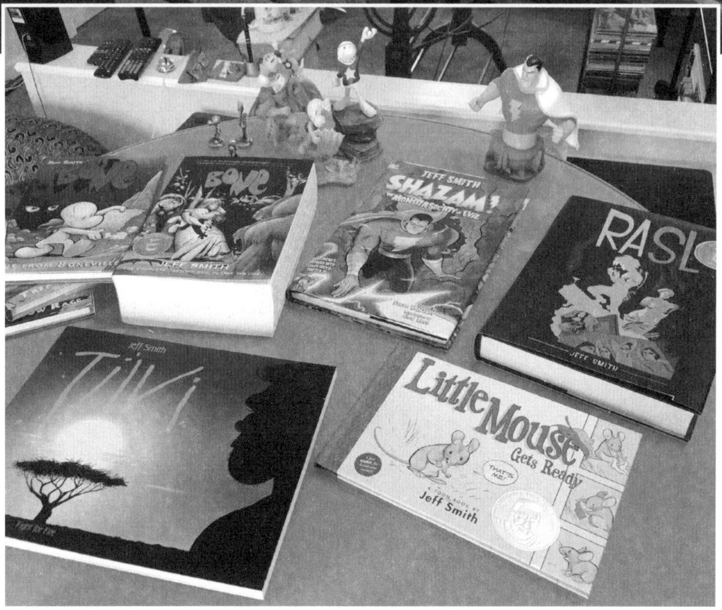
BONE
JEFF SMITH
SHAZAM!
RASL
JEFF SMITH
Jeff Smith
Little Mouse
Gets Ready
Jeff Smith

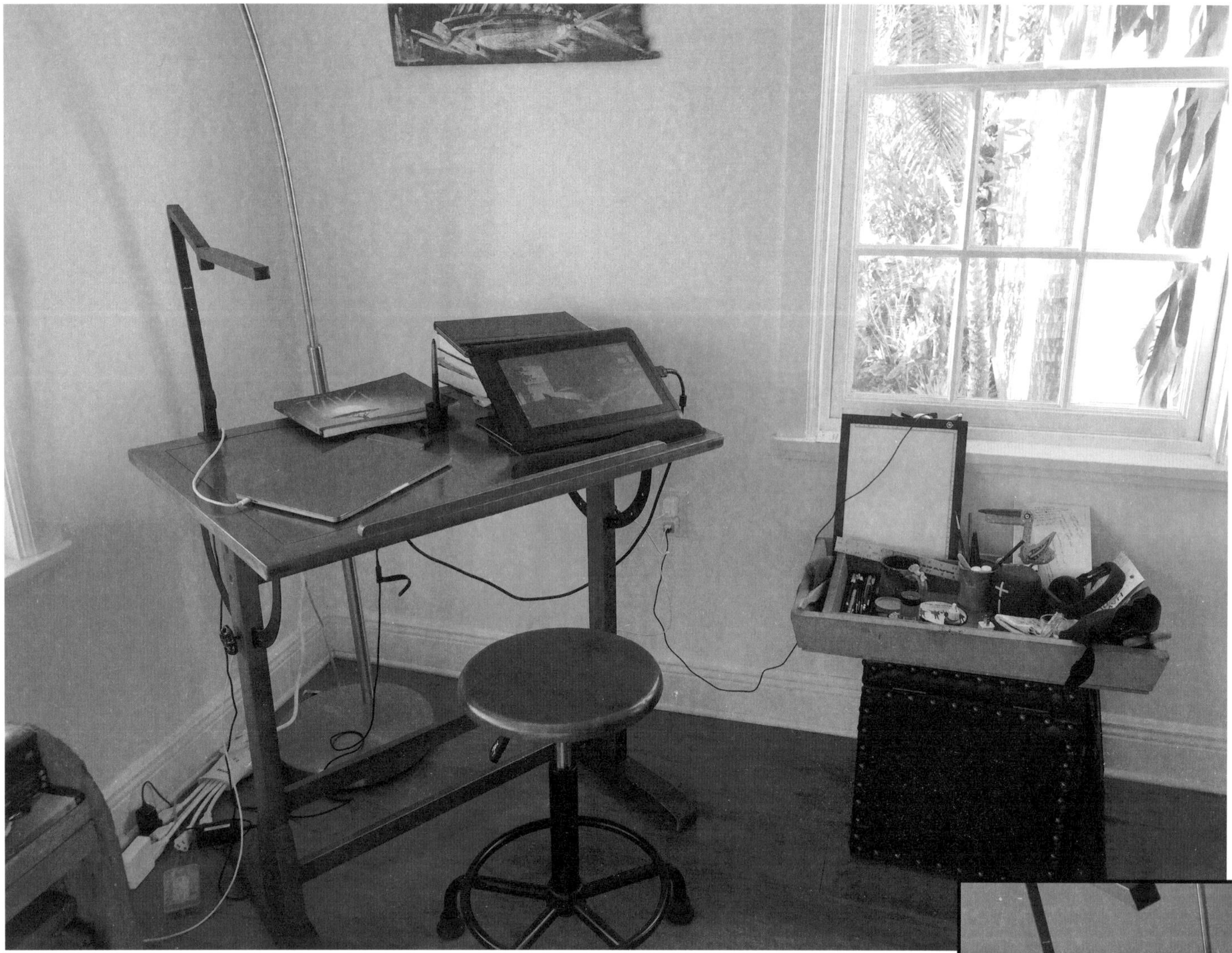

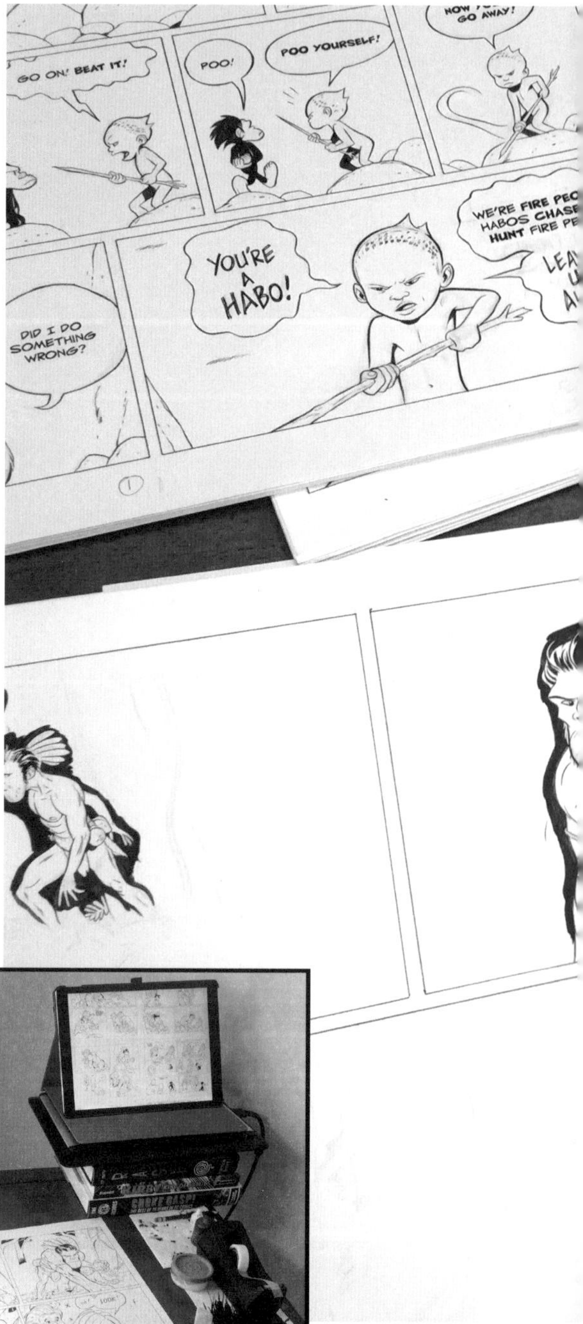
GO ON! BEAT IT!
POO!
POO YOURSELF!
YOU'RE A HABO!
DID I DO SOMETHING WRONG?

This is my workspace in Key West. When we first came down here I set up a tiny drafting table and a stool in the corner, thinking it would be temporary. Eight years later, I'm still sitting at what I affectionately call my *Lil' Hemingway!*

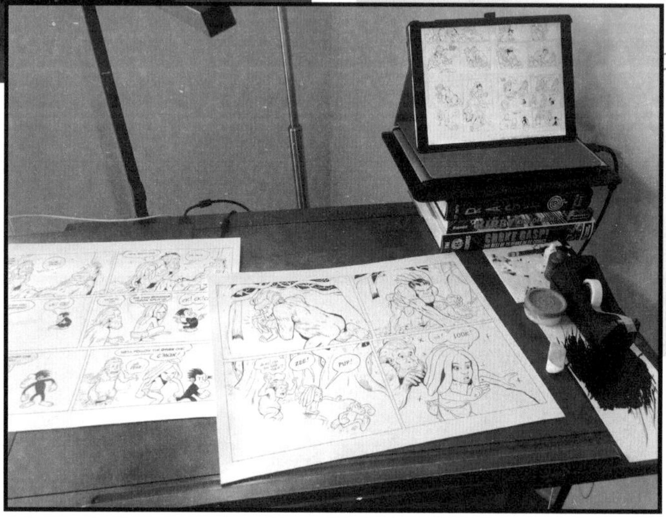

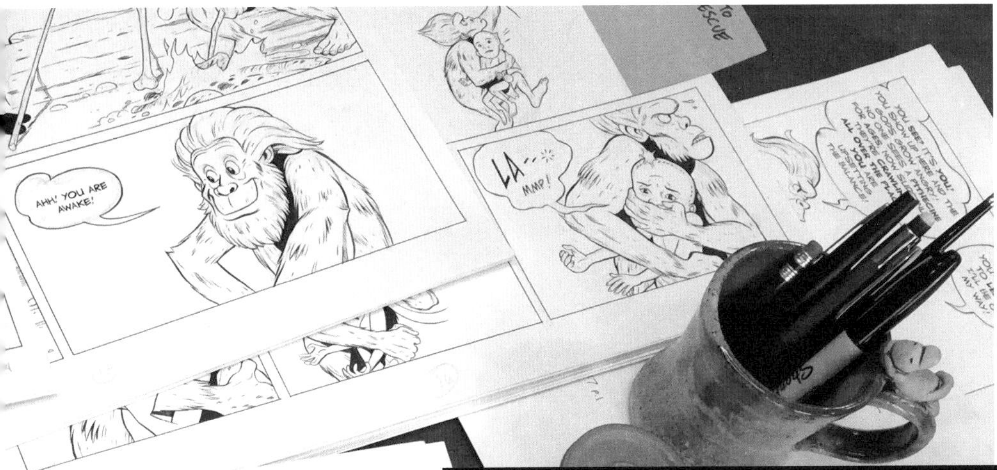
AHH! YOU ARE AWAKE!
LA-
MMP!
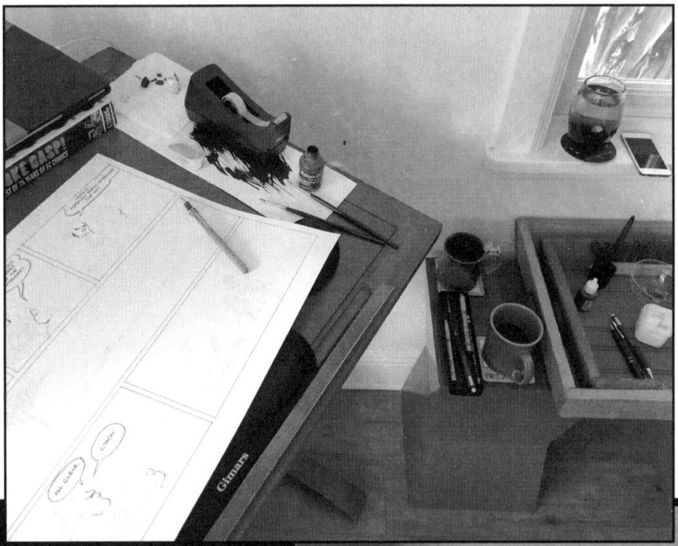
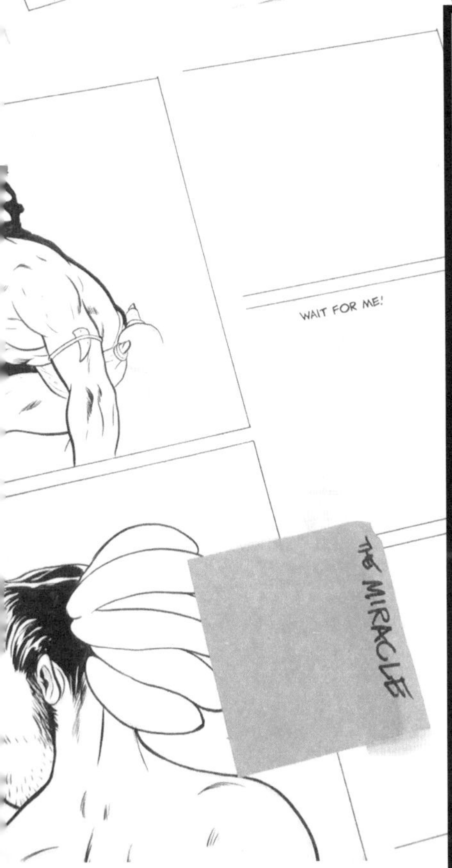
WAIT FOR ME!
THE MIRACLE
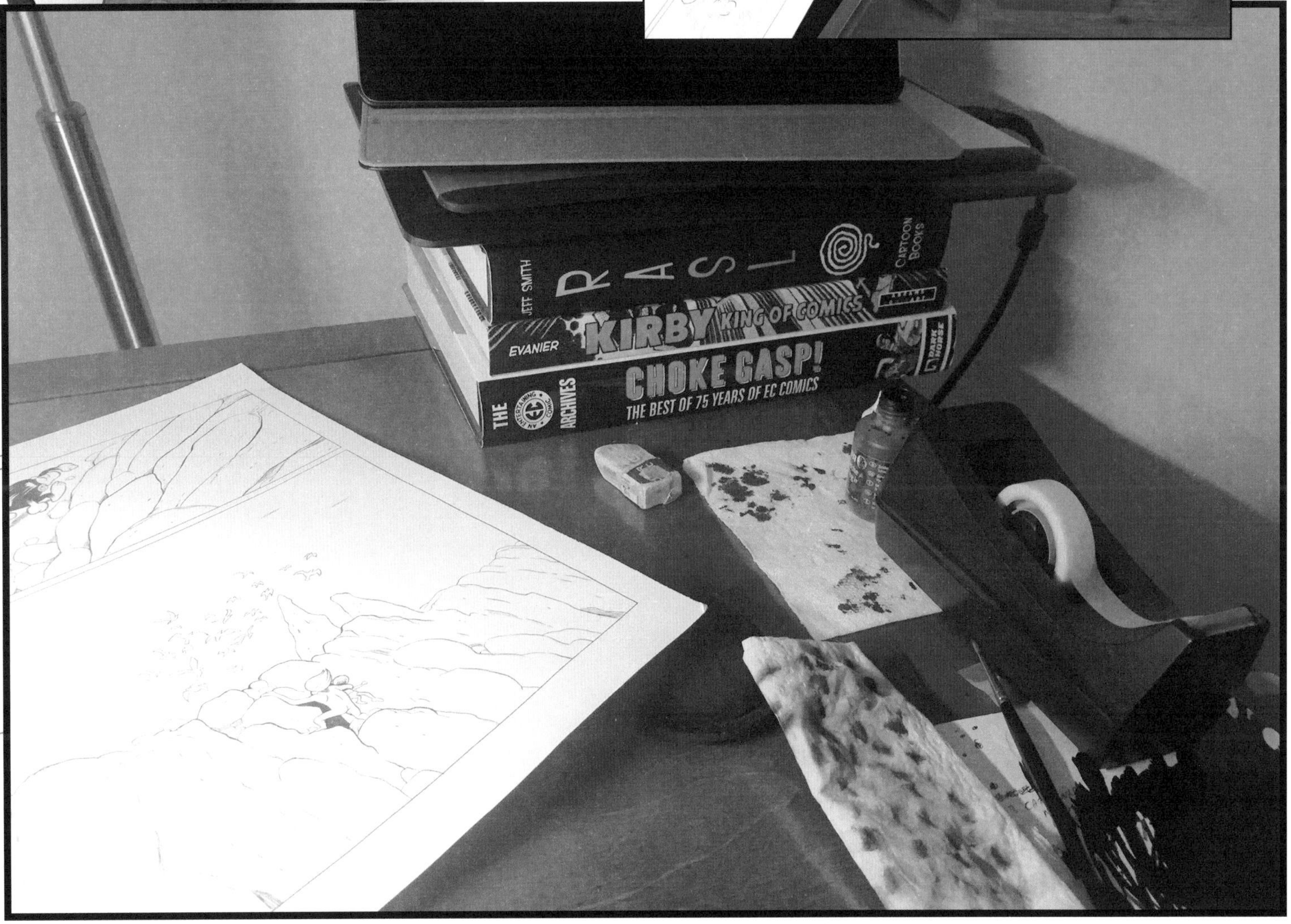
JEFF SMITH
RASL
CARTOON BOOKS
EVANIER
KIRBY KING OF COMICS
THE ARCHIVES
CHOKE GASP!
THE BEST OF 75 YEARS OF EC COMICS

The Campaign

Encouraged to explore Kickstarter as a tool for publicity and self-publishing by Francisca Pulido (of Lady Death and Coffin Comics), as well as Deborah Tucci (of Shi and Crusade Comics), Vijaya and Kathleen Glosan (our Production Manager) got to work setting up a Kickstarter campaign. And what a mess of work that turned out to be! However this was a brilliant, happy and successful bit of promotion! I almost can't believe how good people can be. Our team was overwhelmed but resilient, resourceful, and steadfast. Supporters sent waves of good will in our direction. Thanks, gang!

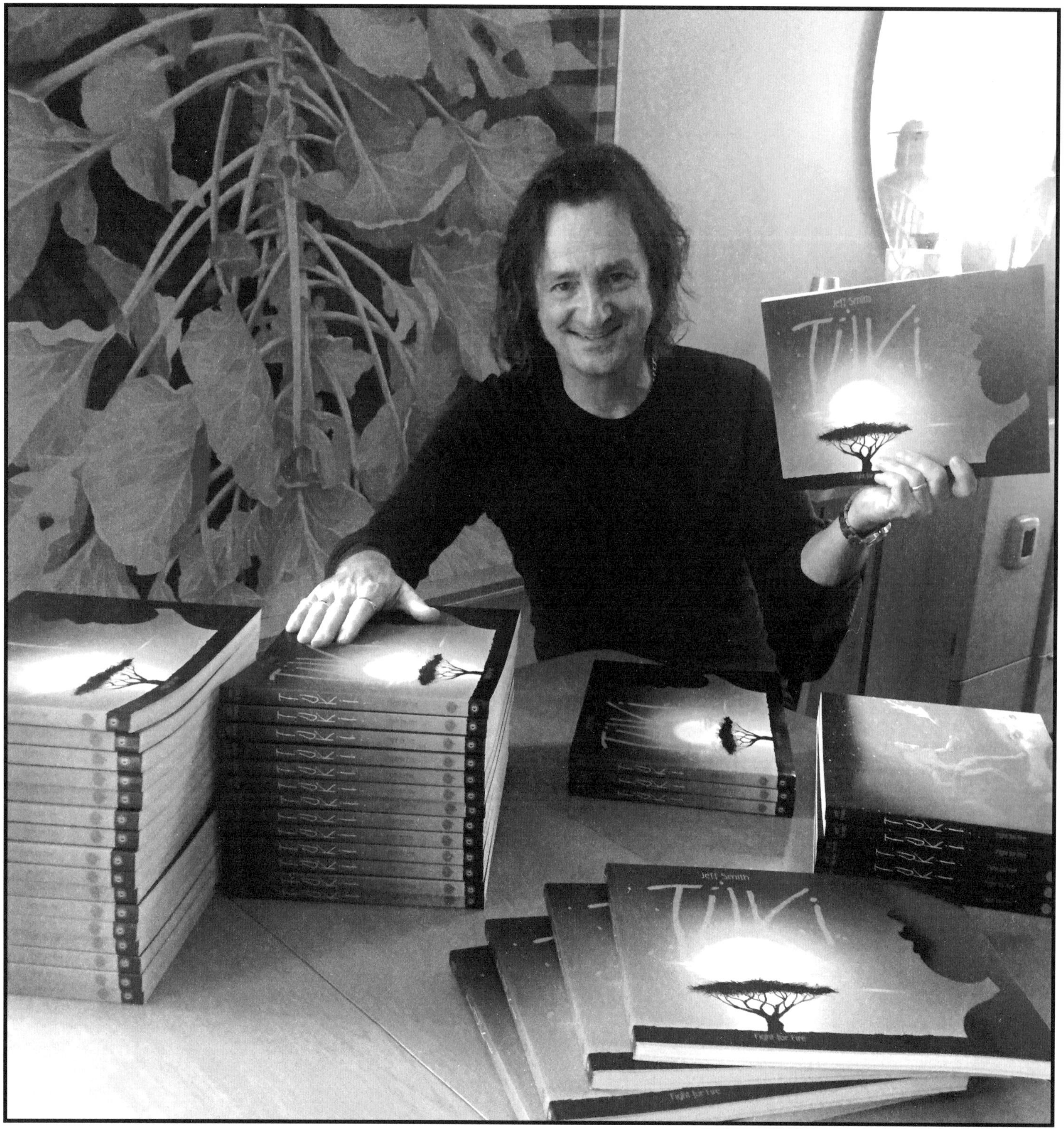
Jeff Smith
Fight for Fire

Rewards!

For anyone who doesn't know, Kickstarter has reward levels. Some of the rewards shown, clockwise from the top right: Signed bookplates with a character sketch; a TUKI key chain with a Homo erectus skull attached (I love this one!); Signed bookplates for regular and special editions.

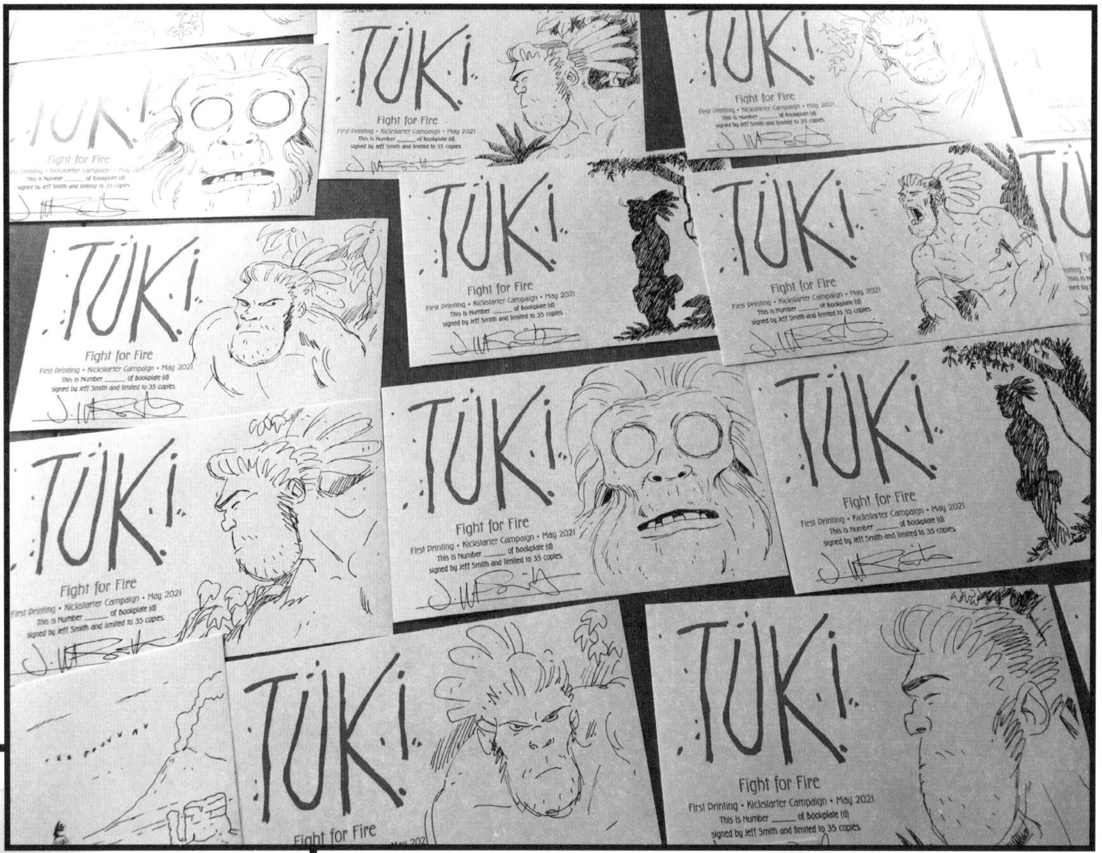
TUKI
Fight for Fire
First Printing • Kickstarter Campaign • May 2021
This is Number _____ of Bookplate (d)
signed by Jeff Smith and limited to 35 copies.

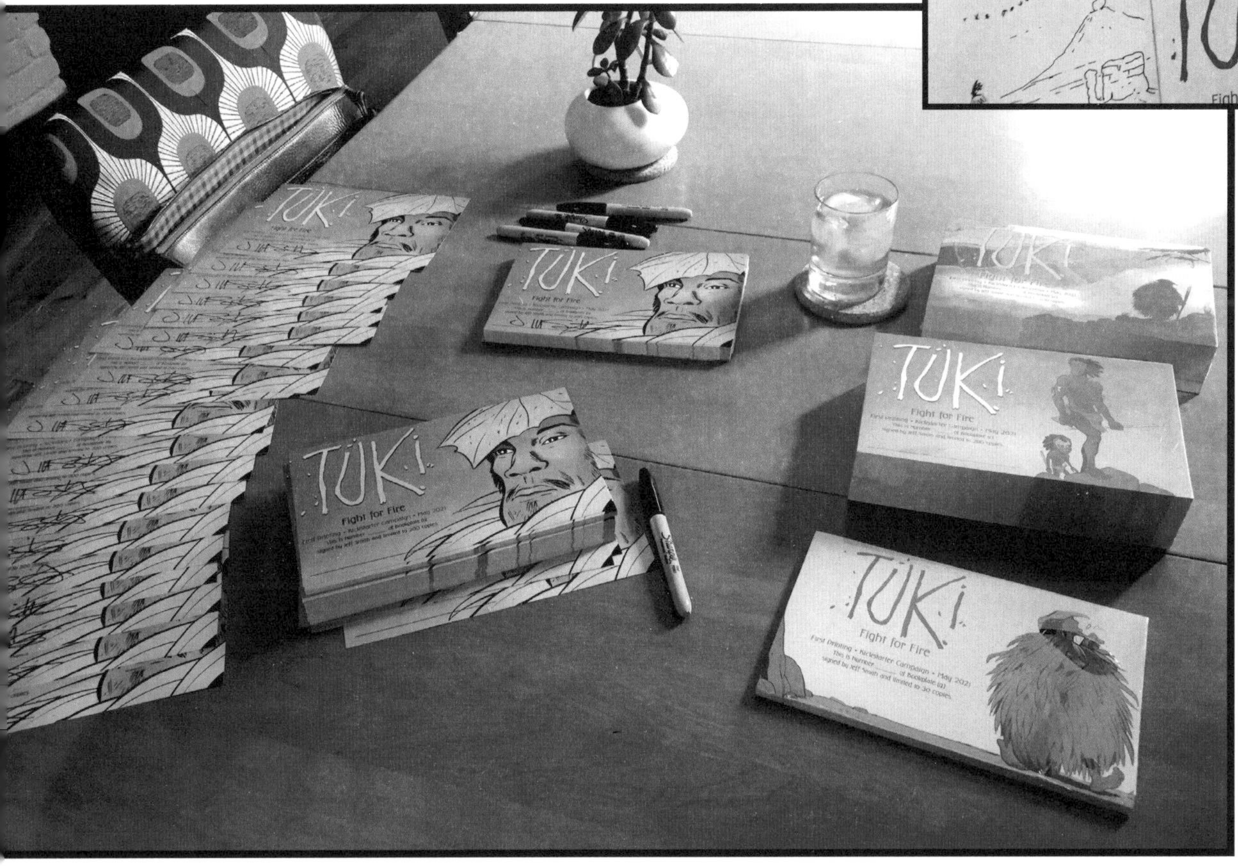
TUKI
Fight for Fire

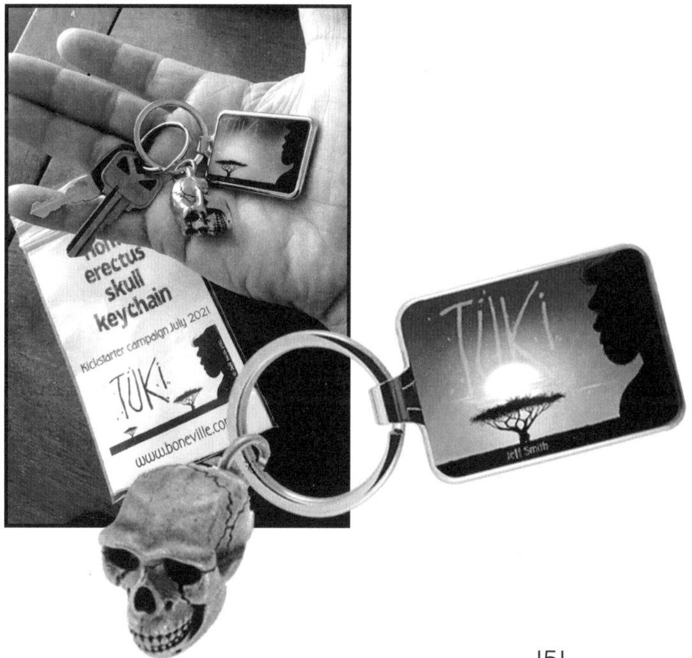
erectus
skull
keychain
Kickstarter campaign July 2021
TUKI
www.boneville.com
TUKI
Jeff Smith

Smile!

Part of the Kickstarter gig is doing video updates. It was a new experience for me, but with responses and questions from readers it felt very much like a two way conversation.

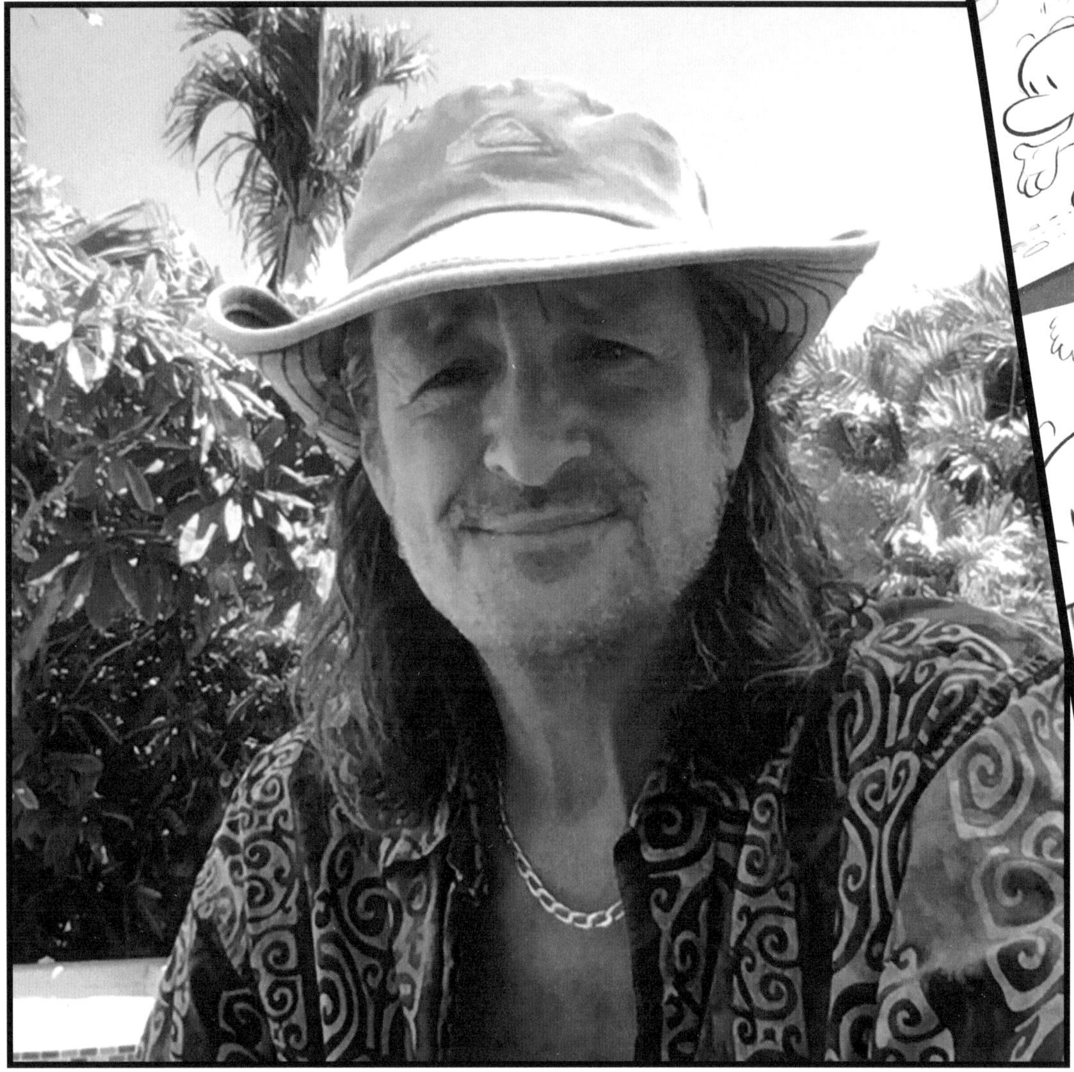

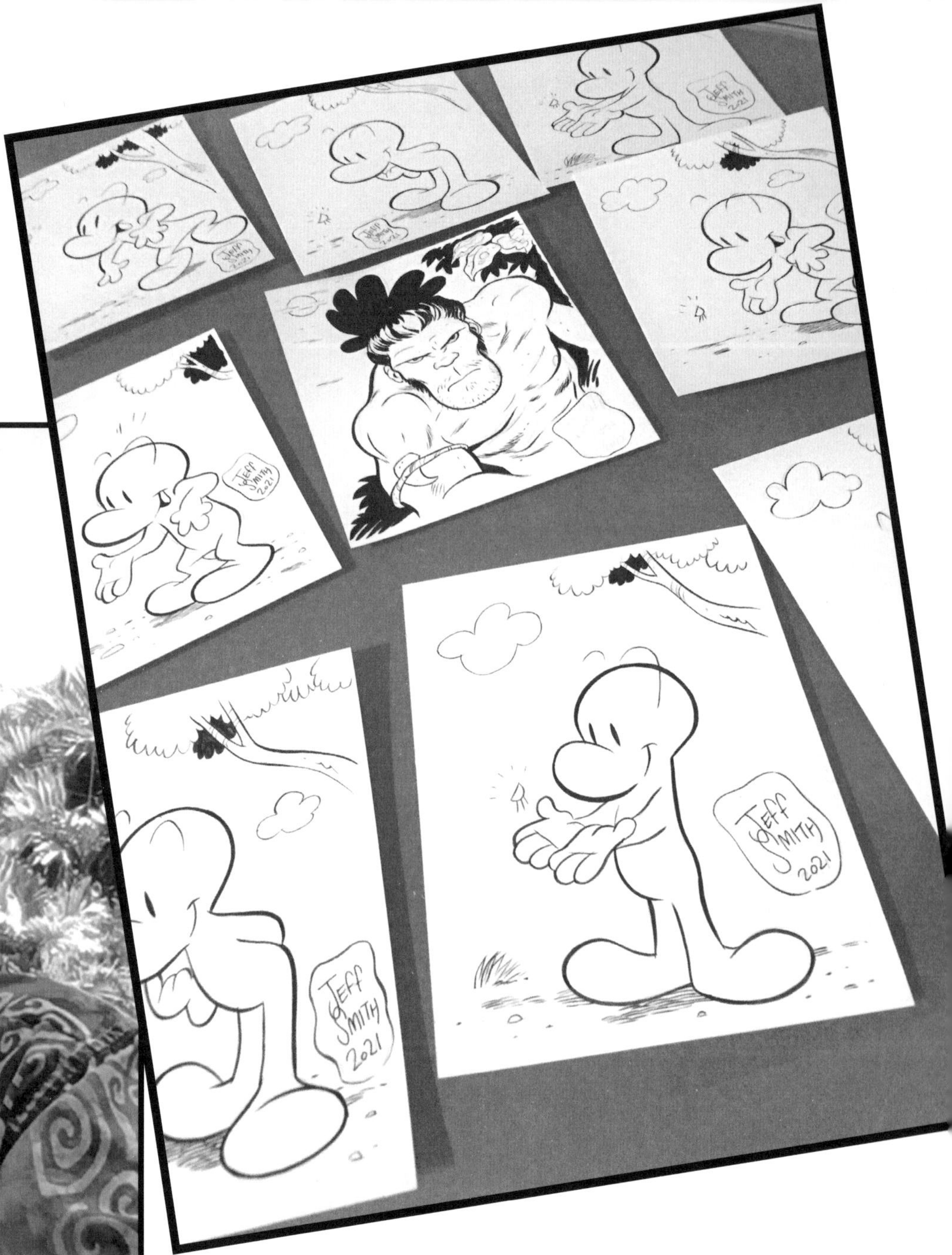
JEFF SMITH 2021
JEFF SMITH 2021

One of the higher tier rewards was an original hand inked drawing limited to 30 to celebrate the 30th anniversary of BONE #1 and Cartoon Books.

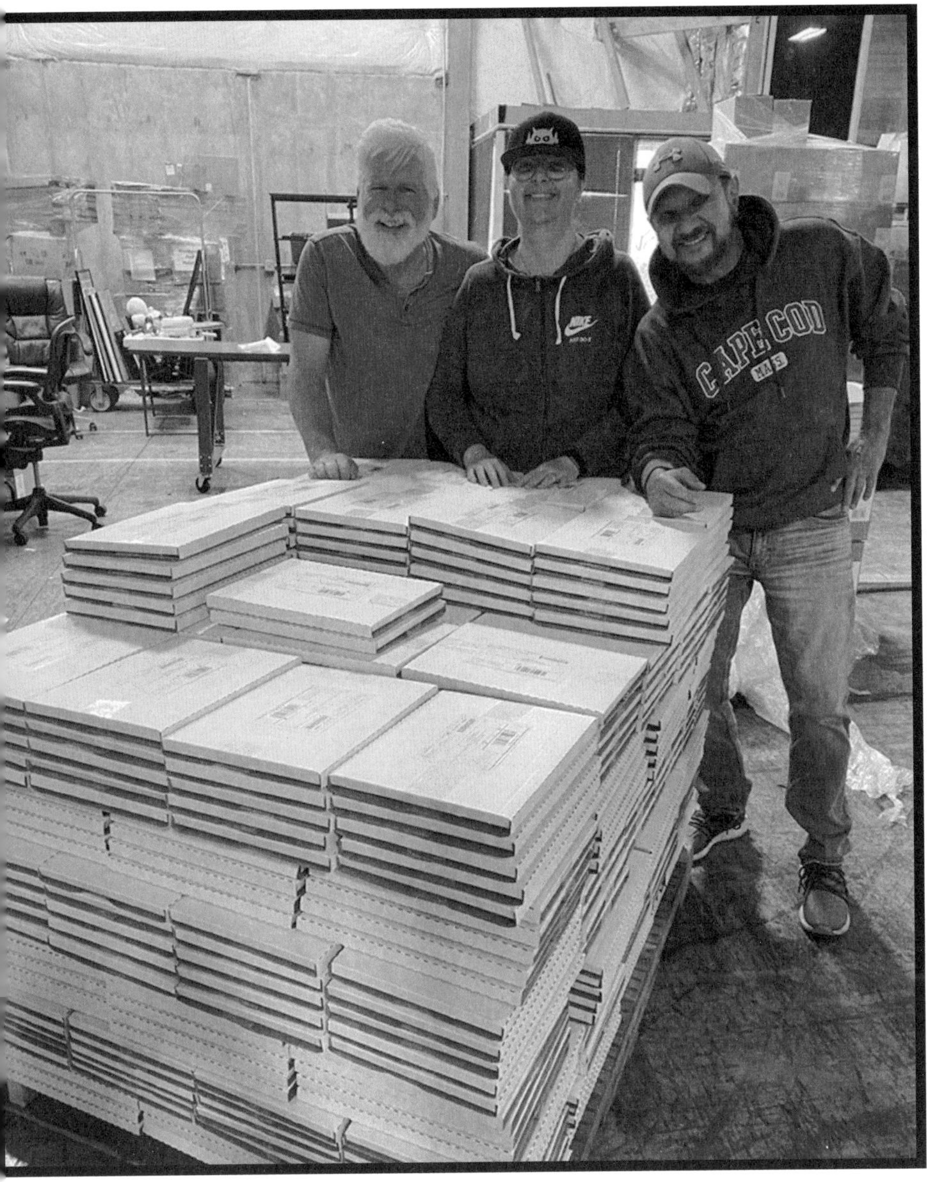
CAPE COD

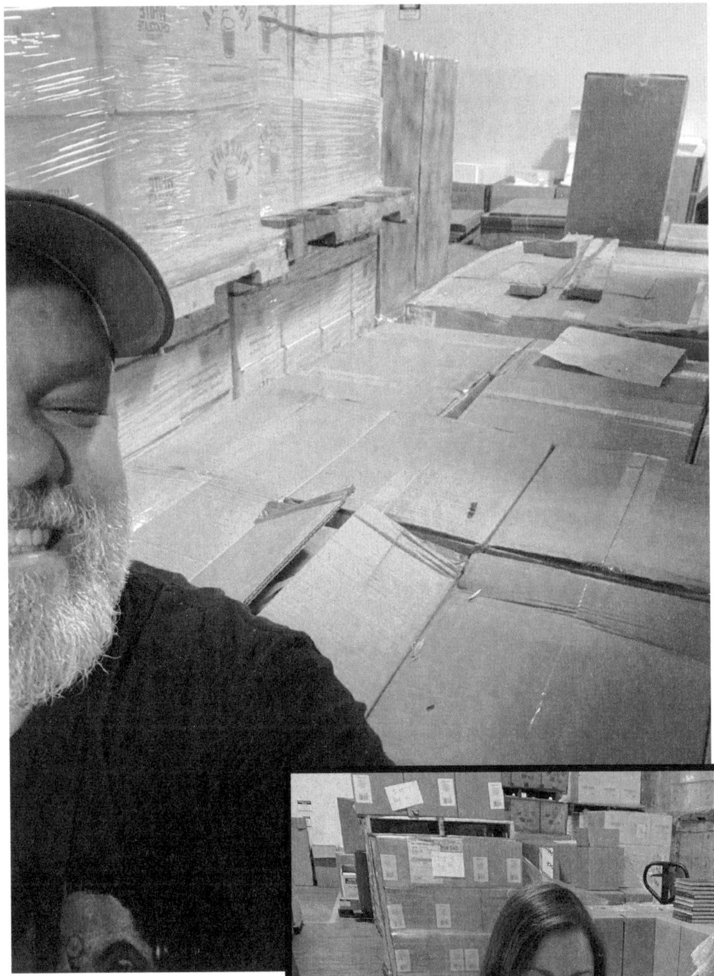

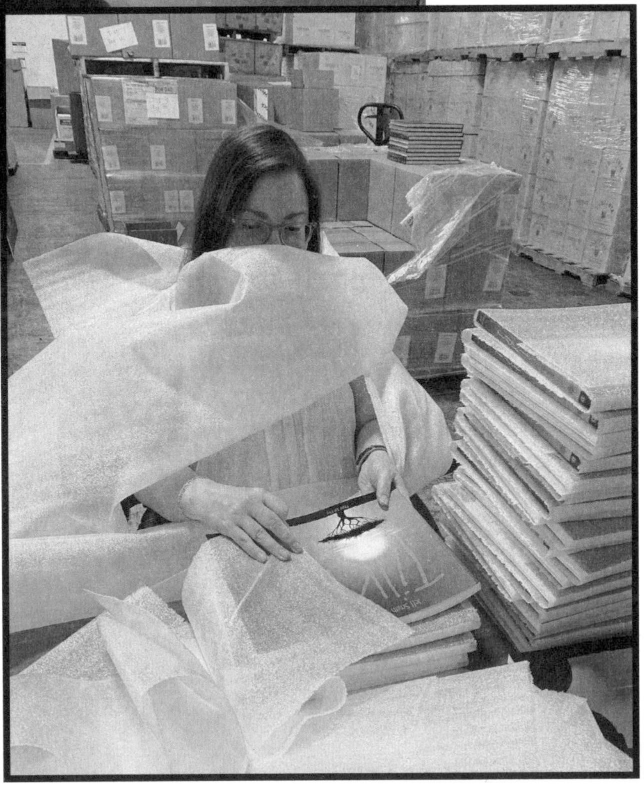

At the Warehouse

Kathleen with back-up Cartoon Bookers Keith Peppers and Tim Destefano filling up another pallet with TUKI books heading out all over the world! Tom Gaadt sitting down on the job (on a massive stack of TUKI books)! That's Kat packing at ludicrous speed!

APPENDIX D
October '95
Africa

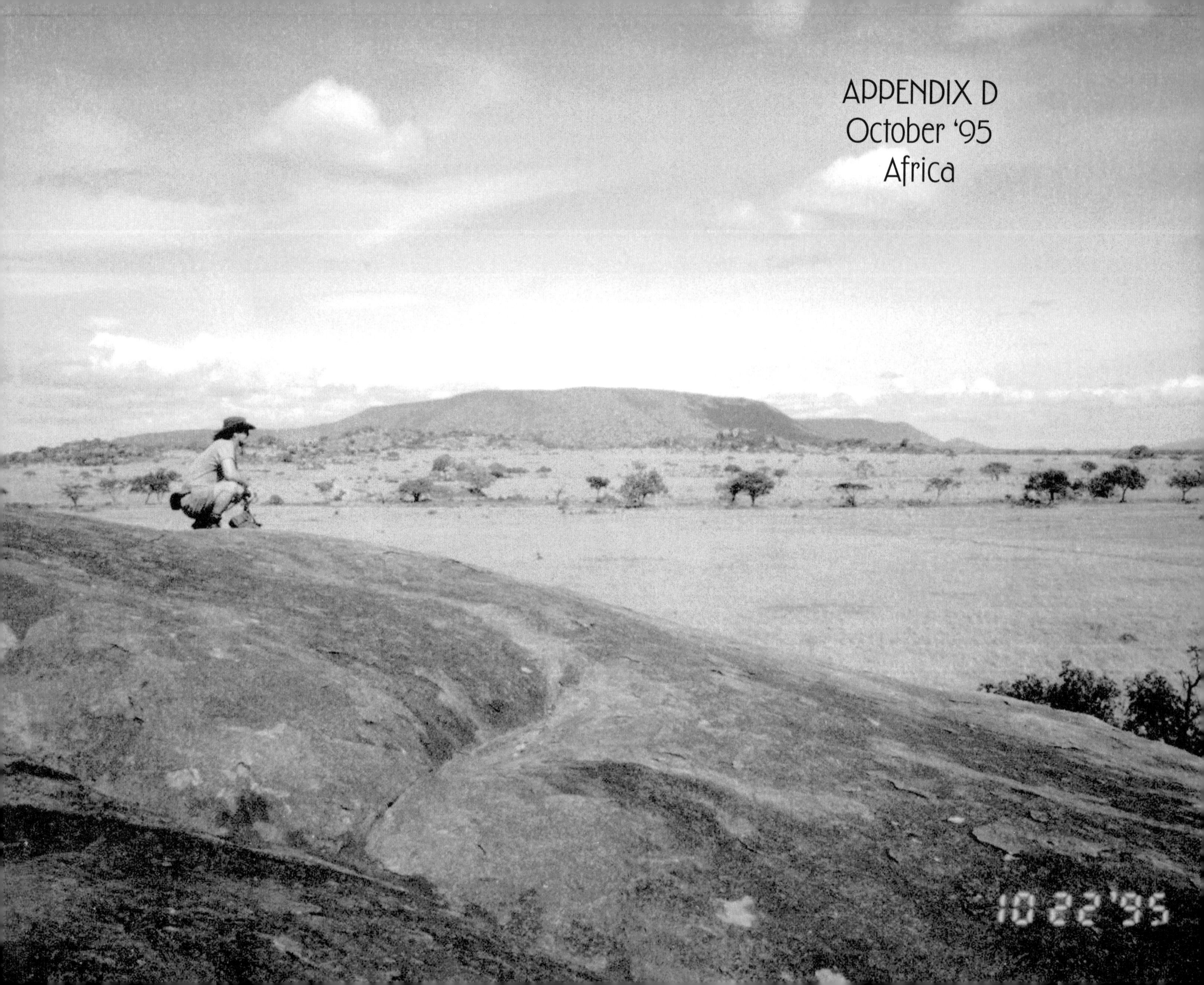
10 22 '95

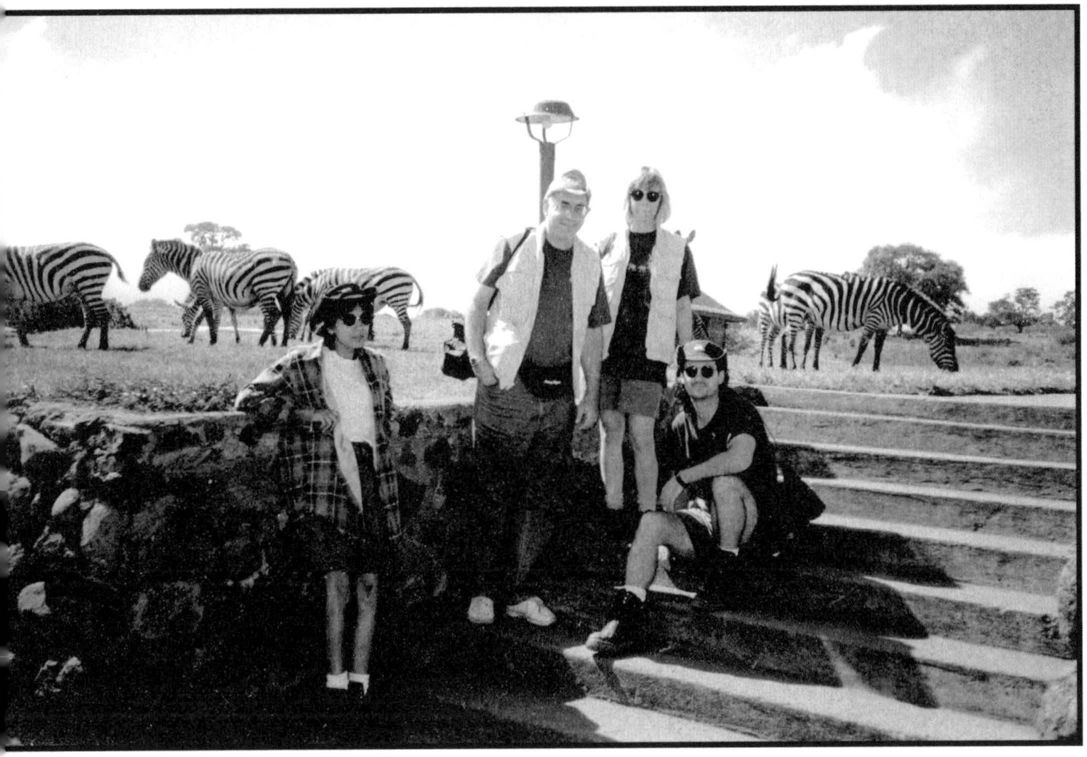

October '95

Vijaya, Larry, Cory & I arrive in Kenya ready to go. We are paired up with two other couples and the eight of us head out into the park. Ten days later we will have traversed the Serengeti, Tarangire, the Great Rift Valley and the Ngorongoro crater. When you go out there. . .It's out there. A hotel is waiting for you at the end of the day, but it is isolated. No fences, just someone walking around with a rifle. The electric generators are turned off at Midnight and let me tell you, that is the darkest dark I have ever experienced. You can't see anything. But you can sure hear things crunching and snapping around in the pure blackness of the jungle twelve feet from your cabin door. Elephants eating trees? Who knows. We heard lions and hyenas yowling back and forth in the distance.

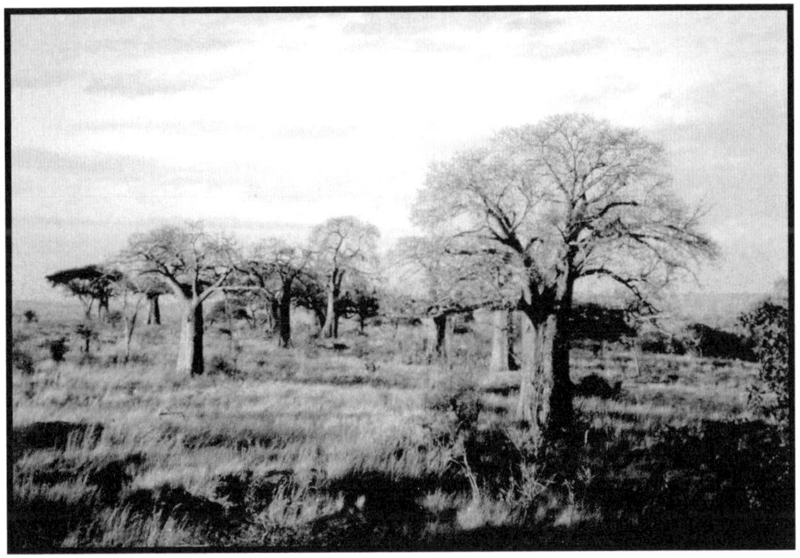

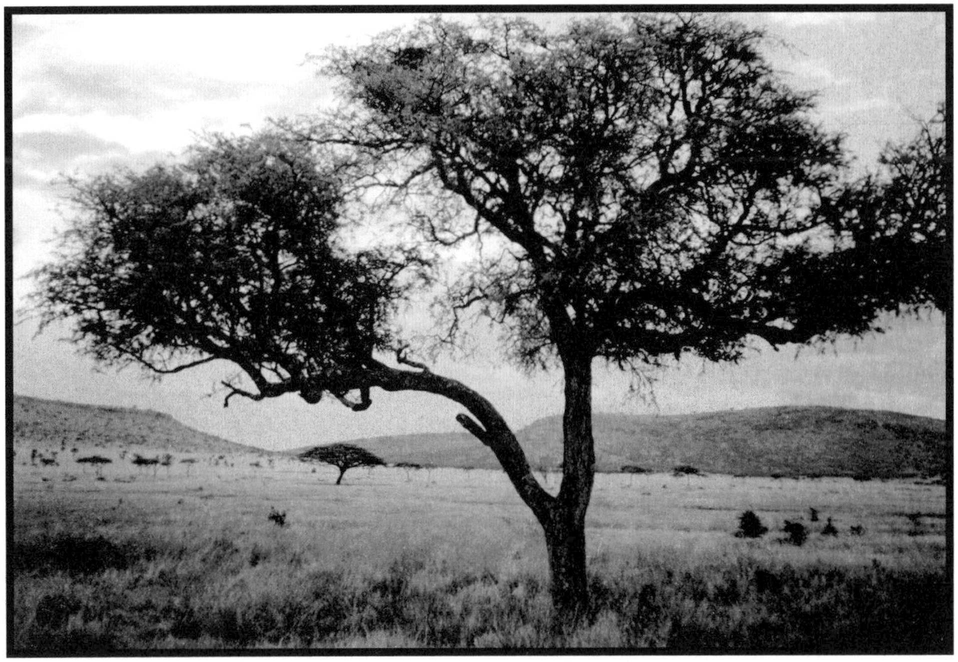

I hadn't the slightest idea for a story about Africa, but I must have had an inkling in the back of my mind, because I remember taking photographs of trees, rocks and landscapes "just in case."

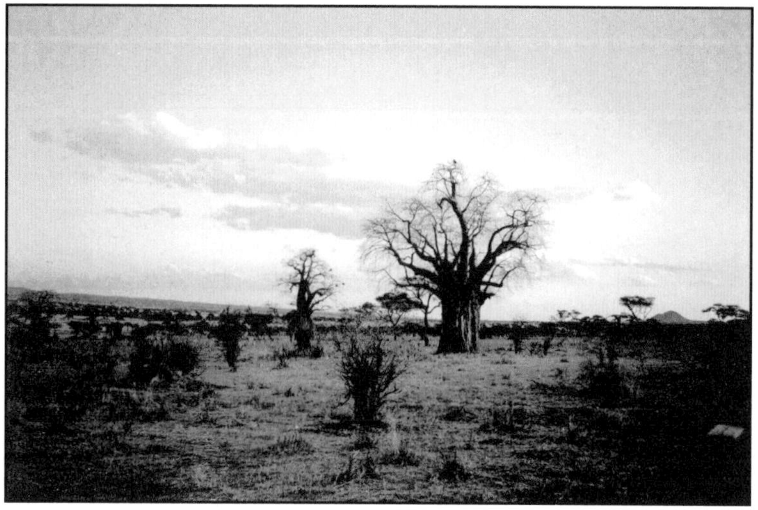

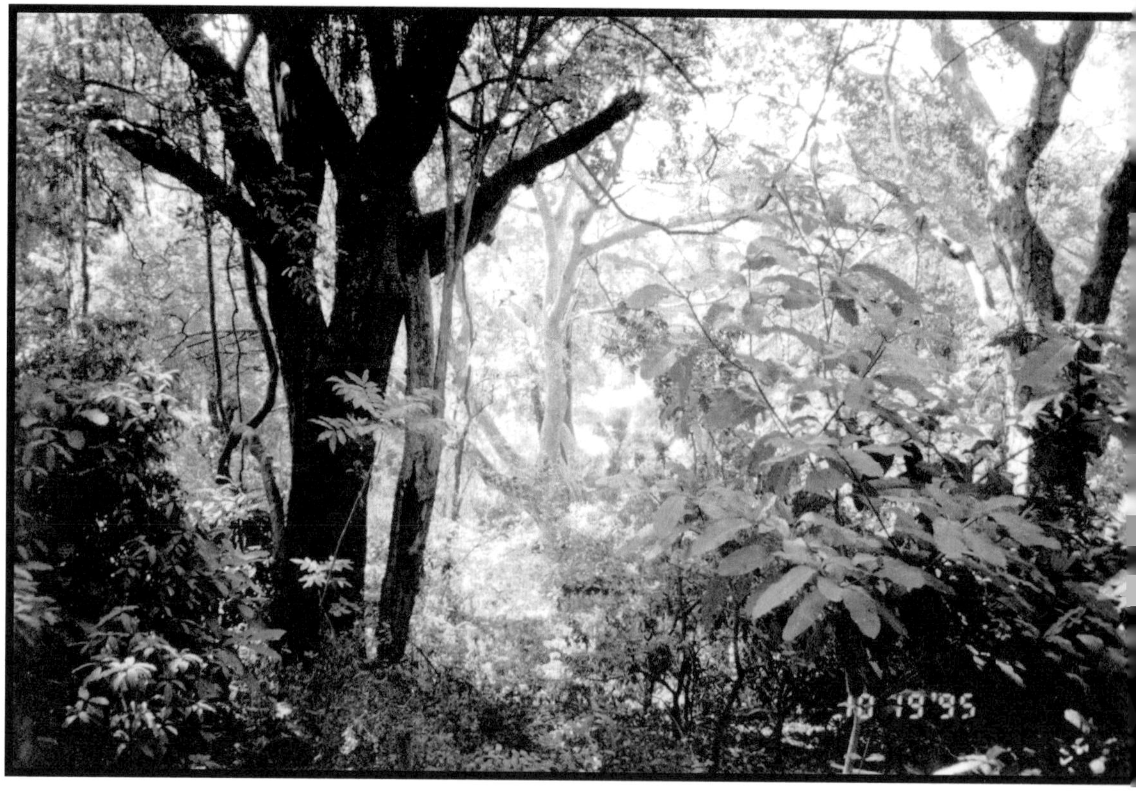

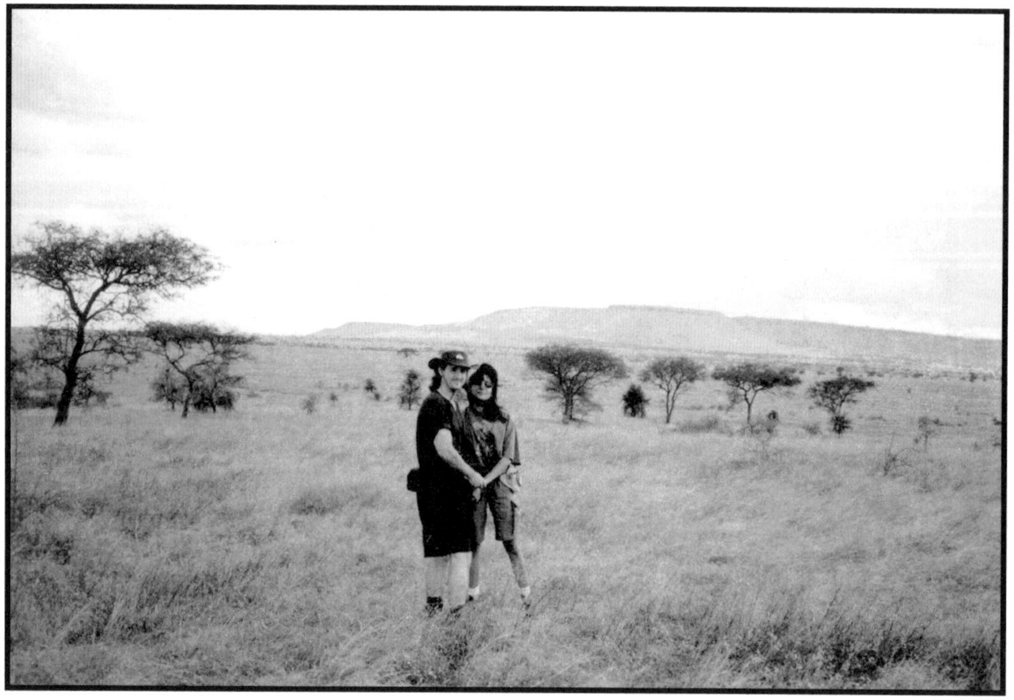

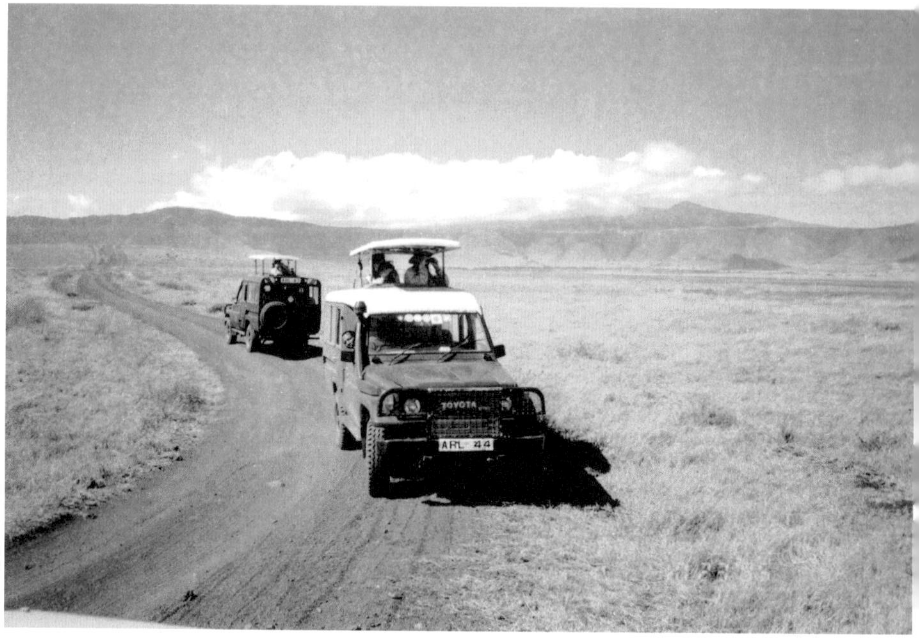

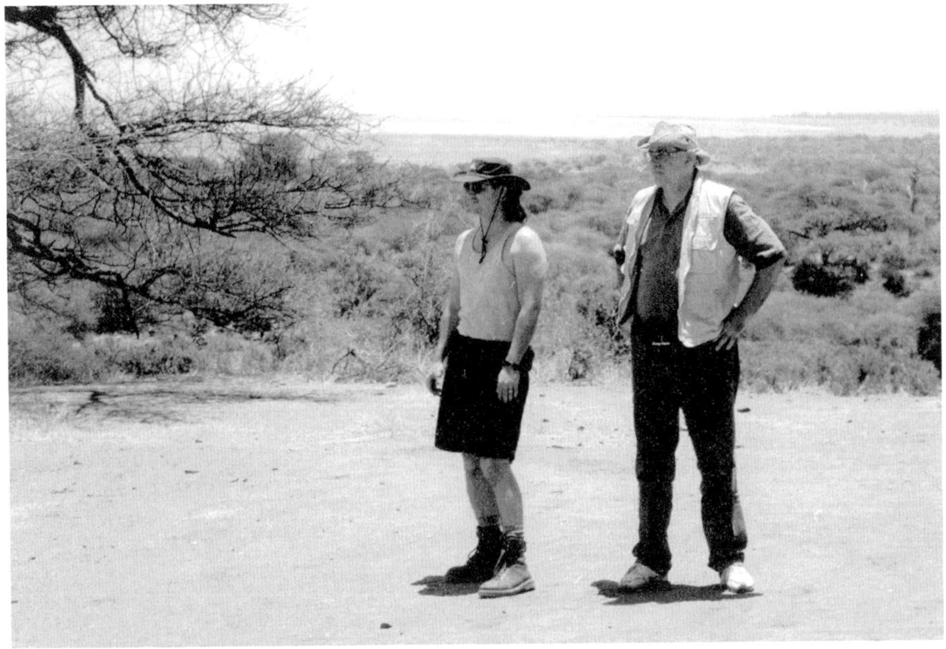

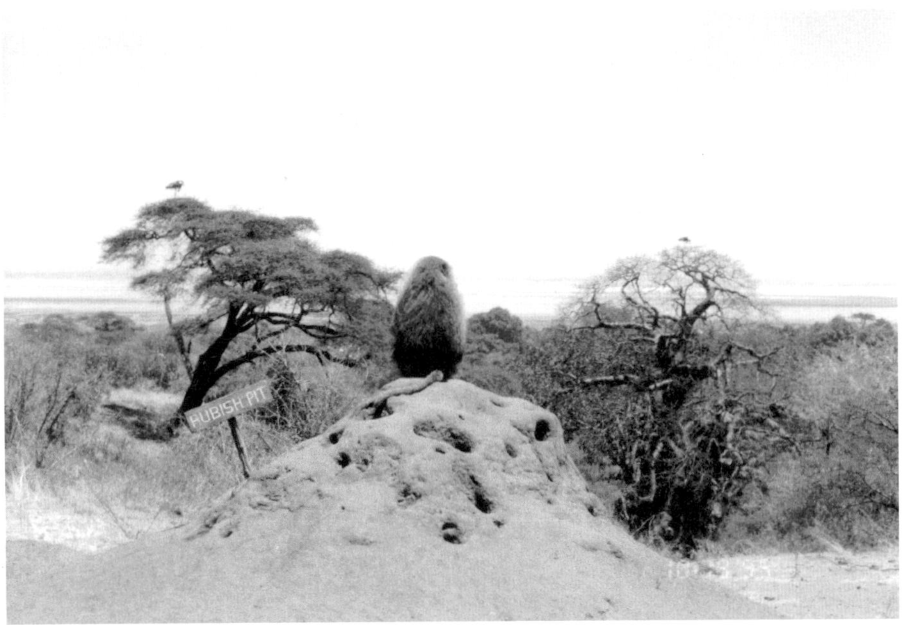
RUBISH PIT

What I learned from a stubborn baboon

One day we brought lunch with us out into the brush. There was a rubbish pit so we could burn our paper bags and leftovers. We got a fire going and started tossing in our trash. Out of nowhere, baboons appeared and the little one darted into the fire to retrieve any bananas that hadn't been eaten. As soon as he emerged from the fire pit, a big baboon snatched the fire roasted banana away. This went on until the big guy had all the bananas, about four I remember, and he sat like a king on the top of the rubbish pit with his back to us enjoying his spoils. Well, we were pretty close to a baboon at this moment and some of the group wanted a picture, but he wasn't having it. He ignored every shout, whistle or hand clap. He was not going to look at us. Then I gave him a bronx cheer, "PPBBTTT!" And his head popped around instantly to see who did it. Larry looked at me and chuckled, "Fart humor goes way back."

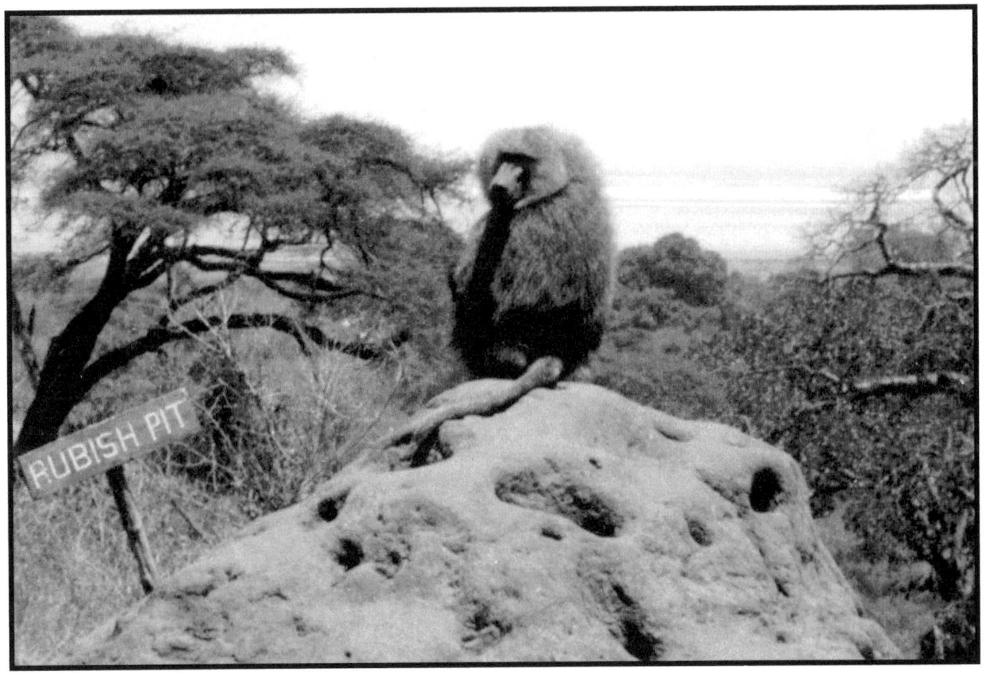
RUBISH PIT

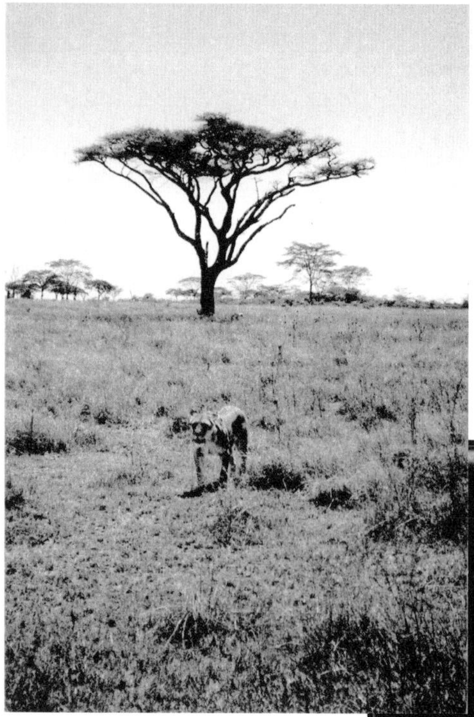

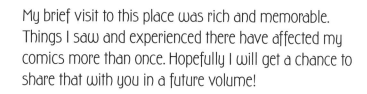

My brief visit to this place was rich and memorable. Things I saw and experienced there have affected my comics more than once. Hopefully I will get a chance to share that with you in a future volume!

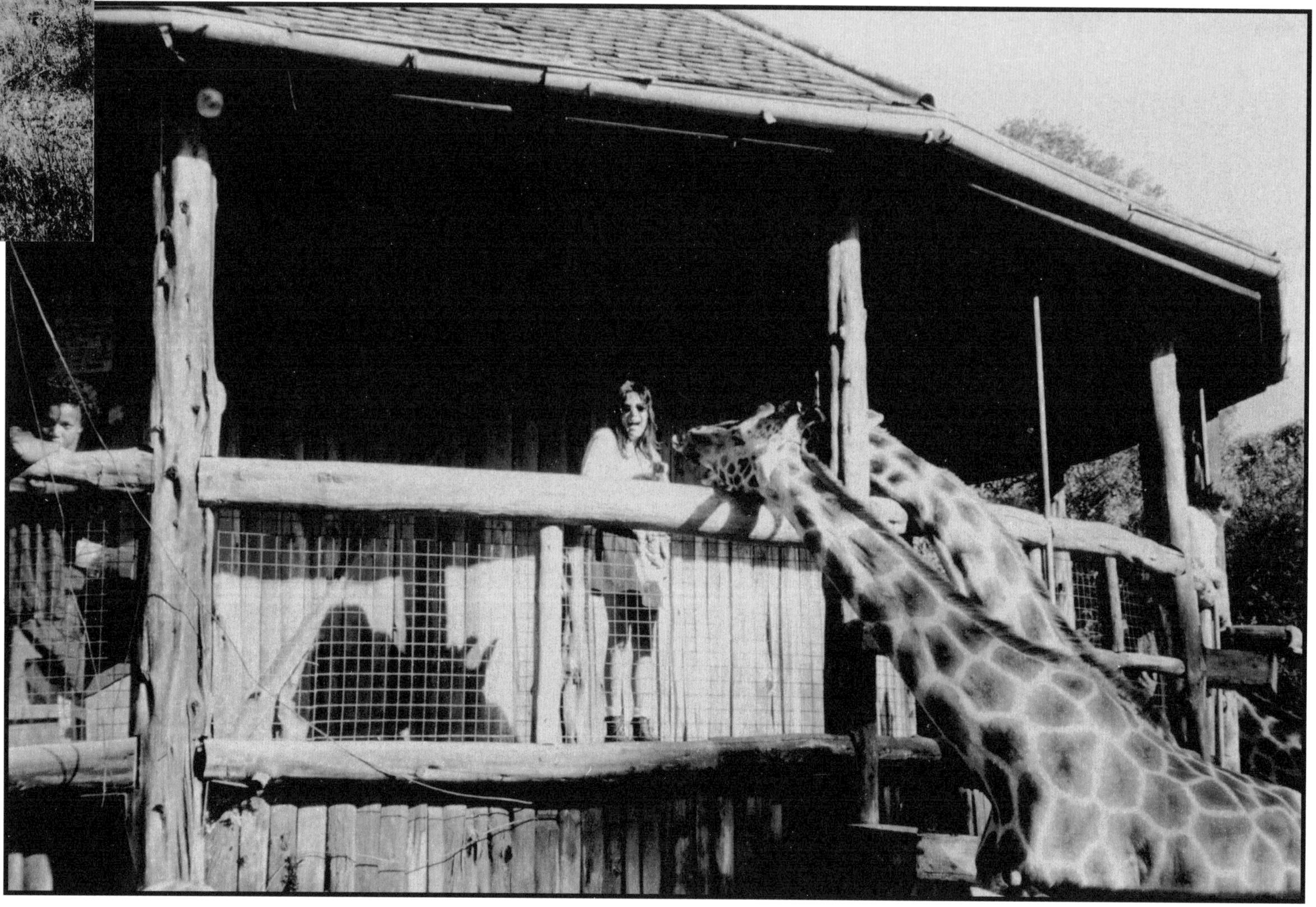

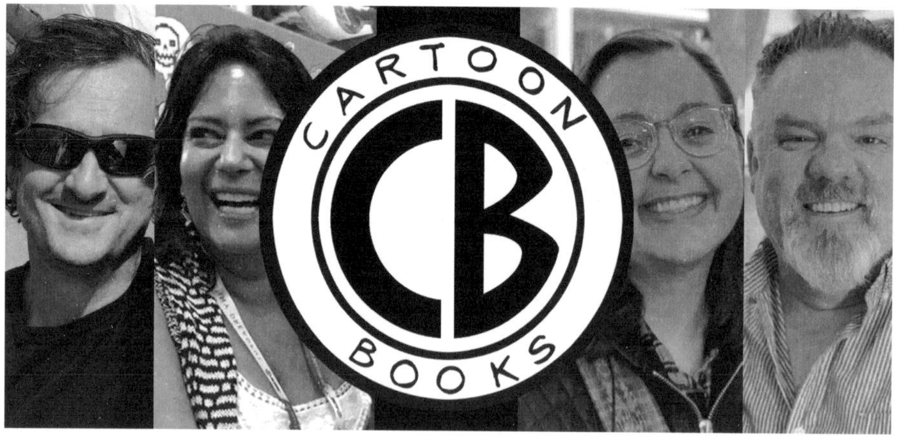
CARTOON
CB
BOOKS

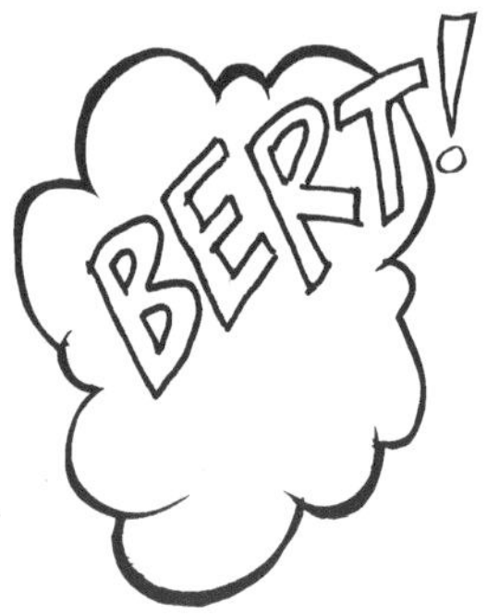
BERT!